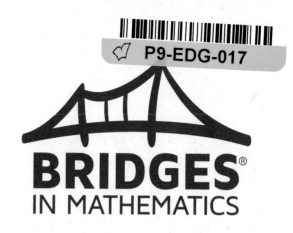

# BRIDGES®
## IN MATHEMATICS

SECOND EDITION
# STUDENT BOOK

GRADE
**3**

Published by  The MATH LEARNING CENTER Salem, Oregon

## Bridges in Mathematics Second Edition Grade 3 Student Book

The Bridges in Mathematics Grade 3 package consists of:

Bridges in Mathematics Grade 3 Teachers Guide Units 1–8

Bridges in Mathematics Grade 3 Assessment Guide

*Bridges in Mathematics Grade 3 Teacher Masters*

Bridges in Mathematics Grade 3 Student Book

Bridges in Mathematics Grade 3 Home Connections

*Bridges in Mathematics Grade 3 Teacher Masters Answer Key*

*Bridges in Mathematics Grade 3 Student Book Answer Key*

*Bridges in Mathematics Grade 3 Home Connections Answer Key*

Bridges in Mathematics Grade 3 Components & Manipulatives

*Bridges Educator Site*

Work Place Games & Activities

Number Corner Grade 3 Teachers Guide Volumes 1–3

*Number Corner Grade 3 Teacher Masters*

Number Corner Grade 3 Student Book

*Number Corner Grade 3 Teacher Masters Answer Key*

*Number Corner Grade 3 Student Book Answer Key*

Number Corner Grade 3 Components & Manipulatives

Word Resource Cards

*Digital resources noted in italics.*

The Math Learning Center, PO Box 12929, Salem, Oregon 97309. Tel 1 (800) 575-8130
www.mathlearningcenter.org

© 2019 by The Math Learning Center
All rights reserved.
Bridges and Number Corner are registered trademarks of The Math Learning Center.

Prepared for publication using Mac OS X and Adobe Creative Suite.
Printed in the United States of America.

To reorder this book, refer to number 2B3SB5 (package of 5).

QBB3901
05122022_LSB
Updated 2019-10-07.

*Bridges in Mathematics* is a standards-based K–5 curriculum that provides a unique blend of concept development and skills practice in the context of problem solving. It incorporates Number Corner, a collection of daily skill-building activities for students.

The Math Learning Center is a nonprofit organization serving the education community. Our mission is to inspire and enable individuals to discover and develop their mathematical confidence and ability. We offer innovative and standards-based professional development, curriculum, materials, and resources to support learning and teaching. To find out more, visit us at www.mathlearningcenter.org.

ISBN 978-1-60262-531-0

# Bridges Grade 3
# Student Book

## Unit 1
### Addition & Subtraction Patterns

## Unit 2
### Introduction to Multiplication

# Unit 3
## Multi-Digit Addition & Subtraction

# Unit 4
## Measurement & Fractions

# Unit 5
## Multiplication, Division & Area

# Unit 6
## Geometry

# Unit 7
## Extending Multiplication & Fractions

# Unit 8
## Bridge Design & Construction: Data Collection & Analysis

**NAME** _____ | **DATE** _____

# Summer Vacation Survey, Part 1

Samir and Sophia interviewed different classmates to find out what they did during summer vacation. Read each question carefully to find out what their classmates did. Then answer each question using words, pictures, or numbers. Show your work.

**1** Fourteen of the people Samir interviewed went swimming, and 9 of the people Sophia interviewed went swimming. How many of Samir and Sophia's classmates went swimming?

$14 + 9 = 23$

**2** Eight of the people Sophia interviewed went to summer camp, and 13 of the people Samir interviewed went to summer camp. How many people went to summer camp?

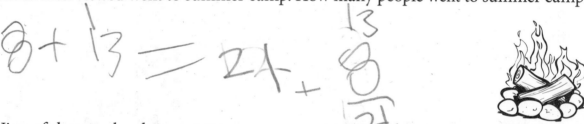

$8 + 13 = 21$

$13 + 8 = 21$

**3** Nine of the people who went to summer camp went to sleepover camp and the rest went to day camp. How many people went to day camp? (Hint: You will need to use the answer to question 2.)

10

**4** Samir and Sophia learned that 17 of their classmates went to the library during summer vacation. Samir interviewed 8 of those 17 people. How many of those people did Sophia interview?

**5** Find each sum or difference.

$7 + 15 = \underline{22}$   $3 + 8 = \underline{11}$   $12 - 7 = \underline{5}$   $16 - 8 = \underline{8}$

**Summer Vacation Survey, Part 2**

Samir and Sophia interviewed their classmates about their favorite summertime activities. They put the results into a bar graph. Use the bar graph to answer the following questions. Use words, pictures, or numbers to show your work.

**1** How many people liked going to the beach best? _____6_____

**2** How many people liked going on a trip best? _____7_____

**3** Nine people liked playing a summer sport and 4 people liked going to the movies. How many more people liked playing a summer sport than going to the movies?

4 + 5 = 0

**4** How many people did Sophia and Samir survey in all? How do you know?

7 + 0 + 4 = 26

**5** Find each sum or difference.

14 − 5 = _____     13 + 5 = __8__     15 − 10 = __5__     9 + 8 = _____

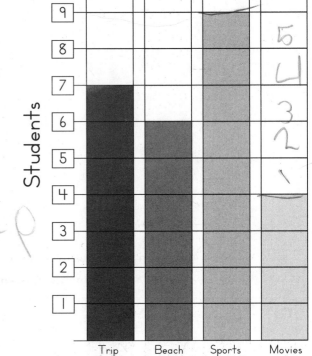

**Title** Favorite Summer Activity

Students

Trip    Beach    Sports    Movies

Activities

**NAME** _kvronh_ | **DATE**

## Story Problems

**1** Conner and Carlos are doing a puzzle. The puzzle has 16 pieces. So far, Conner and Carlos have fit 9 pieces together. How many more pieces do they need to fit together to finish the puzzle?

**a** What is this problem asking you to figure out?

**b** Underline information in the problem that will help you find the answer.

**c** Use this space to solve the problem. Show all your work using numbers, words, or labeled sketches.

Answer _7 pieces_

**2** Simone and Aleshia are saving money to buy a new tent together to take camping. Simone has saved $17 and Aleshia has saved $10. How much have they saved in all?

**a** What is this problem asking you to figure out?

How much have ther saved in alr?

**b** Underline information in the problem that will help you find the answer.

**c** Use this space to solve the problem. Show all your work using numbers, words, or labeled sketches.

$17 + 10 = \boxed{27}$

Answer _____

**3** Write an equation that could represent this picture.

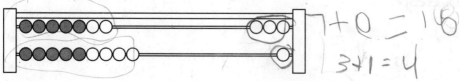

$7 + 0 = 18$

$3 + 1 = 4$

NAME | DATE

 **Addition Table**

## Legend

- Add Zero facts
- Count On facts
- Doubles facts
- Doubles Plus or Minus One facts
- Make Ten facts
- Add Ten facts
- Add Nine facts
- Leftover facts

| | 0 | 1 | 2 | 3 | 4 | 5 | 6 | 7 | 8 | 9 | 10 |
|---|---|---|---|---|---|---|---|---|---|---|---|
| **10** | 0 +10 10 | 1 +10 11 | 2 +10 12 | 3 +10 13 | 4 +10 14 | 5 +10 15 | 6 +10 16 | 7 +10 17 | 8 +10 18 | 9 +10 19 | 10 +10 20 |
| **9** | 0 +9 9 | 1 +9 10 | 2 +9 11 | 3 +9 12 | 4 +9 13 | 5 +9 14 | 6 +9 15 | 7 +9 16 | 8 +9 17 | 9 +9 18 | 10 +9 19 |
| **8** | 0 +8 8 | 1 +8 9 | 2 +8 10 | 3 +8 11 | 4 +8 12 | 5 +8 13 | 6 +8 14 | 7 +8 15 | 8 +8 16 | 9 +8 17 | 10 +8 18 |
| **7** | 0 +7 7 | 1 +7 8 | 2 +7 9 | 3 +7 10 | 4 +7 11 | 5 +7 12 | 6 +7 13 | 7 +7 14 | 8 +7 15 | 9 +7 16 | 10 +7 17 |
| **6** | 0 +6 6 | 1 +6 7 | 2 +6 8 | 3 +6 9 | 4 +6 10 | 5 +6 11 | 6 +6 12 | 7 +6 13 | 8 +6 14 | 9 +6 15 | 10 +6 16 |
| **5** | 0 +5 5 | 1 +5 6 | 2 +5 7 | 3 +5 8 | 4 +5 9 | 5 +5 10 | 6 +5 11 | 7 +5 12 | 8 +5 13 | 9 +5 14 | 10 +5 15 |
| **4** | 0 +4 4 | 1 +4 5 | 2 +4 6 | 3 +4 7 | 4 +4 8 | 5 +4 9 | 6 +4 10 | 7 +4 11 | 8 +4 12 | 9 +4 13 | 10 +4 14 |
| **3** | 0 +3 3 | 1 +3 4 | 2 +3 5 | 3 +3 6 | 4 +3 7 | 5 +3 8 | 6 +3 9 | 7 +3 10 | 8 +3 11 | 9 +3 12 | 10 +3 13 |
| **2** | 0 +2 2 | 1 +2 3 | 2 +2 4 | 3 +2 5 | 4 +2 6 | 5 +2 7 | 6 +2 8 | 7 +2 9 | 8 +2 10 | 9 +2 11 | 10 +2 12 |
| **1** | 0 +1 1 | 1 +1 2 | 2 +1 3 | 3 +1 4 | 4 +1 5 | 5 +1 6 | 6 +1 7 | 7 +1 8 | 8 +1 9 | 9 +1 10 | 10 +1 11 |
| **0** | 0 +0 0 | 1 +0 1 | 2 +0 2 | 3 +0 3 | 4 +0 4 | 5 +0 5 | 6 +0 6 | 7 +0 7 | 8 +0 8 | 9 +0 9 | 10 +0 10 |

NAME _____ | DATE _____

 **Addition Fact Practice**

**1** Complete the Make Ten facts below.

| 5 | ` | 3 | 6 | 7 |
|---|---|---|---|---|
| + 5 | + 9 | + 7 | + 4 | + 3 |
| 10 | 10 | 10 | 10 | 10 |

**2** Solve the Doubles facts below.

| 4 | 8 | 2 | 9 | 3 |
|---|---|---|---|---|
| + 4 | + 8 | + 2 | + 9 | + 3 |
| 8 | 16 | 4 | 17 | 6 |

**3** Solve the Doubles Plus or Minus One facts below.

| 4 | 6 | 6 | 7 | 5 |
|---|---|---|---|---|
| + 5 | + 7 | + 5 | + 6 | + 6 |
| 9 | 14 | 11 | 14 | 11 |

**4** Explain how you can use a Doubles fact to solve each of the following:

**a**  9 + 7

**b**  6 + 8

**c**  3 + 5

**5** Is the sum of 0 and any number always even, always odd, or sometimes even and sometimes odd? Explain.

**6** Write an equation that could represent this picture.

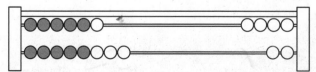

# Work Place Instructions 1A Make the Sum

**Each pair of players needs:**

- 1 deck of Number Cards to share, with the wild cards removed
- their own journals and a pencil

**1** Together, players choose a target number between 8 and 15. Each player writes the target number at the top of a new page in their journal. (If players choose a target number equal to or less than 9, they remove the cards greater than the target number from the deck.)

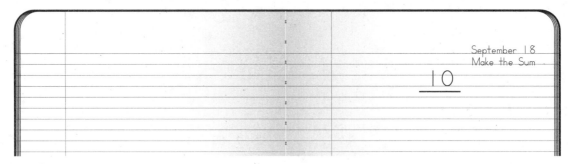

September 18
Make the Sum

10

**2** One player shuffles the cards and places 16 face-down in a 4-by-4 array.

**3** Each player draws 1 card from the deck. The player with the higher number goes first.

**4** The first player turns over 2 cards from the 4-by-4 array.

- If the numbers on the 2 cards add up to the target number, the player keeps the cards and writes an equation in their journal to show the two numbers and the sum.
- If the numbers don't add up to the target number, the player can turn over another card until the sum is equal to or greater than the target number. If the sum is equal to the target number, the player keeps all of the cards and writes an equation in her journal. If the sum goes over the target number, the player turns all the cards back over.

**5** Players replace any cards taken so that there are still 16 cards face-down. Then the next player takes a turn.

**6** The game continues until all the cards are gone, or until there are no more combinations that add up to the target number.

**7** The player with the most cards wins the game.

**8** Players choose a different target number and play again.

## Game Variations

**A** Cards are placed face-up instead of face-down.

**B** Players use a target number lower than 10 or higher than 15. A player turns over 3 or 4 cards at a time and then uses any combination of operations (addition, subtraction, multiplication, division) and each number just once to reach the target number.

**C** Players choose 15 or 20 as the target number. A player turns over 4 cards at a time and uses any combination of operations (addition, subtraction, multiplication, division) and each number just once to reach the target number.

**Addition Mixed Review**

**1** Fill in the missing number in each equation below.

**a** 4 + 6 = _____          **b** 4 + _____ = 11          **c** 9 = _____ + 2

**d** 8 + 9 = _____          **e** 16 = 9 + _____

**2** Explain how you can use a Make Ten fact to help find each sum below.

**a** 8 + 7

**b** 6 + 8

**c** 4 + 9

**3** Complete the equations below by writing three different pairs of numbers with a sum of 12.

**a** _____ + _____ = 12

**b** _____ + _____ = 12

**c** _____ + _____ = 12

**4** Think about the Doubles facts. What is true about all of the sums?

**5** Write an equation that could represent this picture.

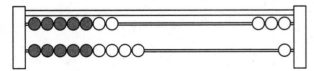

# Subtraction Fact Practice

**1** Solve these Zero facts.

| 6 | 8 | 10 | 13 | 7 |
|---|---|----|----|---|
| − 0 | − 0 | − 0 | − 0 | − 0 |

**2** Solve these Count Back facts.

| 9 | 15 | 7 | 8 | 14 |
|---|----|---|---|----|
| − 2 | − 1 | − 2 | − 3 | − 1 |

**3** Solve these Take All facts.

| 5 | 7 | 16 | 8 | 13 |
|---|---|----|---|----|
| − 5 | − 7 | − 16 | − 8 | − 13 |

**4** Solve these Neighbors facts.

| 8 | 6 | 14 | 17 | 9 |
|---|---|----|----|---|
| − 7 | − 5 | − 12 | − 16 | − 7 |

**5** Jessica has 16 marbles. Nine marbles roll under her bed. How many marbles does Jessica still have in front of her? Show all your work using numbers, words, or labeled sketches.

# Work Place Instructions 1B Target Twenty

## Each pair of players needs:

- 1 deck of Number Cards to share, with wild cards removed
- 2 Target Twenty Record Sheets (1 per player) and a pencil

**1** One player shuffles the cards and places the deck face-down. Each player takes 5 cards.

**2** Each player chooses the 3 cards in their hand that have a sum as close to 20 as possible.

**3** Each player writes an equation on their record sheet showing the 3 numbers and their sum.

**4** Players check each other's work, compute their scores (the difference between 20 and their sum), and record both scores on their record sheets.

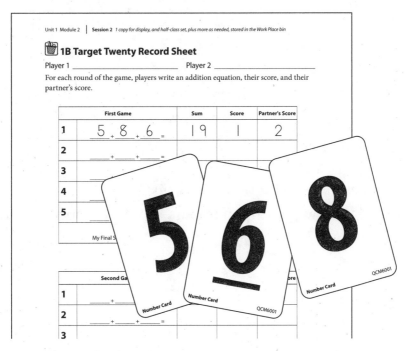

**5** Players put the cards they used face-up in a discard pile. Then each player takes 3 new cards from the deck so they have 5 cards again.

**6** The game continues for a total of 5 rounds.

**7** At the end of the game, players add their own scores. The player with the lower score wins.

## Game Variations

**A** Players return the wild cards to the deck. If a player gets a wild card, they can decide to make it any number between 0 and 10. If a player uses a wild card, they mark a star above the number assigned to the wild card in the equation on their record sheet.

**B** Players can use 30, 40, or 50 as their target number. They will need to use 4, 5, or 6 cards to make these larger numbers.

NAME _____ | DATE _____

 **More Subtraction Fact Practice**

**1** Solve the Take Away Ten facts below.

| 14 | 12 | 18 | 15 | 17 |
|----|----|----|----|----|
| − 10 | − 10 | − 10 | − 10 | − 10 |

**2** Solve the Take Half facts below.

| 8 | 6 | 14 | 12 | 18 |
|----|----|----|----|----|
| − 4 | − 3 | − 7 | − 6 | − 9 |

**3** Solve the Leftover facts below.

| 19 | 20 | 17 | 18 | 15 |
|----|----|----|----|----|
| − 13 | − 8 | − 13 | − 14 | − 4 |

**4** Clarence is 42 inches tall. His brother Charlie is 37 inches tall. How much taller is Clarence? Show all your work using numbers, words, or labeled sketches.

**5** Complete each equation by writing a different pair of numbers with a difference of 9.

**a** _____ − _____ = 9     **b** _____ − _____ = 9     **c** _____ − _____ = 9

# Work Place Instructions 1C Blast Off to Space

## Each pair of players needs:

- 1 clear spinner overlay (players share)
- Blast Off to Space Game Board (1 per player)
- 1C Blast Off to Space Record Sheet (1 per player)
- game markers (8 per player)
- pencil (1 per player)

**1**  Each player places eight rockets (markers) on the launch pads of their choice on their game boards. Players can put more than one rocket on a pad.

**2**  Player 1 spins each spinner once to create a subtraction equation and solves the problem. Player 1 shows how she solved the problem, explaining the strategies she used.

**3**  Then, Player 1 records the equation on her record sheet.

**4**  If there is a rocket on the difference, that rocket can blast off to space!

**5**  Whether or not a rocket blasts off, it is now Player 2's turn. Player 2 repeats steps 3–5.

**6**  Players take turns until one player has launched four rockets.

**7**  Then, players reposition their rockets. Players can use their record sheets to help them think about which numbers might occur more often than others.

> *Jayden  It looks like we've been getting a lot of 8s and 9s*
>
> *Thomas  We've hardly gotten any 3s or 13s.*
>
> *Jayden  I'm going to move my markers to 8 and 9.*
>
> *Thomas  Me too. I'm going to put one on 7 too.*

**8**  The game is over when all of one player's rockets have been blasted into space.

## Game Variations

**A**  Players can use more game markers (10 per person) or fewer (6 per person).

**B**  Players add 5 or 10 to each number they spin.

**More Games Story Problems**

**1** Asha and Oliver are playing Blast Off to Space. In this game, players spin two numbers, find the number that is the difference between the numbers, and 'blast off' a rocket with that number.

**ex** Asha spun a 16 and a 9. What rocket could she blast off for 16 and 9?

Asha can blast off rocket 7, because 16 − 9 = (7)

**a** Oliver spun a 14 and an 8. What rocket could he blast off for 14 and 8?

**b** Asha has a rocket on a 7. What are two numbers she could spin to be able to blast off her rocket on 7?

**2** Raven and Todd are playing a game with marbles. There are 20 marbles in all. The player with the most marbles at the end of the game wins.

**a** After one game, Raven has 13 marbles. How many marbles does Todd have? Show all your work using numbers, words, or labeled sketches.

**b** After another game, Todd has 9 marbles. How many marbles does Raven have? Show all your work using numbers, words, or labeled sketches.

**3** **CHALLENGE** James and Lily are playing basketball. Lily has 57 points. James has 38 points. How many more points does Lily have? Record your work in your math journal, using numbers, words, or labeled sketches. Record the answer here.

**12**

## Addition & Subtraction Equations

**1** Complete the following equations.

$12 = 4 +$ _____          $8 +$ _____ $= 15$          _____ $+ 7 = 13$

$3 = 13 -$ _____          $14 -$ _____ $= 9$          _____ $- 8 = 8$

$8 +$ _____ $= 14$          $5 = 17 -$ _____          $10 = 18 -$ _____

**2** Choose one of the equations above and explain how you figured out the missing number using words, numbers, models, or pictures.

**3** Complete the following equations.

$3 + 7 =$ _____ $+ 6$          $9 + 6 = 10 +$ _____

$5 +$ _____ $= 10 + 2$          _____ $+ 8 = 1 + 10$

# Work Place Instructions 1D Subtraction Bingo

## Each pair of players needs:

- 2 Subtraction Bingo Record Sheets
- 2 colored pencils
- 1 deck of Number Cards

**1** Each player chooses a separate board, either Board A or Board B. One player shuffles the cards and places the deck face-down. Each player takes 5 cards.

**2** Player A chooses 2 cards to add and finds the sum. Then Player A chooses a third card to subtract from the sum. Player A records the subtraction problem under the bingo board.

For example, Player A chooses a 7 and a 9 to add: 7 + 9 = 16. Then, Player A chooses an 8 to subtract from the sum, and solves and records the problem 16 – 8 = 8.

**3** Then, Player A looks for a problem on the bingo board that is equivalent to the subtraction problem he just made. If there is an equivalent problem, Player A explains her thinking to Player B. If Player B agrees, Player A puts an X over the equivalent problem on the game board.

If Player B disagrees with any of Player A's thinking, Player A has to rethink her work until she proves it to Player B.

> *Trina* Hmmm, I got 15 – 8. That's 7. I don't see 15 – 8 on the board anywhere.
>
> *Audrey* That's OK. Do you see anything that equals 15 – 8?
>
> *Trina* I don't see 7 on the board anywhere.
>
> *Audrey* I know, but do you see anything that equals 7? Like 12 – 5? That equals 7.
>
> *Trina* Oh, I get it. OK, I see 13 – 6. That equals 7. Is that what I cross off?
>
> *Audrey* Yes!

**4** Player B repeats steps 3 and 4.

**5** Players continue until one player crosses out 4 problems in a row. They can be vertical, horizontal, or diagonal. Whoever gets 4 in a row first wins the game.

## Game Variations

**A** Players use 3 cards instead of 5 to make the game simpler and less strategic, so they focus on addition and subtraction strategies.

**B** Players continue until one player gets 3 in a row. Or they play until the entire board is crossed out.

**C** Players make problems with all 5 cards. First they add 3 cards together. Then they add the other 2 cards together and subtract this sum from the sum of the first 3 cards.

**D** Players play on the same board, using two different colored pencils. Players try to get 3 problems in a row. In this version, players are also thinking about blocking their partner from getting 3 in a row.

# Addition & Subtraction Mixed Review

**1** Find each sum.

24 + 10 = _____          34 + 10 = _____          24 + 20 = _____

24 + 30 = _____                              34 + 20 = _____

**2** Find each difference.

37 − 10 = _____          37 − 20 = _____          37 − 21 = _____

37 − 22 = _____                              37 − 25 = _____

**3** Complete each equation with a different pair of numbers whose sum is 13.

**a** _____ + _____ = 13

**b** _____ + _____ = 13

**c** _____ + _____ = 13

**4** Write an equation that could represent this picture.

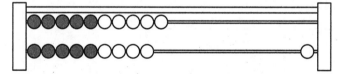

**Adding & Subtracting Two-Digit Numbers**

Write an equation for each problem. Then solve the problem. Show your work using words, numbers, or labeled sketches. Show work in your math journal if you need extra room.

**1** Sam drew a line that was 15 cm long. Then he decided he wanted a longer line, so he added 13 cm to his line. How long was Sam's line when he finished?

Equation _____

**2** Kaya collected 26 pebbles in the park. Her sister Jayla collected 17 pebbles.

**a** If they put their collections together, how many pebbles will they have in all?

Equation _____

**b** If Kaya and Jayla gave their little brother 15 of the pebbles when they got home, how many pebbles would they have left?

Equation _____

**3** **CHALLENGE** Sam drew some more lines.

**a** He drew a second line that was half as long as the first one he ended up with in Problem 1. How long was the second line he drew?

**b** He drew a third line that was five times as long as the first. How long was the third line he drew?

**NAME** _____ | **DATE** _____

 **Adding Lengths** page 1 of 2

The students in Mr. C's class measured some things around their classroom. They want to know what the total length will be if they line up some of the objects end-to-end. Help them with their work. Show your thinking with words, numbers, models, or equations. Use your math journal if you need extra room.

**1** How long are the pencil and the whiteboard eraser lined up end-to-end, 19 centimeters + 15 centimeters?

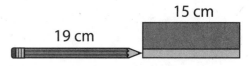

**2** How long are the whiteboard eraser and the piece of paper lined up, 15 centimeters + 28 centimeters?

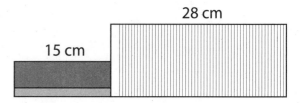

**3** If you put the piece of paper (28 centimeters) besides a chair seat (that was 51 centimeters across), how many centimeters would they measure in all?

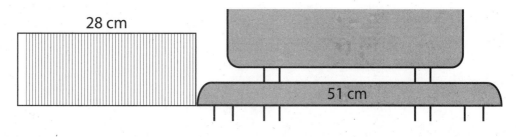

_(continued on next page)_

## Adding Lengths page 2 of 2

**4** The students measured 5 other things in the room, and wondered how long the line would be if they placed all 5 objects end-to-end. The things they measured were 23 centimeters, 13 centimeters, 8 centimeters, 12 centimeters, and 7 centimeters.

| 23 cm | 13 cm | 8 cm | 12 cm | 7 cm |
|---|---|---|---|---|

**5** When the book (22 centimeters) is stacked on top of the stool (99 centimeters), how tall are they together?

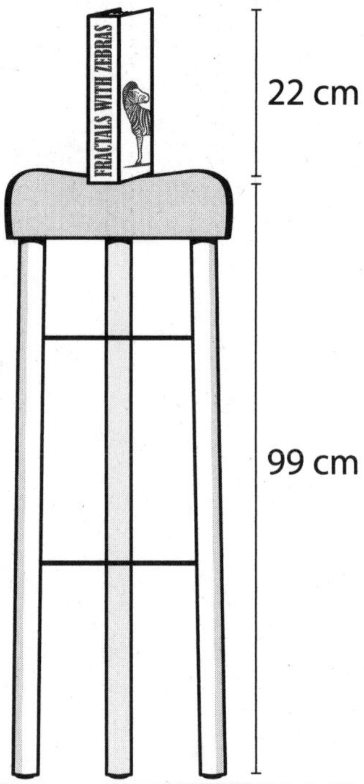

22 cm

99 cm

**6** **CHALLENGE** Add 123 + 36 + 59.

**Counting On & Measuring**

**1**  Count on by 10s to fill in the blanks.

**a**   27      37      _____      57      _____      _____      87      _____      _____      _____

**b**   122      _____      _____      152      _____      _____      _____      192      _____      _____

**2**  Solve the problems below. Show all your work using numbers, words, or labeled sketches. Use your math journal if you need extra room.

**a**   Patrick measured a book that was 27 cm long. Katy measured another book that was 40 cm long. If Patrick and Katy line up the books, how long are the books together?

**b**   Abby measured 6 markers. They were each 25 cm long. If she lined them up in a row end-to-end, how long would the row be?

**c**   Colin measured a poster. The first side of the poster was 88 units long. The second side was 25 units long. How much longer was the first side than the second side of the poster?

**3**  Kendra has 13 marbles in her collection. Kyle has some marbles in his collection. Together, Kendra and Kyle have 30 marbles. Which of the following equations represents this situation?

○  $13 + m = 17$      ○  $30 - 17 = m$      ○  $13 + m = 30$      ○  $m - 17 = 30$

**19**

**NAME** _____ | **DATE** _____

 **Monkeying Around**

**1** During the week, a monkey named Charlie ate 6 bananas, 12 pears, 14 strawberries, and 18 apples. How many pieces of fruit did Charlie eat that week? Show your work using numbers, words, or labeled sketches. Use your math journal if you need extra room.

**2** The monkeys made a path around some bushes. How long is the path? Show your work.

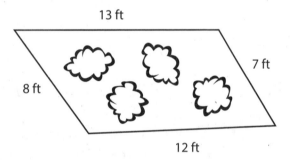

13 ft

7 ft

8 ft

12 ft

**3** Count on by 10s from each number below.

| | | | | | | |
|---|---|---|---|---|---|---|
| 333 | | | | | | |
| 855 | | | | | | |
| 109 | | | | | | |

**4** Solve each problem below. Explain your thinking in numbers, words, or labeled sketches.

| **a**  6 + 2 + 5 + 4 + 8 = _____ | **b**  7 + 1 + 9 + 3 + 10 = _____ |
|---|---|
| | |

#  Work Place Instructions 1E Carrot Grab

## Each pair of players needs:

- 1 Carrot Grab Game Board
- 2 dice numbered 1–6
- 1 spinner overlay
- 2 game marker in different colors
- 20 game markers in a different (third) color

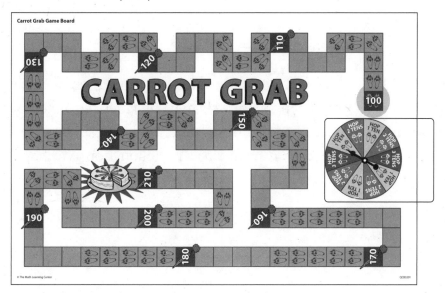

**1** Each player (rabbit) takes a game marker and places it on the board at the beginning of the track.

**2** Player 1 rolls the dice and spins the spinner. He tries to land on a multiple of 10 by hopping the number on the dice and the number of tens on the spinner. The player can split the sum in order to land on the greatest number of carrots. Player 1 takes a game marker for each carrot (multiple of 10) he lands on.

> **Teacher** *Try to land on the multiples of 10, where the carrots are. You can split up the dice hops to help you.*

**3** Player 2 takes a turn, repeating step 2.

**4** As players take turns rolling, spinning, and moving their markers, they try to figure out how to land on a multiple of 10 without counting one by one. Players use combinations to 10 and the patterns on the game board to help.

> **Player 1** *I am on 122 and I rolled 12 and Hop 2 Tens.*
>
> **Player 2** *So you want to go to 130. What is that jump? There are 3 more tracks here, then the blank spaces are 5, so 8?*
>
> **Player 1** *Yeah, and I know that 2 and 8 are 10, so yes, 8 to get to 130. Then I'll hop to 140, 150. Now I need to hop the rest of the 12, so that's 4. I'm on 154. And I get 3 carrots, one for 130, 140, and 150.*

**5** The game is over after both players reach the end of the game board. The player with the most carrots wins the game.

## Game Variation

**A** Players can roll the dice twice to generate four numbers find their sum. Then they jump that amount, still trying to get as many carrots as possible by landing on as many multiples of 10 as possible. In this variation, players do not spin the spinner.

# Counting On & Problem Solving

**1** Count on by 10s to fill in the blanks below.

**a**   54   64   74   84   94   104   204   304   404

**b**   504   404   504   ___   377   300   300   1400   407

**c**   222   223   240   228   262   71   ___   ___   ___

**2** Lydia rides her bike 3 miles from her house to the store. Then she rides her bike 7 miles from the store to her friend's house. Then she rides her bike home. She doesn't know how far it is from her friend's house to her own house, but she knows that she biked 15 miles in all. How far is it from Lydia's friend's house to her own house? Show your work.

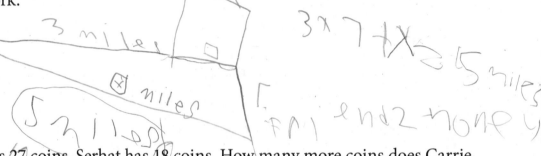

**3 a** Carrie has 27 coins. Serhat has 18 coins. How many more coins does Carrie have? Show your work.

**b** Rachel says this is a subtraction problem. Khan says it is an addition problem. What do you think?

**4** Aaron has 17 cars in his collection. Amira has 12 cars in her collection. How many more cars does Aaron have? Which of the following equations represents this situation?

○ $17 - 12 = c$      ○ $17 + c = 12$      ○ $c + 12 = 29$      ○ $29 - 12 = c$

**More Counting On & Problem Solving**

**1** Count on by tens to fill in the blanks below.

**a**   323    333    _____   _____   _____   373    _____   _____   _____   _____

**b**   738    _____   _____   768    _____   _____   _____   _____   _____   _____

**c**   1,145   _____   1,165   _____   _____   _____   1,205   _____   _____   1,235

**2** Solve the problems below. Show all your work using numbers, words, or labeled sketches. Use your math journal if you need extra room.

**a**   Steven was riding his bike. First he rode to the store which took 15 minutes. Then, he rode his bike to the library, which took 17 minutes. Then, Steven rode home. The whole trip took him 47 minutes. How long did it take Steven to ride his bike home from the library?

**b**   On Monday, Holly rode her bike for 39 minutes. On Tuesday, she rode her bike for 26 minutes. On Wednesday, she rode for 31 minutes. How much longer did Holly ride on Monday than on Tuesday?

**3** Solve the following equations:

13 = _____ + 9          10 + 5 = _____ + 6          _____ = 8 + 7

7 + _____ = 6 + 3          12 = 7 + _____          8 + 9 = 10 + _____

# Work Place Instructions 1F Rabbit Tracks

**Each player needs:**

- 1 Rabbit Tracks Game Board
- 1 spinner overlay
- 2 dice numbered 1–6
- 2 game markers in 2 different colors
- 20 game markers in a different color

**1** Each player (rabbit) takes a game marker and places it on the board at the beginning of the track. Players will take turns.

**2** On each turn, the player rolls the dice and spins the spinner. The player will hop the number of tens shown on the dice and the number of hundreds shown on the spinner. The player can split the sum in order to take hops that will land on carrots, and takes a game marker for each carrot (multiple of 100) they land on.

**3** As players take turns rolling, spinning, and moving their markers, they try to figure out how to land on multiples of 100 without counting ten by ten. Players can use combinations to 100 and the patterns on the game board to help.

> *Player 1 I am on 240. I rolled 6 and 6—I know that's 12. Now I'll spin the spinner… I got Hop 200. The dice shows tens, so that's 12 tens—120. That plus 200 is 320 in all.*
>
> *Player 2 Your next carrot is at 300.*
>
> *Player 1 Yeah, so I'll take a hop of 60 to get to 300. Then I'll hop to 400, 500 — that's my 200. Now I need to hop the rest of the 120, so that's 60. I'm on 560. And I get 3 carrots, one each for 300, 400, 500.*

**4** The game is over after both players reach the end of the game board. The player with the most carrots wins the game. (It is possible for the game to be a tie.)

## Game Variations

**A** Students can use one or two dice numbered 4–9 instead of the 1–6 dice.

**B** Students can loop around the game board and keep collecting carrots until the time has run out.

**Adding & Subtracting**

**1** Solve the following addition and subtraction combinations.

| | | | | |
|---|---|---|---|---|
| 8<br>+ 6 | 10<br>+ 7 | 9<br>+ 9 | 7<br>+ 8 | 5<br>+ 9 |
| 15<br>− 5 | 14<br>− 9 | 10<br>− 8 | 13<br>− 6 | 17<br>− 9 |
| 9<br>+ 7 | 8<br>+ 3 | 30<br>− 10 | 11<br>− 3 | 12<br>− 4 |

**2** Taylor has 27 seashells in his collection. His grandfather gave him 16 more seashells. How many seashells does Taylor have in all? Show your work below and write your final answer on the line.

Answer: _____

**Making Ten & One Hundred**

**1** Solve the following addition and subtraction combinations.

| 8 | 9 | 10 | 3 | 8 | 7 | 7 |
|---|---|----|---|---|---|---|
| + 4 | + 6 | + 8 | + 7 | + 1 | + 6 | + 7 |

| 12 | 9 | 14 | 16 | 20 | 11 | 15 |
|----|---|----|----|----|----|----|
| − 8 | − 4 | − 7 | − 8 | − 17 | − 9 | − 8 |

**2** Solve the following addition and subtraction combinations.

| 8 | 12 | 13 | 21 | 54 | 42 | 83 |
|---|----|----|----|----|----|----|
| + 14 | + 25 | + 27 | − 9 | − 7 | − 6 | − 6 |

**3** Every week, Trevon keeps a reading log. His goal is to read 100 minutes total from Monday to Friday. Here is his reading log so far this week.

**a** How many more minutes does Trevon need to read to meet his goal?

| Day | Minutes Spent Reading |
|-----|-----------------------|
| Monday | 18 |
| Tuesday | 24 |
| Wednesday | 15 |
| Thursday | |
| Friday | |

**b** Write two different equations showing how much time Trevon could spend reading on Thursday and Friday to meet his goal.

# Work Place Instructions 1G Target One Hundred

**Each pair of players needs:**

- 1 deck of Number Cards with the wild cards and 10s removed
- 2 Target One Hundred Record Sheets (1 for each player)

**1** Players shuffle the cards, then take turns drawing 6 cards from the deck.

**2** Each player chooses 4 cards to make two 2-digit numbers that together have a sum as close to 100 as possible.

With these cards, a player could make 63 and 42 (sum of 105) or 64 and 34 (sum of 98).
Since 98 is closer to 100 than 105 is, making 64 and 34 with the cards is a better move.
**Note** The 0 card can be used only in the ones place.

**3** Players write an addition equation with their numbers and their sum on the record sheet.

**4** Players take turns double-checking each other's calculations.

**5** Each player determines their score for the round by finding the exact difference between their sum and 100.

Examples: A sum of 96 has a score of 4, a sum of 107 has a score of 7, and a sum of 100 has a score of 0.

**6** Players record both their own score and their partner's score for the round.

**7** Each player puts the 4 cards they used in the discard pile, and then they take turns getting 4 new cards.

**8** The game continues for four more rounds (five rounds in all).

**9** After five rounds, players add their scores to determine the winner. The player with the lower score wins the game.

## Game Variation

**A** Players can choose to use wild cards. A wild card can be any numeral. When players use a wild card, they need to put a star above the number made from the wild card in the equation on the record sheet.

**Two-Step Problems**

Show your work when you solve these story problems. Use your math journal if you need extra room.

**1** Steve bought 8 cat toys at a craft fair. His aunt went to the same fair and bought 6 more toys for him. Steve gave 5 of the toys to the cat next door and let his cat, Fred, have the rest. How many new toys did Fred get?

**2** Ava had 7 quarters and her brother gave her 4 more. She had a hole in her pocket, and 5 of the quarters fell out on her way to school. How much money did Ava have left when she got to school?

**3** Find each sum or difference.

| 7 | 12 | 15 | 6 | 7 | 9 | 19 |
|---|---|---|---|---|---|---|
| + 8 | − 9 | − 8 | + 5 | + 6 | + 7 | − 12 |

**4** The bus ride from Whitney's school to her house takes 43 minutes. She has been on the bus for 27 minutes. How much longer will Whitney be on the bus before she gets home?

**a** Show one way to solve this problem on the number line.

**b** Show a different way to solve this problem on the number line.

**NAME** | **DATE**

 **Books & Reading Problems**

**1**  Write three different pairs of numbers with a difference of 8.

    **a** _____ – _____ = 8    **b** _____ – _____ = 8    **c** _____ – _____ = 8

**2**  Write three pairs of numbers whose sum is 17.

    **a** ____ + ____ = 17    **b** ____ + ____ = 17    **c** ____ + ____ = 17

Show your thinking when you solve these problems:

**3**  Mr. Morgan had 38 math and science books. 17 of them were math books. How many were science books?

**4**  Jay read 36 more pages than Shannon last week. If Shannon read 125 pages, how many pages did Jay read?

**5**  Jay wanted to read 200 pages last week. How many more pages would he have needed to read to meet that goal?

**More Story Problems**

**1** Samara had a collection of 23 little dolls. She took the dolls to a friend's house and lost 4 of them. Her dad bought a package of 6 more dolls for her. How many dolls does Samara have now? Show your work.

**2** Lola and Serafina were collecting special rocks to give to their brother for his birthday. Lola found 17 rocks, and Serafina found 12. Lola decided to keep 3 of the rocks she found, and Serafina kept 2 of hers. They gave the rest of the rocks to their brother. How many rocks did they give to their brother? Show your work.

**3** Max and Sam are in the same third grade class. Their teacher asked everyone in the class to try to read as much as they could over the weekend and keep track of what they read. On Saturday, Max read 28 pages and Sam read 19 pages. On Sunday, Max read 15 pages and Sam read 26 pages. On Monday, Max and Sam compared the number of pages they read over the weekend. Who read more pages? How many more pages did he read? Show your work.

#  Work Place Instructions 1H Anything But Five

## Each pair of players needs:

- a shared Anything But Five Record Sheet and pencils
- 2 dice numbered 4–9

**1** Both players start the game with 95 points and race to get down to zero points.

**2** On each turn, a player can roll the dice up to three times and subtract the sum or sums from their total points.

- Each time a player rolls the dice, they write an equation on their record sheet that shows the two numbers they rolled and their sum. Players need to write small enough so they can fit three equations in the same box.
- A players can stop rolling after one, two, or three rolls.
- If a player rolls a 5, he or she loses this turn and will not be able to subtract any points.
- When a player decides to stop rolling (if they haven't rolled a 5), they add the sums of all the equations from that turn and then subtract the total from the number of points they have.

Players can use base ten pieces, sketches of base ten pieces, a measuring tape, or mental math strategies to help them with the adding and subtracting, but they must be able to prove to their partner that their results are accurate.

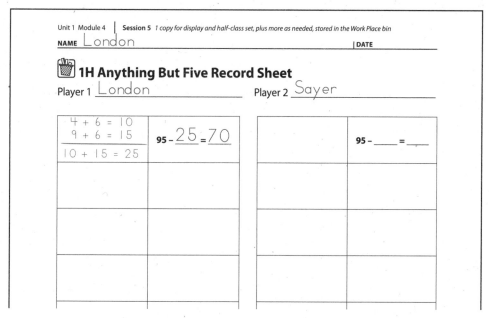

**3** Players take turns rolling and subtracting. The first partner to get to 0 wins.

Players don't need to get exactly to 0. For example, if a player has 6 points left and rolls a 7 and an 8 to make 15, she wins.

## Game Variations

**A** For a more challenging game, players can start at 195 and roll 3 dice. They can decide to simply add the 3 dice for a larger sum, or they can combine 2 of the dice to make a 2-digit number.

**B** For a shorter game, players can start at 50 or 75.

**Alfonso's Money Problem**

Alfonso had $23. He spent $8 at the store during the day. That night, his dad gave him $5 for his allowance. How much money did Alfonso have at the end of the day?

**1** What is this problem asking you to figure out?

**2** Underline any information in the problem that will help you find the answer.

**3** Use this space to solve the problem. Show all your work using numbers, words, or labeled sketches. Write the answer on the line below when you're finished.

_____

**4** **CHALLENGE** Alfonso wants to share his money with his little sister. He wants to give her enough so that they each have exactly the same amount of money. His sister has $9. How much money should Alfonso give her, and how much money will they each have? Show your work. Use your math journal if you need extra room.

NAME _____ | DATE _____

 # Measuring, Rides & Newspapers

**1** Count on by 10s to fill in the blanks below.

| 54 | | | | 94 | | 114 | | 134 | |
|---|---|---|---|---|---|---|---|---|---|
| 29 | | | 59 | | | | 99 | | 119 |
| 236 | | 256 | | | | 296 | 306 | | |

**2** Solve the problems below. Show all your work using numbers, words, or labeled sketches. Label each answer with the correct units. Use your math journal if you need extra room.

**a** Wren measured some items from her room. She measured a book that was 14 inches long, a postcard that was 8 inches long, a CD that was 6 inches long, and a picture that was 13 inches long. Wren lined up all of these items and measured them together. How long were all of the items together?

**b** Over the weekend, Calvin went to an amusement park. He rode the Fantastic Freeway ride for 17 minutes, the Spaceship Speedway ride for 12 minutes, and the Rickety Rackety Rocket Ride for 11 minutes. How long did Calvin spend on these three rides?

**c** Willow delivers newspapers after school. On one street, she delivers 8 newspapers. On another street, she delivers 14 newspapers. On a different street, she delivers 17 newspapers. How many newspapers does Willow deliver on these three streets?

**3** Solve the following equations:

$7 + n = 10$                              $n + 6 = 8 + 4$

$n =$ _____                           $n =$ _____

**Addition & Subtraction: Mixed Review**

## Story Problems

**1** Alejandro is making designs with pattern blocks. His first design has 14 pattern blocks. His second design has 8 pattern blocks. How many more blocks are in his first design than in his second design?

**a** Solve the problem using numbers, pictures, or words.

**b** Write an equation for this problem.

**2** Elizabeth is also making designs with pattern blocks. Her first design has 17 pattern blocks, and her second design has 15 pattern blocks. How many pattern blocks did she use in all?

**a** Solve the problem using numbers, pictures, or words.

**b** Write an equation for this problem.

## Repeated Addition

**3** Solve the following problems:

$5 + 5 + 5 + 5 + 5 =$ _____        $3 + 3 + 3 =$ _____        $6 + 6 + 6 + 6 =$ _____

$2 + 2 + 2 + 2 =$ _____        $9 + 9 + 9 =$ _____        $4 + 4 + 4 + 4 + 4 =$ _____

34

NAME _____ | DATE _____

 ## Missing Numbers Fill In

**1** Fill in the missing numbers in the Make Ten addition facts.

$5 + \underline{\hspace{1cm}} = 10$ $\underline{\hspace{1cm}} + 3 = 10$ $6 + \underline{\hspace{1cm}} = 10$ $10 = \underline{\hspace{1cm}} + 8$

$0 + \underline{\hspace{1cm}} = 10$ $9 + \underline{\hspace{1cm}} = 10$ $10 = \underline{\hspace{1cm}} + 7$ $10 = 4 + \underline{\hspace{1cm}}$

**2** Fill in the missing numbers in the equations below:

$2 + \underline{\hspace{1cm}} = 4$ $16 = \underline{\hspace{1cm}} + 8$ $6 = 3 + \underline{\hspace{1cm}}$ $\underline{\hspace{1cm}} = 9 + 9$

$5 + \underline{\hspace{1cm}} = 10$ $\underline{\hspace{1cm}} + 6 = 12$ $8 = \underline{\hspace{1cm}} + 4$ $7 + 7 = \underline{\hspace{1cm}}$

**3** Fill in the missing numbers to complete the subtraction facts.

$$\begin{array}{r} 15 \\ - \ \square \\ \hline 8 \end{array} \qquad \begin{array}{r} 13 \\ - \ 3 \\ \hline \square \end{array} \qquad \begin{array}{r} 18 \\ - \ \square \\ \hline 9 \end{array} \qquad \begin{array}{r} 11 \\ - \ \square \\ \hline 4 \end{array} \qquad \begin{array}{r} 16 \\ - \ 9 \\ \hline \square \end{array} \qquad \begin{array}{r} \square \\ - \ 3 \\ \hline 8 \end{array}$$

$$\begin{array}{r} 17 \\ - \ \square \\ \hline 9 \end{array} \qquad \begin{array}{r} 12 \\ - \ 3 \\ \hline \square \end{array} \qquad \begin{array}{r} 11 \\ - \ 2 \\ \hline \square \end{array} \qquad \begin{array}{r} 12 \\ - \ \square \\ \hline 9 \end{array} \qquad \begin{array}{r} \square \\ - \ 2 \\ \hline 12 \end{array} \qquad \begin{array}{r} 13 \\ - \ \square \\ \hline 8 \end{array}$$

**4** **CHALLENGE** What is one way the equations in problem 2 are alike?

**More Groups of Stamps** page 1 of 2

For the following questions:

- Write the total cost for each group of stamps.

- Show how you found the total cost. Use numbers, sketches, or words to show your thinking.

| | Cost of Stamps | Your Work |
|---|---|---|
| **1** 4¢ 4¢ 4¢ 4¢ 4¢ / 4¢ 4¢ 4¢ 4¢ 4¢ | 4¢ <br> 10 stamps | 5 × 2 = 10 |
| **2** 5¢ 5¢ 5¢ 5¢ / 5¢ 5¢ 5¢ 5¢ | | 5+5+5+5+5+5+5+5 = 40 |
| **3** 2¢ 2¢ 2¢ 2¢ 2¢ 2¢ 2¢ 2¢ / 2¢ 2¢ 2¢ 2¢ 2¢ 2¢ 2¢ 2¢ | | 16 <br> 2 × 8 = 16 |
| **4** 4¢ 4¢ 4¢ 4¢ / 4¢ 4¢ 4¢ 4¢ | | |

## More Groups of Stamps page 2 of 2

| | | Cost of Stamps | Your Work |
|---|---|---|---|
| **5** | 7¢ 7¢ 7¢ 7¢ <br> 7¢ 7¢ 7¢ 7¢ | | |
| **6** | 9¢ 9¢ <br> 9¢ 9¢ <br> 9¢ 9¢ | | |
| **7** | **CHALLENGE** <br> 11¢ 11¢ 11¢ 11¢ <br> 11¢ 11¢ 11¢ 11¢ <br> 11¢ 11¢ 11¢ 11¢ <br> 11¢ 11¢ 11¢ 11¢ | | |
| **8** | **CHALLENGE** <br> 9¢ 9¢ 9¢ <br> 9¢ 9¢ 9¢ <br> 9¢ 9¢ 9¢ <br> 9¢ 9¢ 9¢ | | |

**NAME** | **DATE**

 **Alexandra's Garden**

For each story problem, show your thinking using numbers, sketches, or words.

**1** Alexandra has a garden. In her garden, she has 6 daisy plants. Each plant has 3 flowers. How many daisy flowers does Alexandra have?

**2** Alexandra also has 5 strawberry plants. Each plant has 6 strawberries on it. How many strawberries does Alexandra have?

**3** Alexandra catches ladybugs for her garden because they will eat aphids that eat her plants. Alexandra has a pepper plant with 4 peppers on it. Each pepper has 4 ladybugs on it. How many ladybugs are on the pepper plant?

**4** Solve the following problems:

$7 + 7 + 7 + 7 =$ _____     $6 + 6 + 6 =$ _____     $9 + 9 + 9 + 9 + 9 =$ _____

**5** **CHALLENGE** Write a multiplication equation to represent one of the problems above.

**38**

**NAME** _____ | **DATE** _____

 **Fruit & Stamps**

**1** Complete the following problems. Show your work using pictures, numbers, or words.

| 3 + 3 + 3 + 3 = _____ | 5 + 5 + 5 + 5 + 5 = _____ | 6 + 6 + 6 + 6 = _____ |
|---|---|---|
| | | |
| | | |

**2** How many apples are in the box? How do you know?

**3** How many lemons are in the box? How do you know?

**4** How many oranges are in the boxes below? How do you know?

**5** In the set of stamps below, each stamp costs the same. Decide how much the stamps should cost. Then, find out how much the entire set of stamps cost. Show your work.

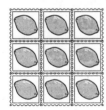

**6** **CHALLENGE** Now make up your own set of stamps. Decide how many stamps you want, how they should be arranged, and how much they cost in all. Show your work.

# Work Place Instructions 2A Loops & Groups

## Each pair of players needs:

- two 2A Loops & Groups Record Sheets
- a die numbered 1–6

**1** Player 1 rolls the die and draws that number of loops. Player 1 rolls a second time to see how many shapes to draw in each loop. Player 1 records the multiplication equation that is represented by the picture.

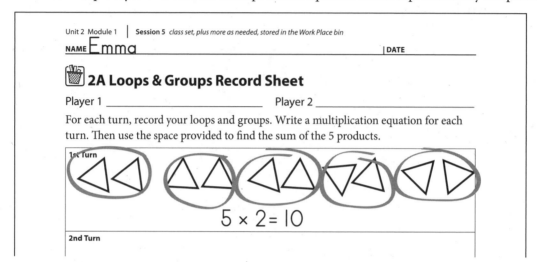

**2** Player 2 repeats step 1 and records their work on their own record sheet.

**3** The game continues for a total of 5 rounds.

**4** At the end of the game, each player finds the sum of their 5 products.

**5** Players share their sums and addition strategies with each other. The player with the highest total wins.

## Game Variations

**A** Players can make a list of numbers from 1 to 36. As they play, players make a tally mark next to each product they get. Players make observations about which products occur the most and least often. Will they be able to put a tally mark next to every number?

**B** Players use a die numbered 4–9. How does the game change with a different die?

# Seascape A: How Long? How Tall?

Chloe the Clownfish is 4 inches long in real life. Use this information to figure out how long, wide or tall some of the other species in Seascape A are.

- Work with a partner.
- Use any materials available to you.
- Show your work in the space provided. Use pictures, numbers, or words to explain your thinking.

**1** The sea anemone is _____ wide.

**2** The parrotfish is __7__ long.

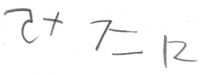

**3** The triggerfish is _____ long.

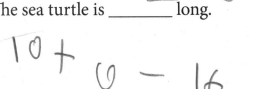

**4** The sea turtle is _____ long.

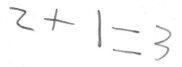

**5** The basket sea star is _____ wide.

**6** The vase sponge is _____ wide.

## Seascape B: How Long? How Tall?

Chloe the Clownfish is 4 inches long in real life. Use this information to figure out how long, wide or tall some of the other species in Seascape B are.

- Work with a partner.
- Use any materials available to you.
- Show your work in the space provided. Use pictures, numbers, or words to explain your thinking.

**1** The brain coral is _____ wide.

**2** The sand tiger shark is _____ long.

**3** Tube sponge A is _____ tall.

**4** Tube sponge B is _____ tall.

**5** The moray eel is _____ long.

**6** Find the length, width, or height of one other living thing in this seascape.

**7** **CHALLENGE** The shorter sea grass is _____ tall.

NAME _____ | DATE _____

## Coral Reef Challenges

Complete the following problems. Show your work using numbers, sketches or words.

**1** Chloe the Clownfish is 4 inches long. She swims past a sea anemone that is 3 times as wide as she is long. How wide is the sea anemone?

3 + 3 + 3 + 3 = 12

**2** Now Chloe swims past a sea turtle that is 3 times as long as the sea anemone is wide. How long is the sea turtle? (You will need to use your answer from problem 1 to answer this question.)

R + 12 + 12 = 36

**3** How much does this set of stamps cost?

3

2 + 1 = = 3  2 ∧ 1 =

**4** For the set of stamps below, decide how much the stamps should cost. Each stamp costs the same. Then, find out how much the entire set of stamps cost. Show your work.

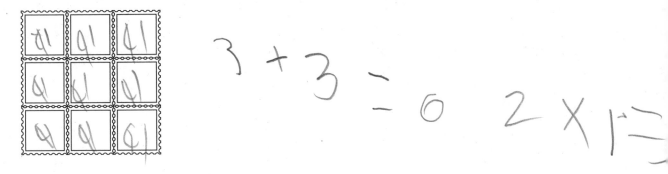

3 + 3 = 6   2 × 1 =

**5** Solve the following equations:

4 + 10 = 14          15 = 8 + 7          13 = 7 + 8

17 − 10 = 7          4 = 13 − 9          13 = 19 − 6

**If You Bake a Cupcake for a Kid ...**

Complete the following problems. Show your work using numbers, sketches, or words.

**1** Mrs. Biddle made some cupcakes for her 3 children. She made 2 cupcakes for each child. How many cupcakes did Mrs. Biddle make?

**2** Then Mrs. Biddle's 3 children all wanted to bring cupcakes to their friends. Mrs. Biddle made 12 more cupcakes. If each child got the same amount of cupcakes, how many cupcakes could each child share?

**3** Next, Mrs. Biddle's 3 children wanted to bring cupcakes to their classes at school. If each child had 20 students in their class, how many cupcakes does Mrs. Biddle need to make?

**4** One large tray of cupcakes has 4 times as many cupcakes as another tray, which has 20 cupcakes on it. Which equation describes this situation?

   ◯  $20 - 4 = c$    ◯  $4 \times c = 20$    ◯  $c + 4 = 20$    ◯  $20 \times 4 = c$

**5** Mrs. Biddle's daughter, Flora, brought a tray of cupcakes to school. The tray had a 4-by-6 array of cupcakes. On the way to school, Flora tripped, and 4 cupcakes fell into a mud puddle. The rest of the cupcakes stayed on the tray. How many cupcakes are still on the tray?

NAME | DATE

 **Toby Goes Shopping**

Toby went shopping with some of his classmates.

**1** Toby's classmates split up into 4 groups of 5 students. Which equation matches that situation?

○ $4 \times 5 = 20$     ○ $4 + 9 = 5$     ○ $4 + 5 = 9$     ○ $5 - 4 = 1$

**2** Use numbers, sketches, or words to show your thinking.

**a** Toby saw fruit at the store. There were 6 rows of 3 peaches in a box. How many peaches were in the box?

**b** Toby's sister picked up a loaf of bread that was 20 inches long. The basket is 3 times as long as the bread. How long is the basket?

**c** Toby bought some stamps. How much did he pay for these stamps?

**d** **CHALLENGE** Toby saw a tray of little pies. How much does the whole tray of pies cost?

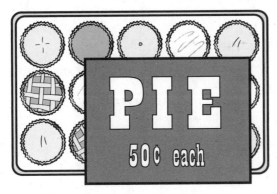

NAME _____ | DATE _____

 **Seascape Challenges**

**1** Chloe the Clownfish is 4 inches long. She swims past a vase sponge that is 7 times as wide as she is long.

**a** How wide is the vase sponge? Use pictures, numbers, or words to show your work.

**b** Write an equation for this problem. _____

**2** Chloe swims through some sea grass. The sea grass is 9 times taller than Chloe's length.

**a** How tall is the sea grass? Use pictures, numbers, or words to show your work.

**b** Write an equation for this problem. _____

**3** Chloe swims away from an octopus. One of its arms is 24 inches long.

**a** How many times longer than Chloe is the arm of the octopus? Use pictures, numbers, or words to show your work.

**b** Write an equation for this problem. _____

**4** Write your own Chloe story problem. Include an equation with the problem and the answer.

**46**

NAME | DATE

# Number Line Puzzles

Fill in the blanks on each of the number lines below.

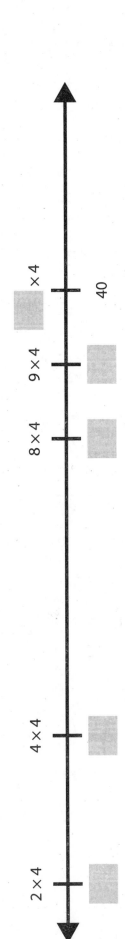

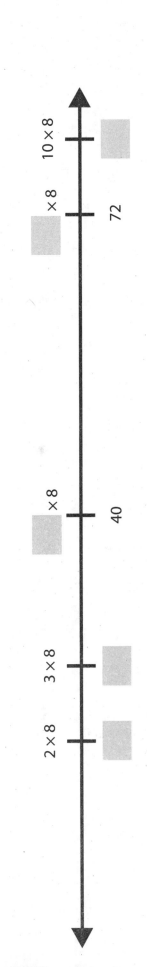

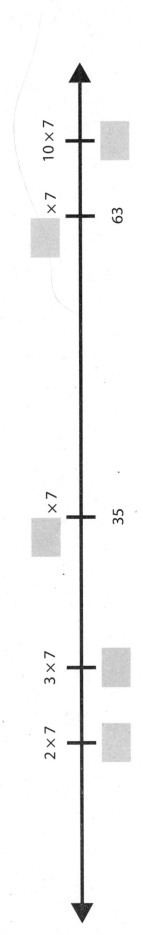

# Work Place Instructions 2B Frog Jump Multiplication

## Each pair of players needs:

- 1 die numbered 1–6
- their own Work Place 2B Frog Jump Multiplication Record Sheets

1    Each player takes a turn rolling the die. The player with the higher roll goes first.

2    The first player rolls the die twice and records the rolls. The first number shows how many jumps to take along the number line. The second number shows the size of each jump.

3    The player predicts (or determines) where they will land after taking the jumps and explains their prediction to their partner.

4    The player makes the jumps and writes a multiplication equation to show the results.

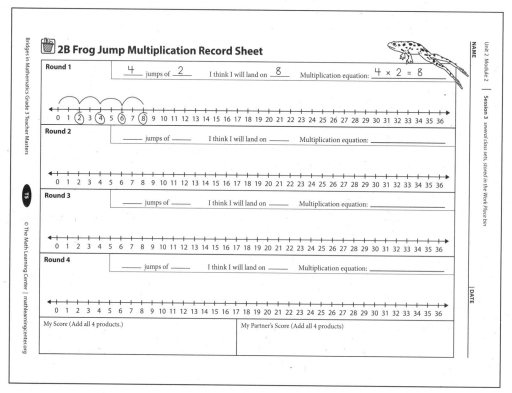

5    Players take turns until each player has had four turns.

6    At the end of the game, players add their four products. The player with the higher sum wins.

**NAME** _____ | **DATE** _____

 ## Windows & Number Puzzles page 1 of 2

## Windows

**1** Find the number of panes in each window. Show your thinking with words, numbers, or pictures. Write an equation that shows your thinking for each window.

**a** Equation _____

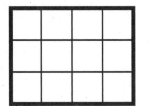

**b** Equation _____

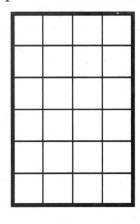

**c** Equation _____

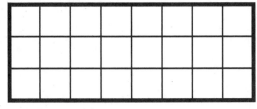

**d** Equation _____

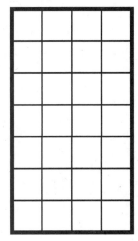

*(continued on next page)*

**NAME** _____ **DATE** _____

## Windows & Number Puzzles page 2 of 2

## Number Puzzles

**2** Find the missing numbers in the equations below.

$2 \times \underline{\hspace{1cm}} = 12$ $\underline{\hspace{1cm}} + 3 = 11$ $10 \times 3 = \underline{\hspace{1cm}}$

$5 + \underline{\hspace{1cm}} = 14$ $17 - 9 = \underline{\hspace{1cm}}$ $\underline{\hspace{1cm}} - 3 = 9$

$6 \times 3 = \underline{\hspace{1cm}}$ $16 - \underline{\hspace{1cm}} = 8$ $\underline{\hspace{1cm}} + 6 = 13$

# More Number Line Puzzles

Use multiplication to help solve these puzzles. Fill in each of the blanks on both lines.

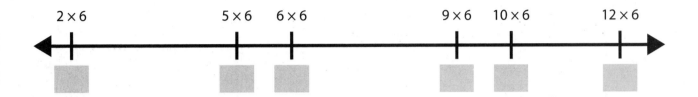

$2 \times 6$       $5 \times 6$   $6 \times 6$      $9 \times 6$   $10 \times 6$    $12 \times 6$

$4 \times 4$   $5 \times 4$   $6 \times 4$      $9 \times 4$   $10 \times 4$   $11 \times 4$

**NAME** _____ | **DATE** _____

 **The Watertown Bank** page 1 of 2

**1** On Wednesday, Wally was cleaning the windows at the bank. He counted the windowpanes as he cleaned, but he kept losing track of how many panes he had counted. Help Wally figure out how many windowpanes there are at the bank. As you solve each problem below, show your work with numbers, sketches, or words.

**a**

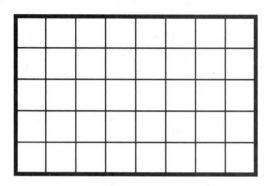

**b**

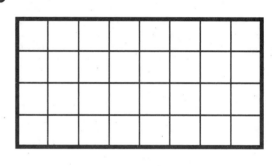

**c**

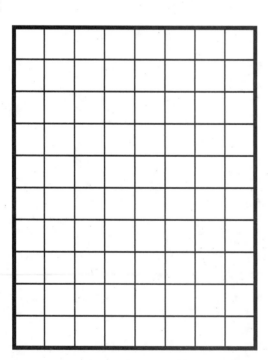

**d**

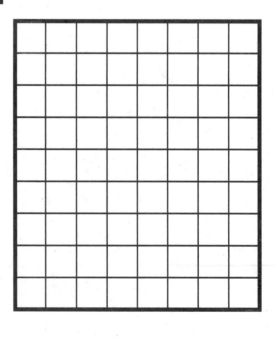

*(continued on next page)*

**52**

NAME | DATE

## The Watertown Bank page 2 of 2

**2** Wally cleaned a window that had 4 windowpanes. Then he cleaned 9 more windowpanes. Which equation describes the number of panes he cleaned?

○ $4 \times 9 = w$            ○ $4 + 9 = w$

○ $9 - w = 4$               ○ $4 \times w = 9$

**3** Wally cleaned a window that had 4 rows of windowpanes with 9 panes in each row. Which equation describes the number of panes in the window?

○ $4 \times 9 = w$            ○ $4 + 9 = w$

○ $9 - w = 4$               ○ $4 \times w = 9$

**More Post Office Mailboxes**

Help Wally figure out how many mailboxes there are on this wall. Use numbers, sketches, or words to show your thinking. Mark your answer clearly.

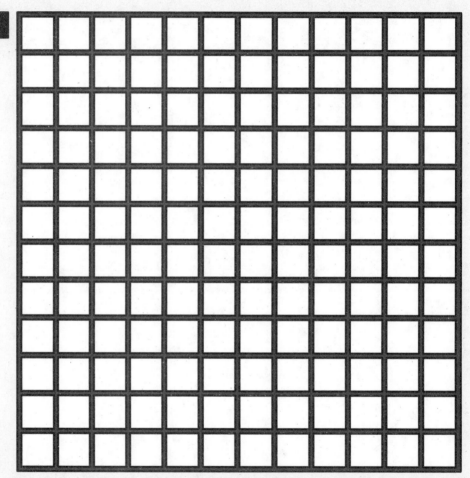

MAILBOXES

**Work Place Instructions 2C Cover Up**

### Each pair of players needs:

- 1 spinner overlay to share
- their own 2C Cover Up Record Sheets

1    Players take turns spinning the same spinner. The player with the higher spin goes first.

2    The first player spins both spinners and draws an array with those dimensions on their grid.

3    The player explains to their partner how to find the product represented by the array (the area of the array).

4    The player writes the total product on the array and writes an equation on the line under the grid.

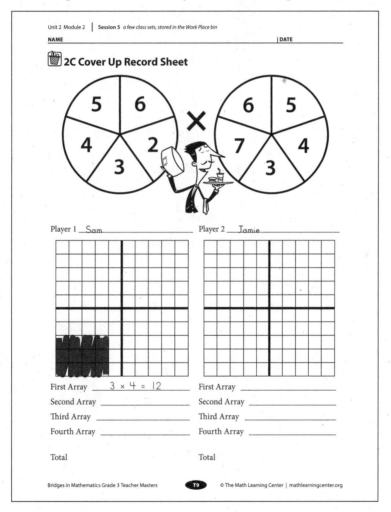

5    Play continues until each player has had four turns.

*If a player spins dimensions for an array that will not fit on the grid, they lose that turn.*

6    At the end of the game, players add their products. The player whose total is closest to 100 wins.

**NAME** _____ | **DATE** _____

 **Watertown Center**

Watertown Center is the biggest building in Watertown. There are many businesses, offices, and stores inside Watertown Center.

**1** On Thursday, Wally was cleaning the windows of Watertown Center. There were so many windowpanes that he had no idea how to count them all. Help Wally figure out how many windowpanes are in the front of Watertown Center. Show your work.

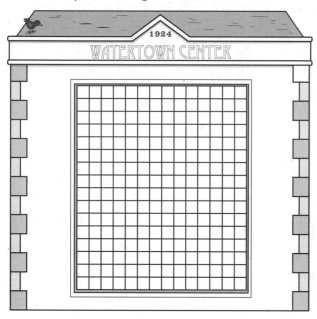

**2** Fill in the missing numbers.

$2 \times 7$    $4 \times 7$    $8 \times 7$    $9 \times 7$    $\boxed{\phantom{0}} \times 7$    $12 \times 7$

70

**3** Solve the following problems.

$2 \times 9 =$ _____        $4 \times 9 =$ _____        $8 \times 9 =$ _____

$10 \times 9 =$ _____        $9 \times 9 =$ _____

**56**

# Multiplication Table

Key:
- [ ] Zero facts (× 0)
- [ ] Ones facts (× 1)
- [ ] Doubles facts (× 2)
- [ ] Doubles Plus One Set facts (× 3)
- [ ] Double-Doubles facts (× 4)
- [ ] Half-Tens facts (× 5)
- [ ] Half-Tens Plus One Set facts (× 6)
- [ ] Double-Double-Doubles facts (× 8)
- [ ] Tens Minus One Set facts (× 9)
- [ ] Tens facts (× 10)

| × | 0 | 1 | 2 | 3 | 4 | 5 | 6 | 7 | 8 | 9 | 10 |
|---|---|---|---|---|---|---|---|---|---|---|---|
| **0** | 0×0 = 0 | 0×1 = 0 | 0×2 = 0 | 0×3 = 0 | 0×4 = 0 | 0×5 = 0 | 0×6 = 0 | 0×7 = 0 | 0×8 = 0 | 0×9 = 0 | 0×10 = 0 |
| **1** | 1×0 = 0 | 1×1 = 1 | 1×2 = 2 | 1×3 = 3 | 1×4 = 4 | 1×5 = 5 | 1×6 = 6 | 1×7 = 7 | 1×8 = 8 | 1×9 = 9 | 1×10 = 10 |
| **2** | 2×0 = 0 | 2×1 = 2 | 2×2 = 4 | 2×3 = 6 | 2×4 = 8 | 2×5 = 10 | 2×6 = 12 | 2×7 = 14 | 2×8 = 16 | 2×9 = 18 | 2×10 = 20 |
| **3** | 3×0 = 0 | 3×1 = 3 | 3×2 = 6 | 3×3 = 9 | 3×4 = 12 | 3×5 = 15 | 3×6 = 18 | 3×7 = 21 | 3×8 = 24 | 3×9 = 27 | 3×10 = 30 |
| **4** | 4×0 = 0 | 4×1 = 4 | 4×2 = 8 | 4×3 = 12 | 4×4 = 16 | 4×5 = 20 | 4×6 = 24 | 4×7 = 28 | 4×8 = 32 | 4×9 = 36 | 4×10 = 40 |
| **5** | 5×0 = 0 | 5×1 = 5 | 5×2 = 10 | 5×3 = 15 | 5×4 = 20 | 5×5 = 25 | 5×6 = 30 | 5×7 = 35 | 5×8 = 40 | 5×9 = 45 | 5×10 = 50 |
| **6** | 6×0 = 0 | 6×1 = 6 | 6×2 = 12 | 6×3 = 18 | 6×4 = 24 | 6×5 = 30 | 6×6 = 36 | 6×7 = 42 | 6×8 = 48 | 6×9 = 54 | 6×10 = 60 |
| **7** | 7×0 = 0 | 7×1 = 7 | 7×2 = 14 | 7×3 = 21 | 7×4 = 28 | 7×5 = 35 | 7×6 = 42 | 7×7 = 49 | 7×8 = 56 | 7×9 = 63 | 7×10 = 70 |
| **8** | 8×0 = 0 | 8×1 = 8 | 8×2 = 16 | 8×3 = 24 | 8×4 = 32 | 8×5 = 40 | 8×6 = 48 | 8×7 = 56 | 8×8 = 64 | 8×9 = 72 | 8×10 = 80 |
| **9** | 9×0 = 0 | 9×1 = 9 | 9×2 = 18 | 9×3 = 27 | 9×4 = 36 | 9×5 = 45 | 9×6 = 54 | 9×7 = 63 | 9×8 = 72 | 9×9 = 81 | 9×10 = 90 |
| **10** | 10×0 = 0 | 10×1 = 10 | 10×2 = 20 | 10×3 = 30 | 10×4 = 40 | 10×5 = 50 | 10×6 = 60 | 10×7 = 70 | 10×8 = 80 | 10×9 = 90 | 10×10 = 100 |

NAME _____ | DATE _____

 **Wendell's Windows**

For Problems 1 and 2, show your work using pictures, numbers, or words. Then write an equation for the problem.

**1** Wally is cleaning the windows of the grocery store. Each window has 7 rows of windowpanes. Each row has 6 windowpanes. How many windowpanes does Wally need to clean in each window?

Equation: _____

**2** Wally's son Wendell helps Wally with the windows. For each day that Wendell helps with the windows, Wally gives him $3. How much money does Wendell have if he helps with the windows for 7 days?

Equation: _____

**3** Complete the Number Line Puzzle below.

**4** Skip-counting:

**a** Fill in the blanks.

| 9 | | 27 | | | 54 | | | 81 |
|---|---|----|---|---|----|---|---|----|

**b** How many 9s are in 63? _____ How do you know?

NAME | DATE

 **Pet Store Price List: Rabbit Food**

**1** Fill in the table.

| Rabbit Food $1.50 per pound | |
|---|---|
| **Number of Pounds** | **Cost** |
| 1 | $1.50 |
| 2 | $3.00 |
| 4 | $6.00 |
| | $9.00 |
| 10 | 15.00 |
| 20 | 2.00 |
| 40 | .00 |

2 50+50 = $

30+30=60
15+15=30

**2** If you paid $16.50 for rabbit food, how many pounds did you buy? Show your thinking.

60 $

NAME _____ | DATE _____

 **Pet Store Lists**

**1** Complete the following price lists.

| Dog Collars $3 each | |
|---|---|
| **Number of Collars** | **Cost** |
| 1 | $3 |
| 2 | |
| | $9 |
| 4 | |
| 10 | |

| Dog Toys $2 each | |
|---|---|
| **Number of Toys** | **Cost** |
| 1 | $2 |
| 2 | |
| | $10 |
| 10 | |
| 20 | $40 |

**2** **CHALLENGE** Now, make up your own price list. Decide what items you are selling and how much each costs, and fill in the table.

| Title: | |
|---|---|
| **Number of** | **Cost** |
| 1 | |
| | |
| | |
| | |
| | |

NAME _____ | DATE _____

 **Array Challenges**

Find the number of squares in each array. You may use any strategy that works for you. Use numbers, sketches, or words to explain how you found the number of squares. If it helps, you can draw on the array. The example may help.

**ex a** How many squares are there in the array below?

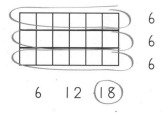

6
6
6

6   12   18

**b** CHALLENGE Write at least one equation that describes the array.

$6 \times 3 = 18$     $3 \times 6 = 18$

**1 a** How many squares are there in the array below?

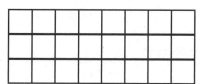

**b** CHALLENGE Write at least one equation that describes the array.

**2 a** How many squares are there in the array below?

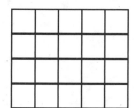

**b** CHALLENGE Write at least one equation that describes the array.

**3** Complete the equations below.

$7 \times \underline{\hspace{1cm}} = 35$         $\underline{\hspace{1cm}} \times 6 = 9 \times 2$         $\underline{\hspace{1cm}} = 10 \times 6$

$5 \times 10 = \underline{\hspace{1cm}} \times 2$         $3 \times \underline{\hspace{1cm}} = 21$         $\underline{\hspace{1cm}} \times 5 = 10 \times 3$

**Multiplication Patterns**

**1 a** Solve the following problems:

$3 \times 5 =$ _____          $5 \times 2 =$ _____          $7 \times 5 =$ _____

$6 \times 5 =$ _____          $4 \times 6 =$ _____          $9 \times 6 =$ _____

$4 \times 3 =$ _____          $3 \times 3 =$ _____          $8 \times 3 =$ _____

**b** Which of the problems above have even products?

**c** Which of the problems above have odd products?

**2** Does $6 \times 7$ have an odd product or an even product? Why?

**3** Write and solve one multiplication problem with an odd product and one multiplication problem with an even product.

**NAME** _____ | **DATE** _____

# Ice Cream Bar Graph

Title _Favorite icecream Flvr_

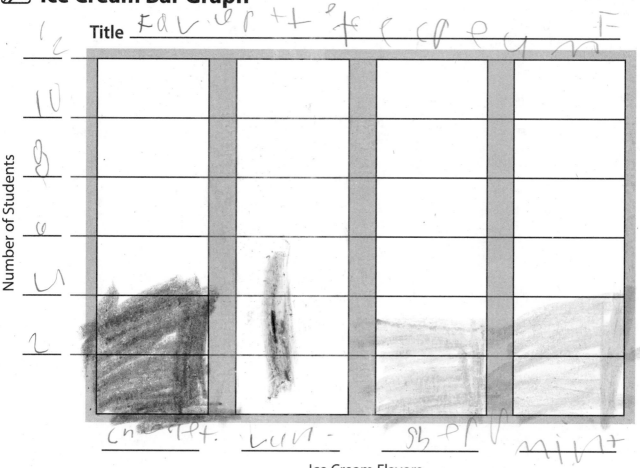

_chocolet._   _van-_   _strbv_   _mint_

Ice Cream Flavors

**1** Which is our class favorite? _____

**2** Which flavor is the least favorite? _____

**3** Write at least 3 other observations about your graph.

**4** This kind of graph is called a bar graph. The other graph you made is called a picture graph. Which kind of graph do you think is better? Why?

# Work Place Instructions 2D Doubles Help

## Each pair of players needs:

- 1 spinner overlay to share
- their own 2D Doubles Help Record Sheets

**1**  Players work together to complete the Doubles facts in the bottom row on the record sheet.

**2**  Players take turns spinning the second spinner. The player with the higher spin goes first.

**3**  The first player spins both spinners to make a multiplication fact.

**4**  The player solves the multiplication fact and writes an equation for that fact in the column on the record sheet that shows the Doubles fact that can be used to solve it.

For example, if a player spins $3 \times 7$, they can write an equation for this fact in the $2 \times 7$ column, because you can use $2 \times 7$ plus another 7 to solve $3 \times 7$.

**5**  Players take turns until one player has written at least one equation in each column.

- If a player spins a fact for a second time, they write an equation for that fact beneath the column.
- Players can write more than one equation in each column by spinning different facts that can be solved using the same Doubles fact to help.
- Writing more than one fact in each column does not improve a player's chance of winning.

**6**  The first player to write at least one equation in each column wins.

If players run out of time before someone writes an equation in each column, the player with equations in the most columns wins.

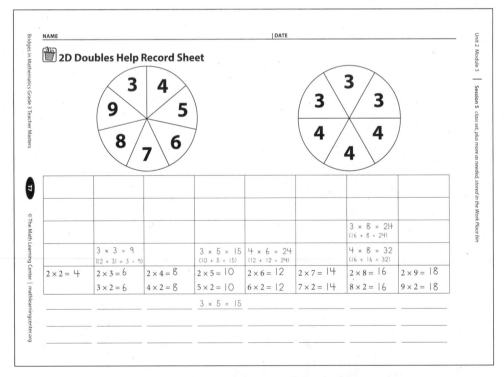

How one player's record sheet might look after 6 turns.

NAME _____ | DATE _____

 **Favorite Ice Cream**

**1** Look at the graphs below and then answer the questions.

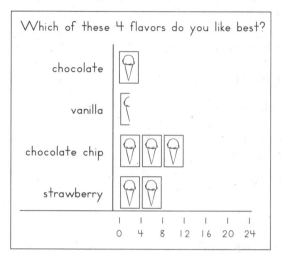

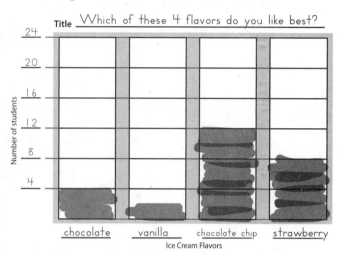

**a** This class took a survey of their favorite ice cream. The results are shown above. Fill in the table:

| Favorite Ice Cream | | | | |
|---|---|---|---|---|
| **Number of Kids** | | | | |
| **Cones** | $\frac{1}{2}$ | 1 | 2 | 3 |

**b** How many kids are in the class? Explain how you know.

**c** How many more students voted for strawberry than vanilla? _____

**d** How many more students voted for chocolate chip than chocolate? _____

**e** How many students did not vote for chocolate chip? _____

**2** Solve the following problems.

_____ × 8 = 32          15 = 9 + _____          8 = 12 − _____          14 − 8 = _____

5 × _____ = 35          9 + _____ = 16          _____ + 13 = 20          9 + _____ = 20

8 × _____ = 56          49 = _____ × 7          18 − _____ = 8          7 = 16 − _____

**NAME** _____ | **DATE** _____

 **Book Bar Graph**

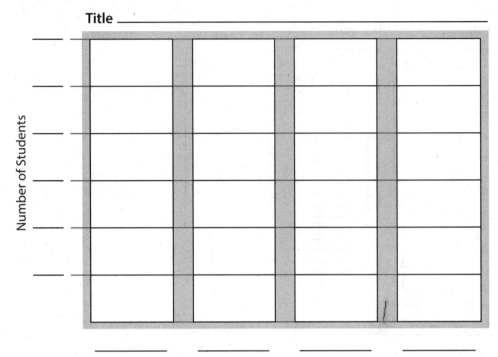

1  Use words or numbers to write at least 4 observations about this graph. Include one word or mathematical symbol from the box in each observation.

2  Name one person who would find it helpful to see your graph. Explain why.

3  This kind of graph is called a bar graph. The other graph you made is called a picture graph. Which kind of graph do you think is easier for people to understand? Why?

**Favorite Books**

**1** Look at the two graphs below and then answer the following questions.

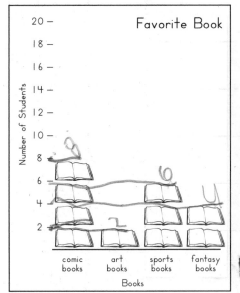 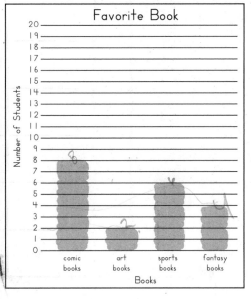 

**a** Do the picture graph and the bar graph above represent the same data?

Yes

**b** How do you know? The hum is smut

**c** Using the picture graph, tell how many students are in the class. Explain how you know.

Look

**d** Using the bar graph, tell how many students are in the class. Explain how you know.

**2** Fill in the blanks:

$2 \times 4$      $4 \times 4$      $8 \times 4$   $9 \times 4$   $\times 4$

40

**NAME** |DATE

 **Library Books Data & Graph**

Woodlawn Elementary School's librarian Mr. Jackson is keeping track of the kinds of books students check out. This chart shows the number of each kind of book the third graders have checked out so far this year.

| Genre | Fiction or Nonfiction | Number of Books Checked Out |
| --- | --- | --- |
| Adventure | F | 32 |
| Art & Crafts | N | 16 |
| Biography | N | 12 |
| Fantasy | F | 10 |
| Fiction | F | 33 |
| Graphic Novels | F | 29 |
| Science | N | 15 |
| Sports | N | 8 |

The third grade teachers want to know more about what their students are reading. Create a bar graph showing the information Mr. Jackson collected. Each cell in the graph stands for 4 books checked out. Label and title your graph.

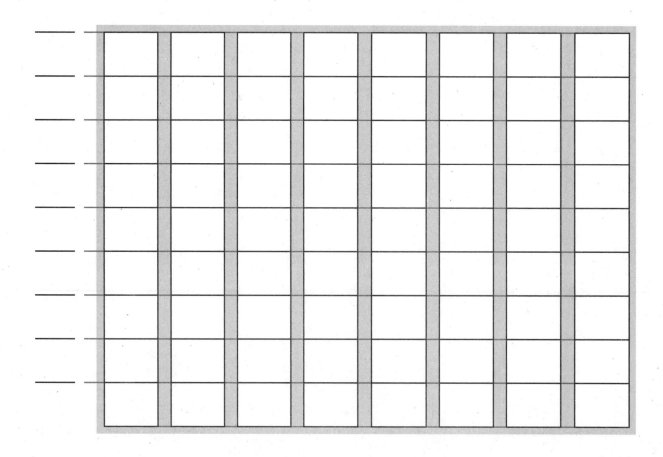

**Library Books Problems**

Use the Library Books Data & Graph you just completed to solve these problems. Show all of your work for problems 3 and 4.

**1** Which kind of book was checked out the most? How many of them were checked out?

**2** Which kind of book was checked out the least? How many of them were checked out?

**3** How many more of the most popular kind of book (see problem 1) were checked out than the least popular kind of book (see problem 2)?

**4** Each kind of book is either fiction or nonfiction.

**a** Which kind of book—fiction or nonfiction—was checked out more?

**b** Exactly how many more of the most popular kind of book (fiction or nonfiction) were checked out?

**5** The librarian noticed that students checked out 21 more of one kind of book than another. Which two kinds of books is the librarian comparing?

**6** **CHALLENGE** There are some kinds of books that students checked out twice as many of as other books. Name as many pairs of books as you can where students checked out two times more of one than the other.

**Gift Wrap Fundraiser**

The students in Ms. Carter's class sold gift wrap to raise money for new playground equipment. The line plot below shows how many rolls of gift wrap the students sold.

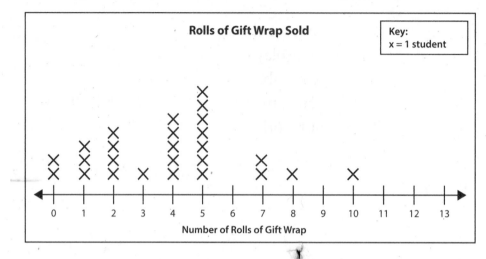

**1** How many students are in the class? Explain how you know.


**2** How many students sold 7 rolls of gift wrap? _____

**3** How many rolls of gift wrap did most of the students sell? _____

**4** Sarah sold more gift wrap than anyone else. How many rolls did she sell? _____

**5** How many rolls of gift wrap were sold in all? Show your work. (Hint: Be careful here. The answer is NOT the total number of Xs on the line plot.)






**6** Fill in the table.

| Cars | 1 | 2 | | | 10 |
|------|---|---|----|----|---|
| Tires | 4 | | 16 | 20 | |

**More Library Books Problems** page 1 of 2

Mr. Jackson is the librarian at Woodlawn Elementary School. He loves to learn about what his students are interested in and like to read so that he can get new books for the library.

**1** Mr. Jackson got some new books for the library, all of which are the same size. He wants to display them for the students and teachers. He put the same number of books on each shelf, as you can see in the picture. How many books are displayed on the shelves in all? Show your work.

**2** The students at Woodlawn love fantasy fiction, so Mr. Jackson ordered some popular series of fantasy books. There are 7 books in the series by one of the most popular fantasy authors. Mr. Jackson decided to buy 4 sets of that series for the library. The students liked those books so much that Mr. Jackson bought 4 sets of another series that includes 5 books. How many new fantasy books did Mr. Jackson buy in all? Show your work.

**3** The students at Woodlawn love science, so Mr. Jackson bought a set of science books for them that included 10 different books. Five of the books were 3 inches thick, 3 were 2 inches thick, and 2 were 1 inch thick. How much space will he need to keep them together on the shelf? Show your work.

*(continued on next page)*

**NAME** | **DATE**

## More Library Books Problems page 2 of 2

The PTA had a fundraiser and they gave some of the money they raised to Mr. Jackson to buy even more books for the library. Mr. Jackson asked some of the teachers to help him decide what to buy. They listed the following books.

| Book | Cost Per Book | Number to Buy |
|------|---------------|---------------|
| The Mystery of the Purple Python | $6 | 3 |
| A Trip to Mars | $7 | 4 |
| The Haunted School Gym | $5 | 4 |
| The Great Book of Food Jokes | $4 | 6 |

**4** After Mr. Jackson figured out how much those books would cost, he saw that he had $85 left to spend. How much money did the PTA give him to start with? Show your work.

**5** Write a story problem about this picture. Solve the problem in your journal, and then trade problems with a classmate. You can add more information—like titles, author names, and prices—to the picture to use in your story problem.

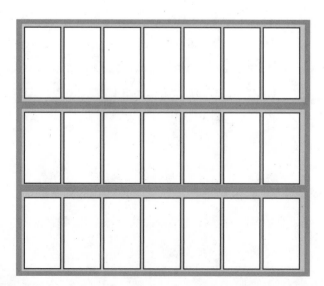

NAME _____ | DATE _____

 **Mr. White's Pencil Survey**

**1** Mr. White did the pencil survey with his class. The line plot below shows his survey results. Study the line plot below and then answer the questions.

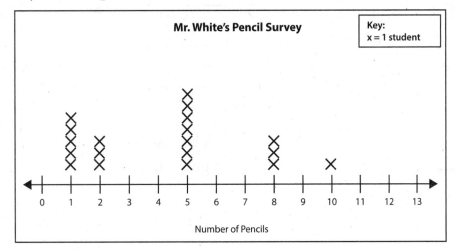

**a** How many students had 3 pencils? _____

**b** How many students had 8 pencils? _____

**c** How many students took part in this survey? _____

**d** How many more students had 5 pencils than had 2 pencils? _____

**e** How many total pencils were found? (Hint: Be careful! The answer is not 19 pencils.)

**2** Fill in the blanks.

3 + _____ = 15        _____ − 5 = 9        16 = _____ + 8        13 = 7 + _____

**3** Solve the following problems.

3 + 3 + 3 + 3 + 3 = _____        8 + 8 + 8 = _____

10 + 10 + 10 + 10 = _____        9 + 9 = _____

**4** Write one of the problems above as a multiplication equation.

**73**

**NAME** _____ |**DATE** _____

 **On Your Own**

**1** Today you will write and design your own problems, based on your work in Unit 2. Read all of the challenges first. You can go in any order—start with whichever challenge you like! Try to write problems that are just right for you to solve, not too easy and not too hard.

**a** Write and solve a multiplication problem involving windowpanes.

Write an equation that describes this problem. _____

**b** Write and solve a multiplication problem involving items at a pet store.

Write an equation that describes this problem. _____

**c** Write and solve a multiplication problem involving coral reef species.

Write an equation that describes this problem. _____

**2** Now solve this story problem: You are playing the Carrot Grab game. You are on 117. You spin "Hop 2 tens" and roll a sum of 8. Where do you land? Describe how you would move in order to get the most carrots.

NAME _____ |DATE _____

##  Multiplication & Division Fact Families

**1** The fact family that belongs with each array is missing an equation. Write the missing equation for each fact family.

| | |
|---|---|
| **ex** $3 \times 4 = 12$ <br> $\underline{4} \times \underline{3} = \underline{12}$ <br> $12 \div 3 = 4$ <br> $12 \div 4 = 3$ | **a** $10 \times 3 = 30$ <br> $\underline{\phantom{0}} \times \underline{\phantom{0}} = \underline{\phantom{0}}$ <br> $30 \div 3 = 10$ <br> $30 \div 10 = 3$ 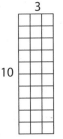 |
| **b** $2 \times 9 = 18$ <br> $\underline{\phantom{0}} \times \underline{\phantom{0}} = \underline{\phantom{0}}$ <br> $18 \div 2 = 9$ <br> $18 \div 9 = 2$ 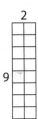 | **c** $5 \times 8 = 40$ <br> $8 \times 5 = 40$ <br> $\underline{\phantom{0}} \div \underline{\phantom{0}} = \underline{\phantom{0}}$ <br> $40 \div 8 = 5$ 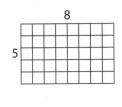 |

**2** Fill in the missing number in each triangle and then write the fact family.

| | |
|---|---|
| **ex** 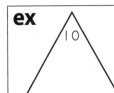 $\underline{2} \times \underline{5} = \underline{10}$ <br> $\underline{5} \times \underline{2} = \underline{10}$ <br> $\underline{10} \div \underline{2} = \underline{5}$ <br> $\underline{10} \div \underline{5} = \underline{2}$ | **a** 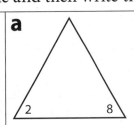 $\underline{\phantom{0}} \times \underline{\phantom{0}} = \underline{\phantom{0}}$ <br> $\underline{\phantom{0}} \times \underline{\phantom{0}} = \underline{\phantom{0}}$ <br> $\underline{\phantom{0}} \div \underline{\phantom{0}} = \underline{\phantom{0}}$ <br> $\underline{\phantom{0}} \div \underline{\phantom{0}} = \underline{\phantom{0}}$ |
| **b** 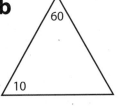 $\underline{\phantom{0}} \times \underline{\phantom{0}} = \underline{\phantom{0}}$ <br> $\underline{\phantom{0}} \times \underline{\phantom{0}} = \underline{\phantom{0}}$ <br> $\underline{\phantom{0}} \div \underline{\phantom{0}} = \underline{\phantom{0}}$ <br> $\underline{\phantom{0}} \div \underline{\phantom{0}} = \underline{\phantom{0}}$ | **c** 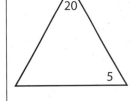 $\underline{\phantom{0}} \times \underline{\phantom{0}} = \underline{\phantom{0}}$ <br> $\underline{\phantom{0}} \times \underline{\phantom{0}} = \underline{\phantom{0}}$ <br> $\underline{\phantom{0}} \div \underline{\phantom{0}} = \underline{\phantom{0}}$ <br> $\underline{\phantom{0}} \div \underline{\phantom{0}} = \underline{\phantom{0}}$ |

# Work Place Instructions 3A Round Ball Tens

## Each pair of players needs:

- 1 Round Ball Tens Record Sheet to share
- 1 spinner overlay
- scratch paper

**1** Player 1 spins each spinner and writes the two numbers on a sheet of scratch paper. If the arrow lands on the line, he spins again.

**2** Player 1 decides which number to use in the tens place and which number to use in the ones place.

In the example below, 4 and 6 could be used to make 46 or 64.

- 46 rounds to 50
- 64 rounds to 60

In this example, 64 was chosen, so 64 was recorded in the basket marked 60.

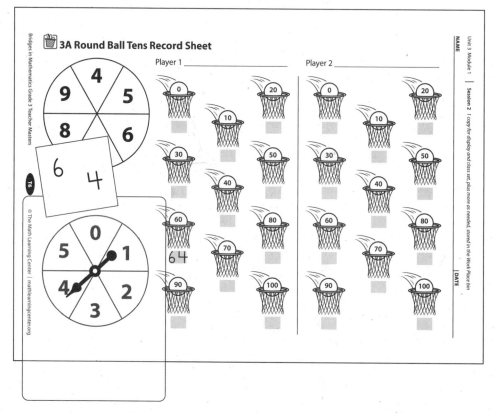

**3** Players continue taking turns spinning both spinners and deciding how to arrange the two numbers.

If both baskets for the numbers spun already have numbers in them, players can write the number they choose next to one of the baskets.

**4** The first player to get at least one number in each basket wins. If players run out of time, the player with numbers in the most baskets wins the game.

## Game Variation

**A** Players can put only one number in or near a basket. If they cannot put either of their numbers in a basket, they lose their turn.

NAME _____ | DATE _____

# Write & Solve Your Own Problems

Fill in the blanks with words that make sense and seem interesting. Solve each problem.
Show your work.

| Fill in the blanks. | Work space |
|---|---|
| **1** Sara has 35 _socks_ in her top drawer. She has 28 _shirts_ in her bottom drawer. How many are there in all? _63_ | 35 20 + 63 |
| **2** Tim spent 26 dollars for a _mathbook_. He spent 18 dollars for a _report_. How much did he spend in all? _44_ | 26 + 18 44 |
| **3** Isabel had 74 _toys_. She gave 26 of them to a friend. How many did she have left? _100_ | 74 + 26 100 |
| **4** Juan baked 4 dozen _____. The dog ate 19 of them. How many are left? _30_ | 48  4 dozen + 19 - 19 30 |
| **5** We saw 102 _____. Then 24 of them flew away. How many were left? _____ | |

#  Work Place Instructions 3B Round & Add Tens

**Each pair of players needs:**
- a record sheet
- a spinner overlay

**1** Players decide who will who will spin and who will record the numbers. Players switch roles for each turn.

**2** Players spin the spinner 4 times to fill in 4 digits on the record sheet.

| Sum of Actual Numbers | Sum of Rounded Numbers | Score |
|---|---|---|
| 3 8 + 5 1 = _____ | ___ ___ + ___ ___ = _____ | |

**3** Players work together to round each number formed to the nearest 10 and fill in the blanks under Sum of Rounded Numbers.

| Sum of Actual Numbers | Sum of Rounded Numbers | Score |
|---|---|---|
| 3 8 + 5 1 = _____ | 4 0 + 5 0 = _____ | |

**4** Players work together to find the sum of the actual numbers and the sum of the rounded numbers.

**5** Players' score is the difference between the sum of the actual numbers and the sum of the rounded numbers.

| Sum of Actual Numbers | Sum of Rounded Numbers | Score |
|---|---|---|
| 3 8 + 5 1 = 89 | 4 0 + 5 0 = 90 | |

**6** Players continue spinning, rounding, and adding until they have played all 5 rounds of the game. Then they add their scores from each round to get their final score.

*Note: Players can work together to play the game a second time and see if they can get a lower score.*

## Game Variations

**A** Students can each use their own record sheet and take turns, each spinning and recording for themselves. Low score wins the game.

**B** Instead of recording the numbers in order as they spin, players can spin all 4 numbers and then use the digits to form the two 2-digit numbers that will yield the lowest score.

**NAME** _____ | **DATE** _____

 ## Adding & Rounding

**1** Solve each problem below. Show your work.

| 92 | 12 | 75 | 145 |
|----|----|----|-----|
| + 48 | + 89 | + 36 | + 230 |

**2** Akiko wants to add 98 and 43. What is an easy way for Akiko to add these two numbers? Solve the problem and show your work.

**3** Jamal is playing Add & Round Tens with a partner. He got a 2, an 8, a 3, and a 7 on his first turn. He wrote them down as he spun them, and wound up with 28 + 37.

   **a** What are his rounded numbers? _____ and _____

   **b** What is the sum of his rounded numbers? _____

   **c** What is the sum of his actual numbers? Show your work.

   **d** What is the difference between the sum of his rounded numbers and the sum of his actual numbers? Show your work.

**4** **CHALLENGE** The next time they played Add & Round Tens, Jamal and his partner decided to change the rules so they can arrange the numbers they spin to make any 2-digit numbers they want. Oh his first turn, Jamal got these four numbers: 2, 4, 7, and 1. Arrange these numbers to get the lowest score possible. (Remember that your score is the difference between the sum of the actual numbers and the sum of the rounded numbers.)

# Work Place Instructions 3C Round Ball Hundreds

## Each pair of players needs:

- 1 Round Ball Hundreds Record Sheet to share
- 1 deck of Number Cards with 10s and wild cards removed
- scratch paper

**1** Players shuffle the remaining cards in the deck and place them face-down in a stack.

**2** Player 1 draws 3 cards off the top of the deck and arranges them to make a 3-digit number. She rounds them to the nearest hundred and records the 3-digit number she made in the appropriate basket.

In the example below, 8, 4, and 6 have been used to make 846. Rounded to the nearest 100, it would be 800, so 846 is recorded in the basket marked 800.

**3** Player 1 puts the used cards in a discard pile and Player 2 draws 3 new cards, arranges them, rounds the number to the nearest hundred, and records this number in the appropriate basket.

**4** Players continue taking turns. They draw 3 cards each time, decide how to arrange the numbers, and round the 3-digit number to determine which basket gets the number.

- If no empty hoops are available for the three possible arrangements of the numbers a player draws, the player misses that turn.
- If players play through the deck, they shuffle the cards and continue playing.

**5** The first player to get a number in every basket wins the game.

**6** When putting the number cards away, players should be sure to return the 0s, 1s, and wild cards to the deck.

## Game Variation

**A** Play Round Ball Thousands. Write another zero at the end of each number on each basketball hoop. Then, draw 4 cards, arrange them as a 4-digit number, round the number to the nearest 1,000, and determine which basket gets the number.

NAME | DATE

 **Rounding**

**1** Round these numbers to the nearest ten.

26 → *30*    73 → *70*    148 → *150*    57 → *60*    261 →

82 → *80*    35 → *40*    912 → *900*    2,179 → *2,100*    444 → *440*

**2** Round these numbers to the nearest hundred.

360 → *400*    452 → *500*    720 → *700*    112 → *400*    680 → *600*

1,241 → *1,000*    870 → *900*    2,550 → *61000*    327 → *100*    5,173 → *2,180*

**3** Round these numbers.

| | to the nearest ten | to the nearest hundred |
|---|---|---|
| 314 | *40* | *60* |
| 5,238 | *30* | *0* |
| 461 | *0* | *40* |
| 7,786 | *0* | *40* |
| 529 | *0* | *40* |
| 8,683 | *0* | *40* |

**4** Solve the following problems.

7 × 6 = _____        _____ × 6 = 24        9 × _____ = 63

2 × 9 = 3 × _____    2 × 8 = _____        6 × _____ = 3 × 10

**NAME** _____ | **DATE** _____

 # Which Makes the Most Sense?

Choose the best estimate for each problem and explain your thinking.
Hint: use rounding to help.

| 49 + 38 | | Why? |
|---|---|---|
| | 70 | 5 ০১ ৪ ০ =৪০ |
| | 80 | |
| | (90) | |

| 98 + 105 | | Why? |
|---|---|---|
| | 150 | 100 + 100 |
| | (200) | |
| | 250 | |

| (55) + (14) | | Why? |
|---|---|---|
| | 60 | |
| | (70) | 60 + 10 = 70 |
| | 80 | |

| 153 + 149 | | Why? |
|---|---|---|
| | (300) | 200 + 100 |
| | 350 | |
| | 400 | |

| 25
+ 73 | | |
|---|---|---|
| | 90 | 30 + 350 |
| | (100) | 50 |
| | 110 | |

| 288
+ 213 | | |
|---|---|---|
| | 400 | 300 + 200 |
| | 450 | |
| | (500) | |

82

## Strategy Match 3

Three students solved the problem 243 + 187. All the students used a number line, but each student solved the problem differently. Match the students' work below to the strategies in the table.

| Solve 243 + 187 = n | |
|---|---|
| **Strategy A** | Add a friendly number that is too big and then go back to adjust. |
| **Strategy B** | Add a friendly number, get to a friendly number, and then add the rest. |
| **Strategy C** | Get to a friendly number right away, add a friendly number, and then add the rest. |

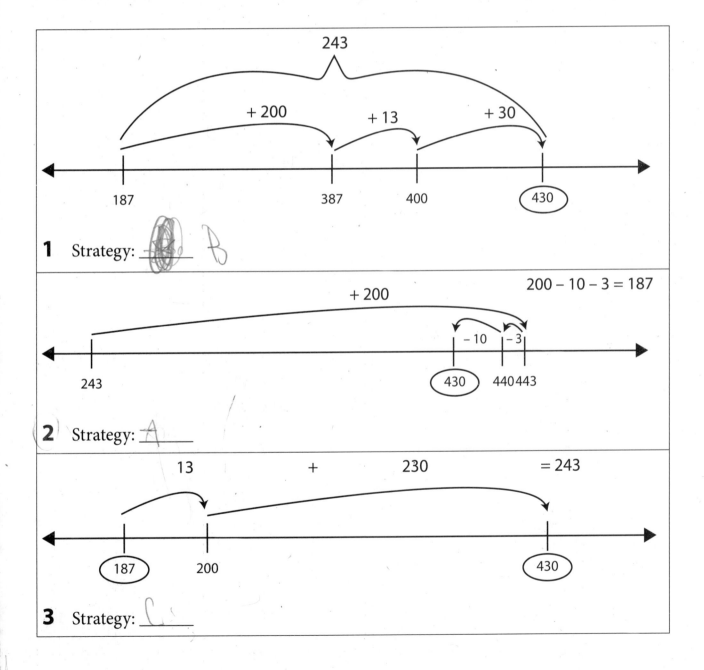

**1** Strategy: _____ B

**2** Strategy: _A_

**3** Strategy: _C_

**Strategy Match 4**

**1** Three students solved a problem using the different strategies shown below.

- Fill in the blanks for each strategy.
- Match the students' work below to the strategies in the table.

| **Solve:** Molly and Sue are playing a game. Molly's score is 82, and Sue's score is 47. How many more points does Molly have? | |
|---|---|
| **Strategy A** | Removal—Take away to a friendly number, then take away a friendly number and adjust. |
| **Strategy B** | Removal—Take away a friendly number and adjust. |
| **Strategy C** | Find the distance (difference) between the numbers. |

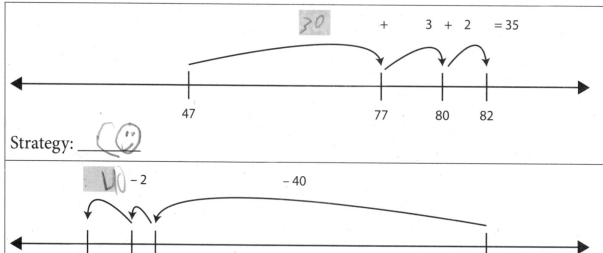

Strategy: _C_

Strategy: _B_

Strategy: _A_

**2** Use the number line below to subtract 76 – 39.

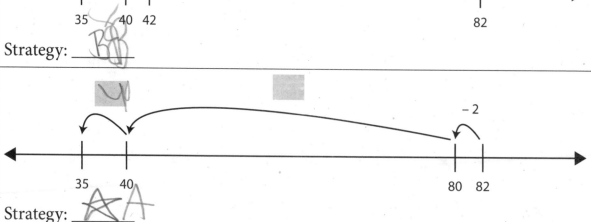

**Strategy Match 5**

Three students solved the problem 91 – 57. All the students used a number line, but each student solved the problem differently. Match the students' work below to the strategies in the table.

| Solve: 91– 57 = n | |
|---|---|
| **Strategy A** | Remove (take away) 57 from 91. |
| **Strategy B** | Find the distance (difference) between the numbers. |
| **Strategy C** | Constant difference—Shift the numbers along the line by the same amount to make the problem easier. |

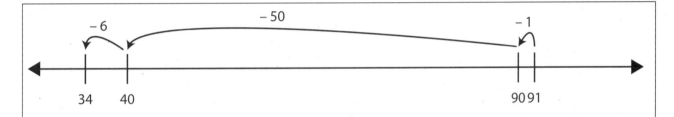

**1** Strategy: _____

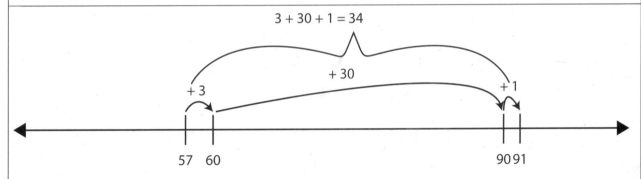

**2** Strategy: _____

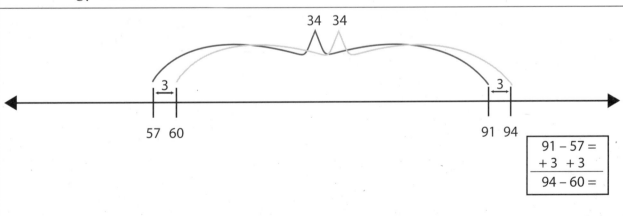

**3** Strategy: _____

**NAME** | **DATE**

 **Strategy Match 6**

Three students solved the problem 71 – 38. All the students used a number line, but each student solved the problem differently.

- Fill in the blanks for each strategy.
- Match the students' work below to the strategies in the table.

| Solve: 71– 38 = *n* | |
|---|---|
| **Strategy A** | Find the distance between 38 and 71. |
| **Strategy B** | Subtract (remove) 38 from 71. |
| **Strategy C** | Add 2 to each number to make the problem easier, then solve the easier problem. |

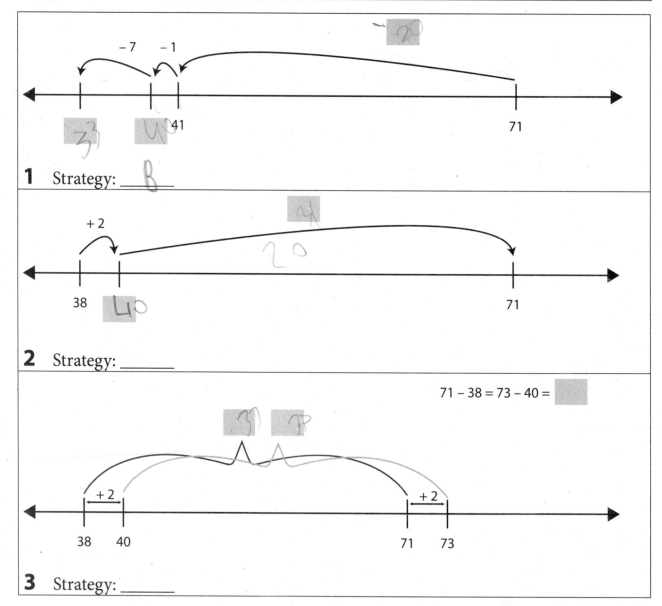

**1** Strategy: _____

**2** Strategy: _____

**3** Strategy: _____

_____  |DATE _____

 ## Strategy Match 7

Three students solved the problem 185 – 148. All the students used a number line, but each student solved the problem differently.

- Fill in the blanks for each strategy.
- Match the students' work below to the strategies in the table.

| Solve: 185 – 148 = *n* | |
|---|---|
| **Strategy A** | Shift the distance between 148 and 185 up 2 to make the problem easier. |
| **Strategy B** | Find the difference between 148 and 185. |
| **Strategy C** | Remove 148 from 185. |

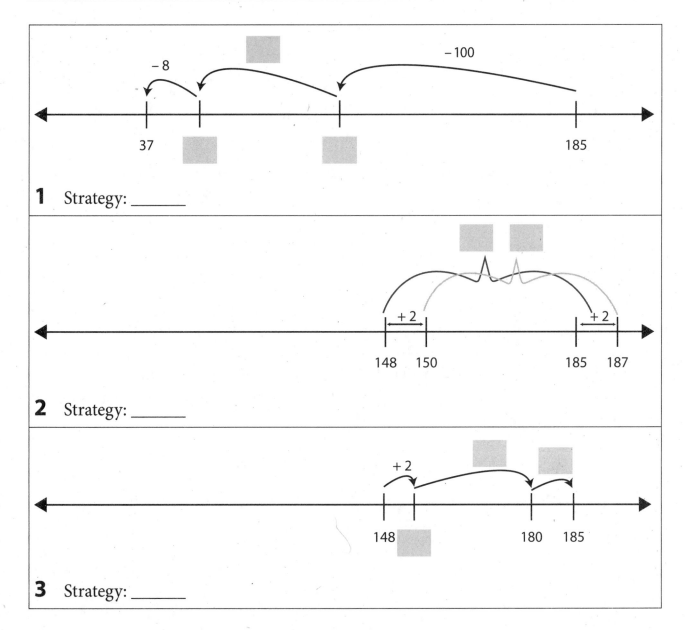

**1** Strategy: _____

**2** Strategy: _____

**3** Strategy: _____

**87**

## Using the Number Line to Find Differences

Use the number lines to solve each problem below.

**ex** Veronica has $76. She wants to buy a bike that costs $162. How much more money does she need?

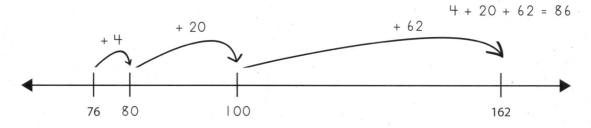

$$4 + 20 + 62 = 86$$

+ 4    + 20    + 62

76   80          100                              162

She needs __$86__ more.

**1** Clive and his family are driving to the beach. They will drive 136 miles total. So far, they have driven 84 miles. How much farther do they have to go? Show your work. Write your answer in the space below.

84                                               136

They have _____ more miles to go.

**2** Shanice is reading a book that is 143 pages long. So far, she has read 56 pages. How many more pages does she have to read? Show your work. Write your answer in the space below.

56                                               143

She has _____ pages left to read.

#  Work Place Instructions 3D Round & Add Hundreds

## Each pair of players needs:

- 1 3D Round & Add Hundreds Record Sheet to share
- 1 spinner overlay
- one 1-6 die

**1** Players decide who will spin and who will record the numbers. Players switch roles for each turn.

**2** Players roll the die to get the first digit of each 3-digit number, then spin the spinner 4 times to fill in the rest of the digits on the record sheet.

| Sum of actual numbers | Sum of rounded numbers | Score |
|---|---|---|
| 276 + 532 = ____ | ____ + ____ = ____ | |

**3** Players work together to round each number formed to the nearest 100 and fill in the blanks under Sum of Rounded Numbers.

| Sum of actual numbers | Sum of rounded numbers | Score |
|---|---|---|
| 276 + 532 = ____ | 300 + 500 = ____ | |

**4** Players work together to find the sum of the actual numbers and the sum of the rounded numbers.

**5** Players' score is the difference between the sum of the actual numbers and the sum of the rounded numbers.

| Sum of actual numbers | Sum of rounded numbers | Score |
|---|---|---|
| 276 + 532 = 808 | 300 + 500 = 800 | 8 |

**6** Players continue spinning, rounding and adding until they have played all 5 rounds of the game. Then they add their scores from each round to get their final score.

Note: Players can work together to play the game again and see if they can get a lower score the second time around.

## Game Variations

**A** Students can each use their own recording sheet and take turns, each spinning and recording for themselves. Low score wins the game.

**B** Instead of recording the numbers in order as they roll and spin, players can roll the die twice, spin 4 times and then arrange the six digits to form the two 3-digit numbers that will yield the lowest score.

**NAME** _____ | **DATE** _____

 **Rounding Review**

When you are rounding, look at the digit one place to the right of where you want to round. If you round to the nearest ten, look at the digit in the ones place. If you round to the nearest hundred, look at the digit in the tens place. If you round to the nearest thousand, look at the digit in the hundreds place.

If the digit is 5 or higher, round up. If it is less than 5, round down.

**1** Underline the number in the *ones* place. Then circle *up* or *down* to show whether you are rounding *up* or *down*. Then round the number to the nearest ten.

**ex** 33<u>4</u> rounds up/(down) to <u>330</u> .

**a** 476 rounds up/down to _____.

**b** 2,053 rounds up/down to _____.

**c** 4,388 rounds up/down to _____.

**2** Underline the number in the *tens* place. Then circle *up* or *down* to show whether you are rounding *up* or *down*. Then round the number to the nearest hundred.

**a** 328 rounds up/down to _____.

**b** 961 rounds up/down to _____.

**c** 4,553 rounds up/down to _____.

**d** 3,348 rounds up/down to _____.

**3** Underline the number in the *hundreds* place. Then circle *up* or *down* to show whether you are rounding *up* or *down*. Then round the number to the nearest thousand.

**a** 4,389 rounds up/down to _____.

**b** 2,503 rounds up/down to _____.

**c** 1,437 rounds up/down to _____.

**d** 6,614 rounds up/down to _____.

**4** Complete the multiplication facts.

$3 \times 3 = $ ___    $4 \times 4 = $ ___    $3 \times 8 = $ ___    $4 \times 10 = $ ___    $3 \times 5 = $ ___    $4 \times 6 = $ ___

$4 \times 7 = $ ___    $3 \times 4 = $ ___    $4 \times 8 = $ ___    $3 \times 7 = $ ___    $4 \times 5 = $ ___    $3 \times 6 = $ ___

**NAME** _____ | **DATE** _____

 **Understanding Place Value**

**1** Brandon, Monica, and Casey are discussing what number this collection represents. Brandon says it is 1,002. Casey says it is 1,200. Monica says it is 1,020.

**a** Who is right? _____

**b** Why?

**c** Write the correct number in words.

**d** Write the correct number in expanded form. _____

**2** Brandon says this is 2,031. Casey says it is 231. Monica says it is 2,301.

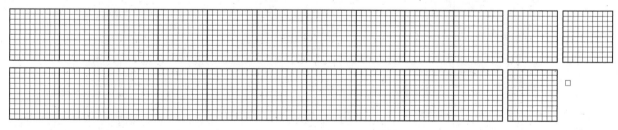

**a** Who is right? _____

**b** Why?

**c** Write the correct number in words.

**d** Write the correct number in expanded form. _____

**91**

# 🔍 Travel Miles Between Cities

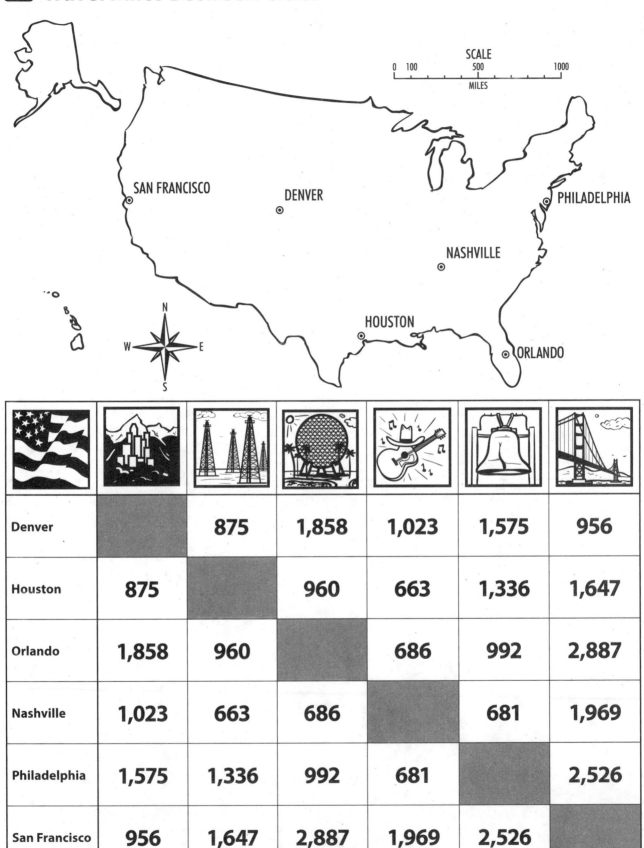

| | | | | | | |
|---|---|---|---|---|---|---|
| **Denver** | | 875 | 1,858 | 1,023 | 1,575 | 956 |
| **Houston** | 875 | | 960 | 663 | 1,336 | 1,647 |
| **Orlando** | 1,858 | 960 | | 686 | 992 | 2,887 |
| **Nashville** | 1,023 | 663 | 686 | | 681 | 1,969 |
| **Philadelphia** | 1,575 | 1,336 | 992 | 681 | | 2,526 |
| **San Francisco** | 956 | 1,647 | 2,887 | 1,969 | 2,526 | |

**NAME** | **DATE**

 **Pages & Miles**

**1** Tasha and her friends are in a reading contest. Last year, the winning team read 2,546 pages. So far, Tasha has read 186 pages. Her friend Lisa has read 203 pages, and her friend Robert has read 215 pages.

**a** Estimate how many more pages they need to read altogether to beat last year's winning team.

**b** Exactly how many pages do they need to read to beat last year's winning team? Show all your work. Make sure your answer comes close to your estimate. If it does not, check your work or solve the problem another way.

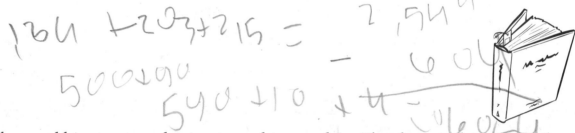

**2** Esteban and his mom are driving to see his grandma. They have to drive 865 miles in all. On Monday, they drove 186 miles. On Tuesday, they drove 267 miles.

**a** Estimate how many miles they will need to drive on Wednesday to get to his grandma's house.

**b** Exactly how many miles do they need to drive on Wednesday to get to his grandma's house? Show all your work. Make sure your answer comes close to your estimate. If it does not, check your work or solve the problem another way.

**Two Travel Miles Problems**

**1** Our family is planning a vacation. My mom and dad don't have much time off, so we are looking for a city close by. We live in Houston and are thinking about going to see the Country Music Hall of Fame in Nashville or going to Disney World in Orlando. What is the difference between the distances we would have to travel to each city?

**2** Rachel is traveling from Denver to Nashville to see her cousin. If she has already traveled 356 miles, how many more miles does she need to travel?

NAME _____  | DATE _____

 # Round & Subtract

**1** Rounding numbers can help you make good estimates. Round each pair of numbers to the nearest ten and then subtract the rounded numbers to estimate the difference.

| Numbers to Subtract | Rounded to the Nearest Ten | Estimated Difference |
|---|---|---|
| **ex**  867 – 485 | $870 - 490$ | |

The difference between 867 and 485 is about ___380___.

| Numbers to Subtract | Rounded to the Nearest Ten | Estimated Difference |
|---|---|---|
| **a**  608 – 263 | | |

The difference between 608 and 263 is about _____.

| Numbers to Subtract | Rounded to the Nearest Ten | Estimated Difference |
|---|---|---|
| **b**  732 – 546 | | |

The difference between 732 and 546 is about _____.

**2** Now round to the nearest hundred and then subtract to estimate the difference.

| Numbers to Subtract | Rounded to the Nearest Hundred | Estimated Difference |
|---|---|---|
| **a**  1,508 – 620 | | |

The difference between 1,508 and 620 is about _____.

| Numbers to Subtract | Rounded to the Nearest Hundred | Estimated Difference |
|---|---|---|
| **b**  2,482 – 936 | | |

The difference between 2,482 and 936 is about _____.

**NAME** | **DATE**

 # Round, Estimate & Find the Sum

Before you start adding numbers, it is a good idea to estimate what their sum will be.
That way, you can tell if your final answer is reasonable. Round each pair of numbers to
the nearest ten and then add the rounded numbers to estimate the sum. Then use the
standard algorithm to find the exact sum.

| | | Round, Add & Estimate | Exact Sum *(Use the algorithm)* |
|---|---|---|---|
| **ex** | 348<br>+ 173 | 350<br>+ 170<br>520<br><br>The sum will be about __520__ | 348<br>+ 173<br>521 |
| **1** | 267<br>+ 338 | 270<br>+340<br><br>The sum will be about _____ | 267<br>+ 338 |
| **2** | 438<br>+ 583 | 440<br>580<br><br>The sum will be about _____ | 438<br>+ 583 |
| **3** | 842<br>+ 159 | 840<br>+159<br>994<br><br>The sum will be about _____ | 842<br>+ 159 |
| **4** | 528<br>+ 454 | 520<br>454<br><br>The sum will be about _____ | 528<br>+ 454 |

**96**

NAME _____ | DATE _____

 **Addition Methods**

Use the standard algorithm to solve each problem. Then solve it a different way. Label your method. Circle the strategy that seemed quicker and easier.

| | | Standard Algorithm | Different Strategy |
|---|---|---|---|
| **ex** | 25<br>+ 26 | $\begin{array}{r} {}^1 25 \\ + 26 \\ \hline 51 \end{array}$ | $25 + 25 = 50$<br>$50 + 1 = 51$<br><br>Strategy: <u>Doubles</u> |
| **1** | 51 + 29 = | | Strategy: _____ |
| **2** | 198<br>+ 56 | | Strategy: _____ |
| **3** | 348 + 578 = | | Strategy: _____ |
| **4** | 34<br>56<br>+ 29 | | Strategy: _____ |

## More Addition Strategies

Use the standard algorithm to solve each problem. Then solve it a different way. Label your method. Circle the strategy that seemed quicker and easier.

| | Standard Algorithm | Different Strategy |
|---|---|---|
| **a** $\begin{array}{r} 63 \\ +36 \\ \hline \end{array}$ | | Strategy: _____ |
| **b** $149 + 253 =$ | | Strategy: _____ |
| **c** $53 + 28 + 72 =$ | | Strategy: _____ |
| **d** $\begin{array}{r} 379 \\ +272 \\ \hline \end{array}$ | | Strategy: _____ |
| **e** $\begin{array}{r} 512 \\ +365 \\ \hline \end{array}$ | | Strategy: _____ |

NAME _____ | DATE _____

# Running Robots

**1** Fill in the bubble to show the best estimate for each problem:

| a | 78<br>− 29 | ○ 30<br>○ 40<br>◉ 50<br>○ 60 | b | 202<br>− 169 | ◉ 30<br>○ 40<br>○ 50<br>○ 60 |

**2** Solve each subtraction problem below. You may use the regrouping strategy (standard algorithm) or any other strategy for addition that is efficient for you. Be sure to show your work.

**a** Nina and Ricardo designed robots. Nina's robot can run for 235 minutes before the batteries need to be recharged. Ricardo's robot can run for 187 minutes before the batteries need recharging. How much longer can Nina's robot run than Ricardo's?

**b** Kiran and Brenda also designed robots. Kiran's robot can walk 307 meters before the batteries need to be recharged. Brenda's robot can walk 268 meters before the batteries need to be recharged. How much farther can Kiran's robot walk than Brenda's?

NAME | DATE

 ## Subtraction Strategies

Use the standard algorithm to solve each problem. Then solve it a different way. Label your method. Circle the strategy that seemed quicker and easier.

| | Standard algorithm | Different Strategy |
|---|---|---|
| **ex** $\begin{array}{r} 200 \\ -137 \end{array}$ | $\begin{array}{r} \cancel{200} \\ -137 \\ \hline 63 \end{array}$ | $200 + 3 = 203$ <br> $137 + 3 = 140$ <br> $203 - 140 = 63$ <br><br> Strategy: constant differences |
| **1** $\quad 75 - 24 =$ | 75 <br> 24 | Strategy: _____ |
| **2** $\begin{array}{r} 243 \\ -129 \end{array}$ | | Strategy: _____ |
| **3** $\quad 512 - 339 =$ | | Strategy: _____ |
| **4** $\begin{array}{r} 649 \\ -326 \end{array}$ | | Strategy: _____ |

**100**

**NAME** _____ **| DATE** _____

 # More Subtraction Strategies

Use the standard algorithm to solve each problem. Then solve it a different way. Label your method. Circle the strategy that seemed quicker and easier.

| | Standard algorithm | Different Strategy |
|---|---|---|
| **1** 91<br>− 45 | | Strategy: _____ |
| **2** 253 − 149 | | Strategy: _____ |
| **3** 265 − 174 | | Strategy: _____ |
| **4** 374<br>− 251 | | Strategy: _____ |
| **5** 592<br>−246 | | Strategy: _____ |

**NAME** _____ | **DATE** _____

 # Bike-a-thon

Akira and Taro are participating in a bike-a-thon to raise money for people who lost their homes in an earthquake. For every mile they ride, they will earn $1 to help rebuild and refurnish homes. Show your work with numbers, sketches, or words as you help Akira and Taro figure out how far they have ridden and how much money they have earned. Then, write an equation for each problem.

**1** In one week, Akira rode her bike 87 miles. Taro rode his bike 51 miles. How many more miles did Akira ride?

Equation: _____

**2** After two weeks, Akira and Taro biked a total 276 miles. After 3 weeks, they had biked a total of 413 miles. How many miles did they ride in the third week? (Hint: How much farther had they biked at the end of the third week than at the end of the second week?)

Equation: _____

**3** Akira and Taro want to raise $537. After four weeks, they have raised $498. How much more money do they need to earn?

Equation: _____

**Karate Problems**

Answer, and explain using numbers, sketches, or words.

**1** In a class of 30 students, the karate instructor wants to work with small, equal groups of students.

    **a** If there are 3 groups, how many students are in each group?

    **b** If there are 5 groups, how many students are in each group?

    **c** If there are 6 groups, how may students are in each group?

    **d** If there are 10 groups, how many students are in each group?

    **e** If there are 2 groups, how many students are in each group?

    **f** If there are 15 groups, how many students are in each group?

**2** **CHALLENGE** Write your own story problem to match this expression: $60 \div 3$. Then solve your own problem and show the answer. Be sure to label your answer with the correct units. Use your math journal if you need extra room.

The answer to my problem is _____

NAME _____ | DATE _____

 **Roll, Tell & Record the Time**

**1**

**2**

**3**

**4**
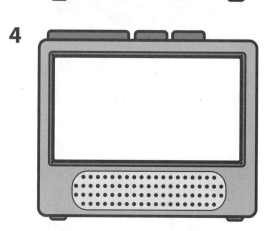

**5**

**6**
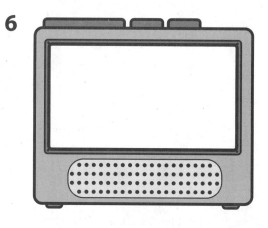

**7**

**8**

# Work Place Instructions 4A Tic-Tac-Tock

**Each pair of players needs:**

- 2 Tic-Tac-Tock Record Sheets (1 for each player)
- 2 blue 1–6 dice
- 1 green 1–6 die
- 1 white 4–9 die
- 1 student clock

**1**  Players record their name and the date at the top of a record sheet and decide in a fair way who goes first.

**2**  Player 1:

- Rolls the 2 blue dice and finds the sum of the numbers rolled.
- Tells her partner how she found the sum.
- Sets the hour hand to that number (the sum).
- Rolls the green 1–6 die and the white 4–9 die together and multiplies them to find the product of the numbers rolled.
- Tells her partner how she found the product.
- Sets the minute hand to that number and reads the time aloud.

> **Player 1**  *I got 2 + 4 on the blue dice. Four and 2 more is 6, so I have to set the hour hand to 6. Then, I got 3 and 6 with the other dice. 3 × 6 is, let's see ... 6, 12, 18. It's 18. So the minute hand goes on 18, but there's no 18 on the clock.*
>
> **Player 2**  *Right, but remember with minutes, you can use the numbers to count by 5s. So, the 1 is 5 minutes, the 2 is 10 minutes, the 3 is 15 minutes. So, 18 minutes would be between the 3 and the 4.*
>
> **Player 1**  *Oh, right, I remember. OK, the minute hand is at 18 and the hour hand is at 6. It is 6:18.*

**3**  When players agree on the time, Player 1 looks for a clock on her record sheet that she can fill in. The time must match the description below the clock.

There may be more than one description that matches the time rolled, but a player can fill in only one clock per turn. If there is no clock to fill in, the player must wait until the next turn to fill in a clock.

**4**  Player 2 takes a turn, following the directions in Steps 2 and 3.

**5**  Players take turns rolling the dice, finding the time, and recording it on their record sheets in an appropriate box. They are trying to fill three clocks in a row. Rows can be horizontal, vertical, or diagonal.

**6**  The first player to fill in three clocks in a row on their record sheet wins the game.

## Game Variations

**A**  Play for blackout: race to fill all 9 clocks instead of just a row of 3 clocks.

**B**  Play with one record sheet instead of two. This version of the game is closer to tic-tac-toe because players can use strategies, along with luck, to block one another.

**C**  Make a new game sheet with your own descriptions for each clock. Make sure your descriptions are possible. For example, there is no way get the time 1:47 because you can't add to get 1 or multiply to get 47 with the dice in this game.

## Telling Time on Two Kinds of Clocks

**1** Read each of these clock faces and write the time on the digital clock.

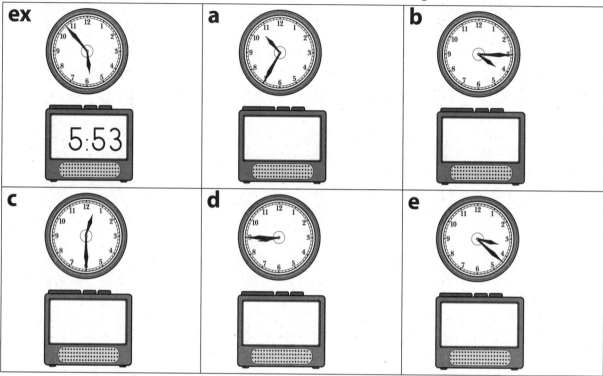

**2** Draw the hour and minute hands on the clock faces to show the times below.

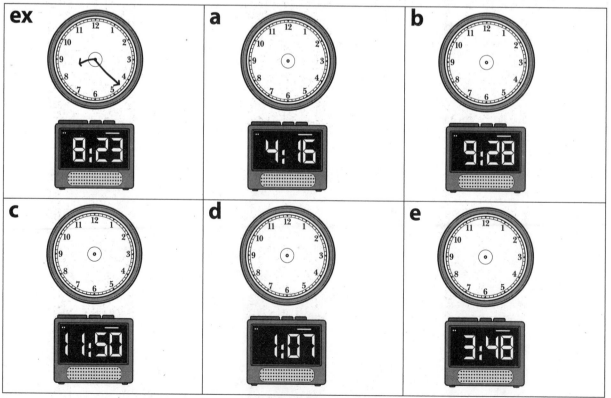

NAME _____ | DATE _____

## 🔍 **What Is the Time?** page 1 of 2

1   Use the timelines to model and solve problems a and b below.

**a**   Tifani's school ended at 3:30. She went to soccer practice after school for 1 hour and 15 minutes. Then it took her 10 minutes to walk home. When did she arrive home?

Tifani arrived home at _____.

**b**   Craig starts walking to school at 7:45 am. It takes him 20 minutes to walk to school. School starts at 8:30 am. How much time does Craig have before school starts?

Craig has _____ before school starts.

2   Sara is only allowed to spend 5 hours a week watching television. Look at the chart to see how much she has used so far this week. How much time does she have left to watch television this weekend? Show all your work.

| Day | Time |
|-----------|------------|
| Monday | 45 minutes |
| Tuesday | 60 minutes |
| Wednesday | 90 minutes |
| Thursday | 45 minutes |
| Friday | 30 minutes |

Sara has _____ left to watch television this weekend.

NAME _____ | DATE _____

## What Is the Time? page 2 of 2

**3** Show your work for the problems below. You can draw and use timelines to help if you like.

**a** Noah started playing his guitar at 3:22 p.m. He played for 46 minutes. When did he stop playing?

Noah stopped playing his guitar at _____.

**b** Jennifer usually starts her homework at 6:30 p.m., but she was 8 minutes late. She worked on her homework for 27 minutes. What time did she finish her homework?

Jennifer finished her homework at _____.

**c** **CHALLENGE** Jeremy started exercising at 4:45 p.m. and he stopped at 5:38 p.m. How long did he exercise?

Jeremy exercised for _____.

**NAME** _____ | **DATE** _____

## Telling Time on Analog & Digital Clocks

**1** Fill in the bubble that shows the time on the clock.

**a** ○ 1:55
○ 2:11
○ 2:55
○ 11:10

**b** ○ 3:45
○ 9:03
○ 9:15
○ 10:15

**c** ○ 6:35
○ 6:40
○ 7:30
○ 8:30

**d** ○ 4:40
○ 8:15
○ 8:20
○ 3:40

**2** Draw lines to show match the clocks that show the same time.

**a**

**b**

**c**

**3** **CHALLENGE** Sam leaves school at 3:15. It takes Sam 2 minutes to walk 1 block, and he lives 13 blocks away from school. Draw hands on the clock face and write the time on the digital clock to show when he gets home from school if he doesn't stop along the way. Show all your work.

**Alex Walks Home from School**

**1** Alex started walking home from school at 3:15. He got home 20 minutes later. What time did he get home?

**a** What is this problem asking you to figure out?

**b** Underline any information in the problem that will help you find the answer.

**c** Use this space to solve the problem. Show all your work using numbers, words, or labeled sketches. You can use the clocks or the timeline to help. Write the answer on the line below when you're finished.

Answer _____

**2** **CHALLENGE** Social studies started 55 minutes before Alex started walking home from school at 3:15. What time did social studies start?

NAME _____ | DATE _____

 **Mass of Clay**

**1** Mr. Frisbie's third graders are studying mass. Yesterday, Mr. Frisbie divided the class into 5 groups. He gave the kids in each group identical lumps of clay, and asked them to find the mass of each lump, and the mass of all the lumps put together. The kids recorded the information on this table. Use the information on the table to solve the problems below. Show your work using pictures, numbers, and words.

| Group Number | Mass of Each Lump of Clay in Our Group (in grams) | Mass of All the Lumps of Clay in Our Group Put Together (in grams) |
| --- | --- | --- |
| Group 1 | 15 g | 90 g |
| Group 2 | 17 g | 102 g |
| Group 3 | 19 g | 114 g |
| Group 4 | 20 g | 120 g |
| Group 5 | 14 g | 84 g |

**a** How much clay did Mr. Frisbie's class use for their experiments yesterday?

**b** What else has about the same mass as the clay they used?

**c** If Mr. Frisbie started with a kilogram of clay, how much clay is left? (1 kilogram = 1,000 grams)

**d** How many students are in Group 1?

**e** How may students are in Group 4?

**2** CHALLENGE How many students are in Mr. Frisbie's class? Show your work.

**NAME** _____ | **DATE** _____

 **Estimate, Measure & Compare the Mass** page 1 of 2

**1** In the table below:

**a** Write the name of an item in the first column. Estimate the mass and record it in the second column.

**b** Find the actual mass of the item and record the measurement. Round your measurement to the nearest gram.

**c** Find the difference between your estimate and the actual measurement. Record the difference in the last column.

**d** On the second page, continue estimating, finding the mass, and finding the difference for all the items. Use what you know about the mass of the first item to estimate the others.

| Item | Your Estimate (in grams) | Actual Measure (in grams) | The Difference (in grams) |
|---|---|---|---|
| Pencil | | | |
| Rock | | | |
| | | | |
| | | | |

*(continued on next page)*

**112**

NAME _____ | DATE _____

## Estimate, Measure & Compare the Mass page 2 of 2

| Item | Your Estimate (in grams) | Actual Measure (in grams) | The Difference (in grams) |
|---|---|---|---|
| | | | |
| | | | |
| | | | |
| | | | |

**2** Answer the questions.

**a** When people measure the mass of an object, they are finding out (circle one):

how long it is                              how heavy it is

how much matter is in it                   how wide it is

**b** To find the mass of an object, you need (circle one):

a ruler             a balance             a bathroom scale    a measuring cup

**c** If you want to find how long a skateboard is, you would use (circle one):

a ruler             a balance             a bathroom scale    a measuring cup

**3** When you finish, choose additional items in the classroom you want to measure and record them in your math journal.

**113**

**Grams & Kilograms**

There are 1,000 grams in 1 kilogram.

**1** John's cat weighs 5 kilograms. How many grams is that?

**2** Carly's dog weighs 18 kilograms. How many grams is that?

**3** Ramona weighs 27 kilograms. How many grams is that?

**4** John's cat had kittens. One of them weighed 500 grams. How many kilograms is that?

**5** Frank was measuring out some peanuts. He wanted exactly 1 kilogram of peanuts. So far, he has 300 grams. How many more grams does he need to get exactly 1 kilogram of peanuts? Show all your work.

**6** One baby chick weighs about 50 grams. How many baby chicks would it take to make 1 kilogram? Show all your work.

**NAME** _____ | **DATE** _____

 **Which Container Is Best?** page 1 of 2

**For each problem below:**
- Estimate and record which containers you think will hold the amount of water needed. (It's OK if you choose more than one container that might work.)
- Test your estimates using your liquid measuring cups.
- Decide which beverage container actually works best.
- Record your recommendation.

Sarah needs to bring some water for several different activities this week. Help her choose the best container for each activity.

**1** For a car trip to her grandma's on Monday, Sarah needs to bring about 500 milliliters of water to drink.

    **a** Estimate: Which of the containers look like they would hold about 500 milliliters?

    **b** Container _____ holds about 500 milliliters.

**2** For her track meet on Saturday, Sarah needs to bring about a liter of water to drink.

    **a** Estimate: Which of the containers look like they would hold about 1 liter? Are there any combinations of two or more containers that might hold 1 liter?

    **b** Container(s) _____ hold(s) about 1 liter.

**3** For ballet class on Wednesday, Sarah needs to bring about 800 milliliters of water to drink.

    **a** Estimate: Which of the containers look like they would hold about 800 milliliters? Are there any two containers that look like they would hold 800 milliliters combined?

    **b** Container(s) _____ hold(s) about 800 milliliters.

*(continued on next page)*

## Which Container Is Best?  page 2 of 2

### Last Month

**4**  On the way home from each track meet last month, Sarah bought a 2-liter bottle of juice. How many total milliliters of juice did she drink if there were 6 track meets last month? Show your work.

**5**  Last week Sarah made punch for her friends. The recipe called for 200 milliliters of orange juice, 300 milliliters of cranberry juice, and half a liter of sparkling cider to make enough punch for 4 people. Sarah had 8 people at the party. How much punch did she make? Show your work.

**6**  Two weeks ago, Sarah bought a container of milk that held 2 liters. She drank a 250-milliliter glass of milk every day. How many days did it take her to use the entire container of milk? Show your work.

**7**  Sarah had a cold last month, so she took 5 milliliters of cough syrup every day. Her bottle of cough syrup held 75 milliliters How many times could she take the cough syrup before the bottle was empty? Show your work.

NAME _____ | DATE _____

 **Liquid Volume**

There are 1,000 milliliters in 1 liter. Use this information to help solve the problems below. Show your work for each problem.

**1 a** John's bucket of water has 5 liters. How many milliliters is that?

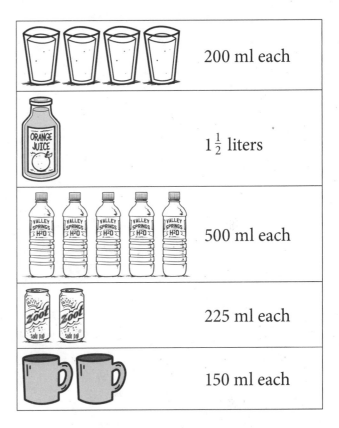

| | |
|---|---|
| | 200 ml each |
| | $1\frac{1}{2}$ liters |
| | 500 ml each |
| | 225 ml each |
| | 150 ml each |

**b** John poured 2 liters of water out of his bucket. How many milliliters does he have left in the bucket?

**2** Ramona has a juice bottle that has $1\frac{1}{2}$ liters. How many milliliters is that?

**3** Sarina was measuring out some milk. She wanted exactly 1 liter of milk. So far, she has 300 milliliters. How many more milliliters does she need to get exactly 1 liter of milk?

**5** Suki drank $4\frac{1}{2}$ liters of liquid today. Look at the table above and decide which items she drank. (Hint there is more than one correct answer.)

**4** One small bottle of shampoo holds about 50 milliliters. How many bottles of this size would it take to make 1 liter?

# Work Place Instructions 4B Measurement Scavenger Hunt

## Each pair of players needs:

- 2 Measurement Scavenger Hunt Record Sheets (1 for each player)
- 1 clear spinner overlay

## Each pair of players also needs access to:

- Measuring tape marked with millimeters
- Pan balance scale
- Metric masses: 7 boxes of 100 paperclips, 1 bag of 50 one-gram cubes, a container of loose 1-gram cubes
- Modeling clay
- 1-quart/1-liter measuring cup
- Pitcher or container with a pour spout, filled with about 1 liter of water
- Several different unmarked containers of different volumes
- Dish towel or paper towels

**1**    Players each record their name and the date on individual record sheets.

**2**    Working together, players spin the measurement spinner to find out if they are going to measure mass, volume, or length. Then they spin the quantity spinner to find out how much mass, volume, or length they are looking for. They record the results in the first two columns on the table on their record sheets.

| 1 | Volume | 750 | grams (milliliters) millimeters | greater than | I would dump some out and try again. |
| 2 | Length | 100 | grams milliliters (millimeters) | less than | I would measure again. |

**3**    Then the scavenger hunt begins! Because this activity is about estimating, players take a guess before finding the actual mass, volume, or length of whatever they are measuring.

**4**    If players spin mass, they will use modeling clay.
- Players make a ball of clay to try to approximate the mass they spun.
- Then, they find the actual mass of the ball of clay they made by placing it on one side of the pan balance scale, and using the metric masses on the other.

**5**    If players spin volume, they will use water.
- Players pour water from the pitcher into one of the containers to try to approximate the amount they spun.
- Then they pour water from the container into the measuring cup to find its actual volume.

**6**    If players spin length, they find an object in the classroom.
- Players look for an object in the classroom that is approximately the length they spun on the quantity spinner. For example, if they spin 750, they find an object that they think is about 750 millimeters long.
- Then, they measure the object to find out how long it actually is.

**7**    Players record the results on their record sheets.

**8**    Players repeat Steps 2–7 until their record sheets are filled.

**NAME**                                                                                    | **DATE**

 # More or Less?

**1**  Look at the following items and circle what you believe to be the correct answer.

| | | | |
|---|---|---|---|
| A balloon has a mass of | more than | (less than) | a kilogram. |
| Two hamburgers have a mass of | more than | less than | a kilogram. |
| A glass of juice holds | more than | less than | a liter. |
| A leaf has a mass of | more than | less than | a gram. |
| A washing machine holds | (more than) | less than | a liter. |
| A bottle of ketchup holds | more than | less than | 3 liters. |
| A loaf of bread has a mass of | more than | (less than) | a kilogram. |
| A handful of popcorn has a mass of | (more than) | less than | a gram |
| Five boxes of 100 small paperclips have a mass of | more than | (less than) | a kilogram. |
| A can of soda holds | more than | (less than) | a liter. |
| A bathtub holds | (more than) | less than | 20 liters. |

**2**  Make up some of your own more than and less than questions.

| | | | |
|---|---|---|---|
| has a mass of | more than | less than | |
| has a mass of | more than | less than | |
| has a mass of | more than | less than | |
| holds | more than | less than | |
| holds | more than | less than | |
| holds | more than | less than | |

# Work Place Instructions 4C Target One Thousand

**Each pair of players needs:**

- 1 deck of Number Cards with the 10s and wild cards removed, shuffled
- 2 Target One Thousand Record Sheets (1 for each player)

**1** Players take turns drawing 8 Number Cards from the deck.

**2** Each player chooses 6 cards to make two 3-digit numbers that together have a sum as close to 1,000 as possible.

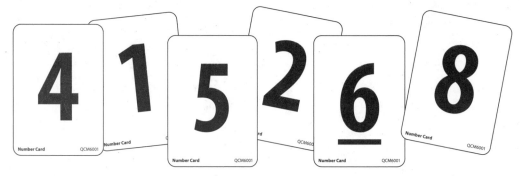

With these cards, a player could make 156 + 824 (sum of 980) or 156 + 842 (sum of 998). Since 998 is closer to 1,000 than 980 is, making 156 and 842 with the cards is a better move.

**3** Players write an addition equation with their numbers and their sum on the record sheet.

**4** Players take turns double-checking each other's calculations.

**5** Each player determines their score for the round by finding the exact difference between their sum and 1,000.

**6** A sum of 980 has a score of 20. A sum of 1,002 has a score of 2. A sum of 1,000 has a score of 0.

**7** Players record both their own score and their partner's score for the round.

**8** Each player puts the 6 cards they used in the discard pile, and then takes turns getting 6 new cards.

**9** The game continues for two more rounds (three rounds in all).

**10** After three rounds, players add their scores to determine the winner. The player with the lower score wins the game.

## Game Variations

**A** Players can review 2-digit addition by playing Target One Hundred (Work Place 1G).

**B** Players can challenge themselves by playing Target Ten Thousand and making addends out of all 8 cards.

**C** Players can choose to use wild cards. A wild card can be any numeral. When players use a wild card, they put a star above the number made from the wild card in the equation on the record sheet.

**120**

**Bird Measurement Problems** page 1 of 2

Solve the problems on this sheet and the next. Show your thinking using words, numbers, or sketches.

1   A bird named Sal has a mass of 149 grams. Sal landed on a leaf next to a bird named Ted with a mass of 398 grams. How much mass do they have together? Be sure to label your answer with the correct units.

Together, Sal and Ted have a mass of ___547___ ___grums___
                                                    Units

2   How much more mass does Ted have than Sal? Be sure to label your answer with the correct units.

Ted has ___249___ ___grums___ more mass than Sal.
                  Units

3   If Sal leaves his nest at 1:30 and flies for 2 hours and 10 minutes, what time does he come back?

Sal comes back at _____.

4   If Ted leaves his nest at 8:50 and flies for 30 minutes, what time does he come back?

Ted comes back at _____.

*(continued on next page)*

## Bird Measurement Problems page 2 of 2

**5** Ted jumped into a beaker of water that held 313 ml of water. When he flew back out, there was only 189 ml of water left. How much water had splashed out of the beaker?

_____ _____ had splashed out of the beaker.
　　　　　　　　Units

**6** Ted's nest has three times as much mass as Ted. How much mass does Ted's nest have?

Ted's nest has a mass of _____ _____
　　　　　　　　　　　　　　　　　Units

**7** Sal's nest has three times as much mass as Sal. How much mass does Sal's nest have?

Sal's nest has a mass of _____ _____
　　　　　　　　　　　　　　　　Units

**8** **CHALLENGE** Sal's mother has a mass of 450 grams, which is 6 times the mass of his baby brother, Sammy. How much mass does Sammy have?

Sammy has a mass of _____ _____
　　　　　　　　　　　　　　　Units

#  Mr. Measure

Mr. Measure is a measuring man. He uses his ruler, meter stick, scale, pan balance scale, and other tools to measure. Help Mr. Measure find measurements in the problems below. Use the correct unit in your answer. Use numbers, sketches, or words to show your work.

**1** Mr. Measure measures rainfall for two months. In the first month, there was 129 ml of rain. In the second month, there was 285 ml of rain. How many milliliters of rain fell in these two months?

**2** Mr. Measure found the mass of 2 rocks. A gray rock has a mass of 276 g. A black rock has a mass of 413 g. How much more mass does the black rock have?

**3** It takes Mr. Measure 30 seconds to measure the height of each of his houseplants. How long does it take Mr. Measure to measure the height of 9 houseplants?

**4** **CHALLENGE** How many minutes does it take Mr. Measure to measure his houseplants?

**NAME** _____ | **DATE** _____

## More Measurement Problems page 1 of 2

Solve the following problems. Show your thinking using words, numbers, or sketches. Label your answers with the correct units.

**1** There were 5 lizards sitting on one side of a pan balance scale. Together, the lizards had a mass of 234 grams. One lizard with a mass of 25 grams got off the balance and a different lizard with a mass of 43 grams got on. Now, how much mass do the 5 lizards on the balance have?

$$209$$
$$43$$
$$\overline{\phantom{0}232}$$

The 5 lizards on the pan balance scale have a mass of ___232 grams___.

**2** There are 4 puppies and each puppy has a mass of about 3 kilograms. The mother dog has a mass that is 5 times as much as one of her puppies. How much mass do all 5 dogs—the 4 puppies and their mother—have together?

$$5 \times 3 = 15$$

The 5 dogs together have a mass of ___15 kilograms___.

**3** The dog's water dish had 23 milliliters of water. The owner added water so that there was 4 times that amount. The dog drank 39 milliliters of that water. How much water was left in the dish?

$$\times \begin{array}{r} 3\,9 \\ 2\,3 \\ \hline 1\,6 \end{array}$$

$$\begin{array}{r} 16+ \\ 4 \\ \hline 20 \end{array}$$

There was ___20 milliliters___ of water left in the dish.

## More Measurement Problems page 2 of 2

**4** Abby is four times taller than her dog, Gabi. Gabi is 51 centimeters tall. How tall is Abby when she is wearing shoes that are 6 centimeters tall?

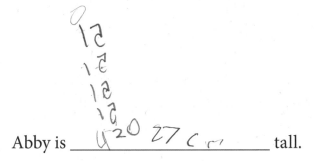

Abby is ___ 420 27 c m ___ tall.

**5** Use the number line provided to model and solve each of these problems.

**a** The Math Club started baking at 3:35 p.m. and baked for 3 hours and 30 minutes. What time did they finish?

The Math Club finished baking at _____.

**b** The Math Club started setting up for the bake sale the next day at 11:45 a.m. They were ready to start the bake sale at 1:30 p.m. How long did it take them to set up?

It took the Math Club _____ to set up.

**NAME** _____ | **DATE** _____

 **Millie Millipede**

Although Millipede means thousand legs, millipedes actually have less than 400 legs. Millie is a millipede who has about 200 legs. Help Millie solve the problems below. Use the correct unit in your answer. Use numbers, sketches, or words to show your work.

**1** One day, Millie Millipede started walking in her garden at 11:15. She walked for 1 hour and 30 minutes. What time was it when she stopped walking?

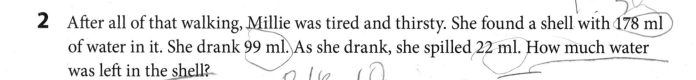

**2** After all of that walking, Millie was tired and thirsty. She found a shell with 178 ml of water in it. She drank 99 ml. As she drank, she spilled 22 ml. How much water was left in the shell?

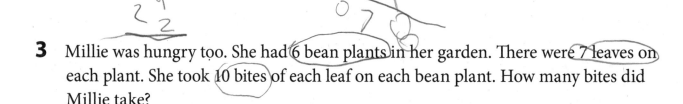

**3** Millie was hungry too. She had 6 bean plants in her garden. There were 7 leaves on each plant. She took 10 bites of each leaf on each bean plant. How many bites did Millie take?

**4** Then, Millie was tired. She fell asleep for 2 hours. When she woke up, it was 3:45. What time did she fall asleep?

**Arnie Orangutan**

Orangutans are members of the ape family. They live mostly in trees and use their long arms to swing from branch to branch. Solve the problems below about Arnie the Orangutan. Use numbers, sketches, or words to show your work. Be sure to label each answer with the correct units.

**1** Arnie Orangutan collected 26 kilograms of bananas. He ate 6 kilograms. Then, he divided the rest between his 4 babies. How many kilograms of bananas did each baby get?

**2** Arnie Orangutan found a pool of water with about 400 liters of water. He drank 18 liters of water. Then, he jumped in the pool and took a bath. When he finished, there were only 296 liters of water left. How much water splashed out while he was in his bath?

**3** Arnie Orangutan loves to swing from tree branch to tree branch. On Monday, he swung 286 meters. On Tuesday he was tired and only swung 25 meters. On Wednesday, he swung 5 times as far as he swung on Tuesday. How far did Arnie swing on Monday, Tuesday, and Wednesday all together?

**4** On Thursday, Arnie started swinging at 11:30. He swung for 3 hours and 20 minutes. What time did he stop swinging?

**NAME** _____ | **DATE** _____

 # Choose a Measurement Unit

**1** A box of cereal has 10 servings. Each serving is 240 grams (g).

    **a** How many grams of cereal are in the box? Show your work.

    **b** Is that more or less than 2 kilograms? (Hint: 1 kilogram = 1,000 grams)

**2** Circle the appropriate words to fill in the blanks.

    **a** A work boot is heavy! I would measure its _____ with _____.

      | (mass) length volume | liters kilograms grams |

    **b** An elephant is tall. I would measure its _____ with _____.

      | mass (height) volume | centimeters kilograms meters |

    **c** A pencil box is short! I would measure its _____ with _____.

      | mass (length) volume | liters (centimeters) meters |

    **d** An eyedropper doesn't hold much. I would measure its _____ with

    _____.

      | mass (length) volume | liters kilograms (milliliters) |

    **e** A marking pen is light! I would measure its _____ with _____.

      | mass length (volume) | (liters) kilograms grams |

    **f** That pitcher holds lots. I would measure its _____ with _____.

      | mass (length) volume | liters kilograms (meters) |

    **g** An eel is long! I would measure its _____ with _____.

      | mass length (volume) | liters kilograms (meters) |

    **h** A pool holds lots of water! I would measure its _____ with _____.

      | mass length (volume) | (liters) kilograms meters |

NAME _____ | DATE _____

 **Comparing Unit Fractions**

**1** Fill in the shapes to show each fraction.

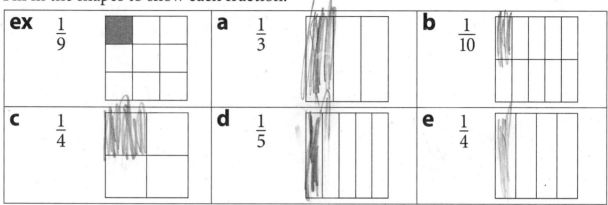

| **ex** $\frac{1}{9}$ | **a** $\frac{1}{3}$ | **b** $\frac{1}{10}$ |
| **c** $\frac{1}{4}$ | **d** $\frac{1}{5}$ | **e** $\frac{1}{4}$ |

**2** Look at the fractions you shaded in above. Use them to help complete each number sentence by writing <, >, or =.

| **ex** $\frac{1}{3}$ > $\frac{1}{9}$ | **a** $\frac{1}{5}$ < $\frac{1}{3}$ | **b** $\frac{2}{9}$ > $\frac{1}{9}$ |
| **c** $\frac{1}{10}$ < $\frac{1}{9}$ | **d** $\frac{1}{5}$ < $\frac{1}{10}$ | **e** $\frac{1}{2}$ > $\frac{1}{3}$ |

**3** Use what you know about fractions to complete each number sentence by writing <, >, or =.

| **a** $\frac{1}{100}$ < $\frac{1}{50}$ | **b** $\frac{7}{25}$ > $\frac{5}{25}$ | **c** $\frac{1}{4}$ > $\frac{1}{16}$ |

**4** My friends and I are sharing a watermelon. I got $\frac{1}{3}$ of the watermelon and my friend Michelle got $\frac{1}{6}$ of the watermelon. Who got more? Explain your answer.

   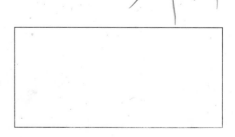

**5** Divide the shape and shade in the fraction.

**a** $\frac{1}{4}$

**b** $\frac{3}{4}$

**NAME** _____ | **DATE** _____

## 🔍 More Pattern Block Fractions

**1** Today, we're going to call the hexagon from our pattern blocks one whole. Tell what fraction of the whole each of the blocks below is, and explain how you know.

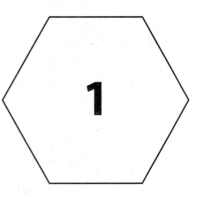

**a** If the hexagon is 1, the trapezoid is _____ because

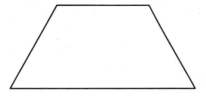

**b** If the hexagon is 1, the blue rhombus is _____ because

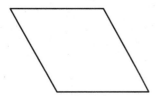

**c** If the hexagon is 1, the triangle is _____ because

**2** Write >, =, or < in the circle between each pair of fractions to show how they compare. Use your pattern blocks to help. The first one is done for you.

$\frac{1}{2}$ ⟩ $\frac{2}{6}$   $\frac{1}{3}$ = $\frac{2}{6}$   $\frac{3}{6}$ < $\frac{2}{3}$   $\frac{2}{2}$ = $\frac{3}{3}$

$\frac{2}{3}$ > $\frac{1}{2}$   $\frac{2}{3}$ < $\frac{5}{6}$   $\frac{3}{6}$ > $\frac{1}{2}$   $\frac{4}{6}$ = $\frac{2}{3}$

# Work Place Instructions 4D Hexagon Spin & Fill

## Each pair of players needs:

- 2 Hexagon Spin & Fill Record Sheets (1 per player)
- 1 spinner overlay
- container of pattern blocks

**1** Players write their names and the date on their record sheets. Both partners fill out a record sheet.

**2** Player 1 spins the spinner and takes the pattern block(s) to represent the fraction spun. She places the block or blocks on the first hexagon on the record sheet.

**3** If she can, Player 1 trades pieces so she always has the fewest pattern blocks possible.

> **Player 1** I landed on $\frac{4}{6}$, so I'll put down 4 triangles. Oh, but 3 triangles cover half of the hexagon, so I'll trade them in for a trapezoid, because that's the same as half a hexagon.

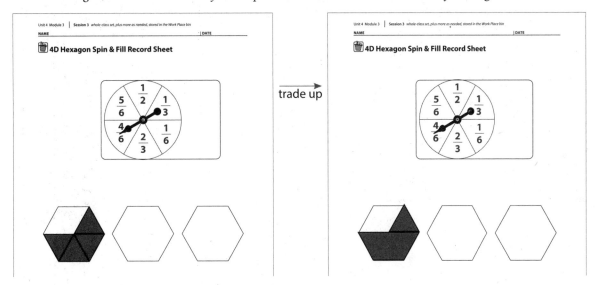

**4** Players alternate turns, repeating steps 2 and 3.

**5** Players continue playing until they fill up all three hexagons on their entire record sheet. They should always try to trade to have the fewest pattern blocks. Players should also fill the first hexagon before moving to the second hexagon and then fill the second hexagon before moving to the third hexagon.

**6** The player who fills the entire sheet first wins.

Players can have a "leftover piece" at the end of the game. For example, if they need to fill in $\frac{1}{6}$ of the last hexagon, but they spin $\frac{1}{2}$, they can use a $\frac{1}{6}$ green triangle to fill the last hexagon and have a $\frac{1}{3}$ blue rhombus left over.

## Game Variations

**A** Players can write equations that represent the fractional amounts that made up each cookie before they traded up.

**B** Players can also spin twice. They add the two amounts and take that amount in pattern blocks. They place them on the record sheet, making sure to trade up so that they always have the fewest pieces.

**C** The game is played according to the usual rules, except at the end, players have to fill the three hexagons exactly. If they spin a piece that is too large, they miss that turn and keep spinning until they spin the piece or pieces that exactly fill the last hexagon.

**131**

**NAME** _____ | **DATE** _____

 **Comparing Fractions**

**1** Circle your answers.

**a** Which is longer, **half of recess** or **half of Saturday**?

**b** Which is longer, **half of a minute** or **half of an hour**?

**c** Which is more, **half of an apple** or **half of a watermelon**?

**d** Which is more, **half of a cookie** or **half of a cake**?

**e** Which is heavier, **half of a kilogram** or **half of a gram**?

**f** Which is heavier, **half of a book** or **half of feather**?

**g** Which holds more, **half of a water bottle** or **half of a swimming pool**?

**h** Which is more, **half of a liter** or **half of a milliliter**?

**2** Write the correct symbol: < or > or =

$\frac{1}{2}$ ▢ $\frac{1}{3}$        $\frac{1}{4}$ ▢ $\frac{1}{3}$        $\frac{1}{8}$ ▢ $\frac{1}{7}$

**3** Choose one pair of fractions from problem 2. Discuss your answer. How do you know which is more?

**4** My friends and I are sharing a watermelon. I got $\frac{1}{4}$ of the watermelon, and my friend Michelle got $\frac{2}{4}$ of the watermelon. Who got more? Explain your answer.

**5** Divide the shape into the number of parts you need, and shade in the fraction.

**a** $\frac{1}{6}$        **b** $\frac{1}{3}$

**The Broken Ruler, Part 1**

**1** Find, mark, and label the measurements on the rulers below. The first one has been done for you.

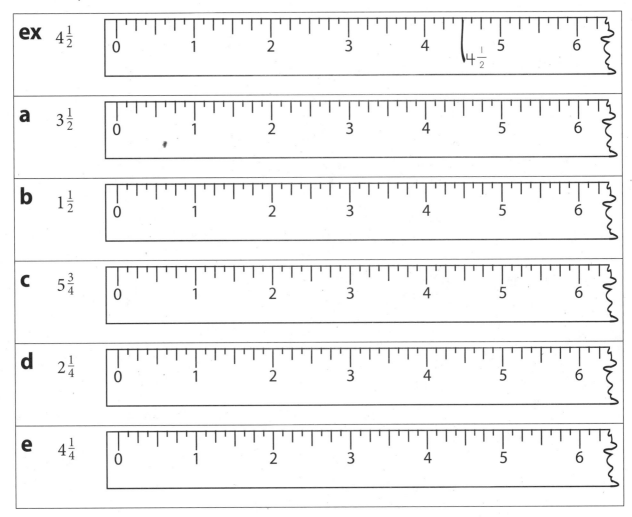

**2** Share your work with a partner. Does he or she agree with each of the marks you made on the rulers? If not, decide who's correct and fix your work.

**3** **CHALLENGE** What other fractions do you know? Mark and label them on this ruler.

**NAME** | **DATE**

## 🔍 Number Line Sketches page 1 of 2

**1** Use your double number line to model the word problems below. Then sketch your solution on the number line. Write an equation to explain your thinking.

**a** Today you jogged $\frac{1}{3}$ of a mile before stopping to chat for a moment with your friend. Then you continued to jog another $\frac{1}{3}$ of a mile before stopping for a drink of water. How far did you jog in all?

**b** During P.E., teams of 3 people run a relay. Each person runs $\frac{1}{4}$ of the way around the track. Where does the race end?

**c** My mom bought a long length of ribbon to make bows for my sister and me. We each get $\frac{2}{6}$ of the ribbon. How much of the total ribbon is used?

*(continued on next page)*

## Number Line Sketches page 2 of 2

**d** On the ranch, fences are located every $\frac{1}{6}$ of a mile. If I stop at the fifth fence, how much of a mile did I travel?

**e** In our city, drinking fountains are located every $\frac{1}{8}$ of a mile. If I go a mile, stopping at every fountain, how many times will I stop?

**2** I'm walking my dog $\frac{3}{6}$ of the way to the park this morning. Another fraction name for $\frac{3}{6}$ is _____.

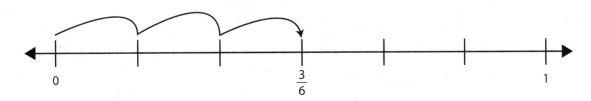

**3** **CHALLENGE** Write your own fraction word problem below using a number line to model your answer. Write an equation to show your computation.

NAME | DATE

 **The Broken Ruler, Part 2**

**1** These rulers have been broken at both ends so they fit on the page. Find, mark, and label the measurements on each. The first one has been done for you.

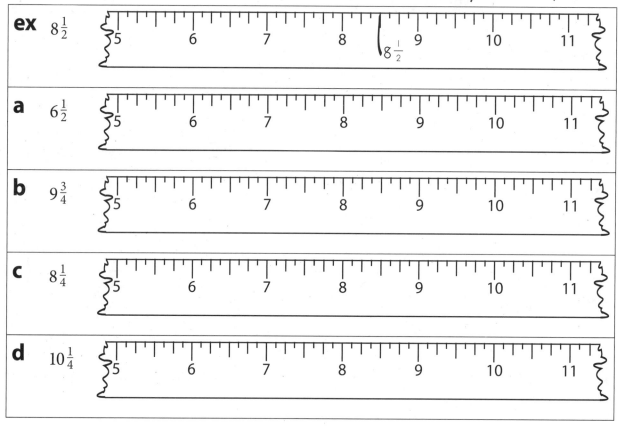

**2** Share your work with a partner. Does he or she agree with each of the marks you made on the rulers? If not, decide who's correct and fix your work.

**3** **CHALLENGE** What other fractions do you know? Mark and label them on this ruler.

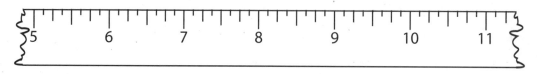

**Mass, Volume & Length Review**

**1** Anabel's turtle has a mass of 413 grams. Her frog has a mass of 288 grams. Does the mass of both pets put together equal a kilogram? If not, how much less than a kilogram is the mass of both pets added together? Show your work using numbers, sketches, or words.

**2** Raphael had a bottle of water with 1,000 milliliters of water in it. He drank 376 milliliters of water. Then, he went for a run. After his run, Raphael drank 574 more milliliters of water.

**a** How much water did Raphael drink in all? Show your work using numbers, sketches, or words. Be sure to label the answer with the correct unit.

**b** How much water was left in Raphael's water bottle? Show your work using numbers, sketches, or words. Be sure to label the answer with the correct unit.

**3** What unit do you use? Circle the unit you would use for each type of measurement.

| Mass | liters | grams | centimeters |
|---|---|---|---|
| Volume | milliliters | inches | grams |
| Length | kilograms | milliliters | centimeters |

NAME _____ | DATE _____

 **Beanstalk Data**

**1** Use your beanstalk measurements to answer the questions below.

**a** My beanstalk is _____ inches tall.

**b** How many leaves are on your beanstalk? _____

**c** The longest leaf is _____ inches long.

**d** The widest leaf is _____ inches wide. Measure this to the nearest quarter-inch.

**2** Put a red dot on the smallest leaf on your beanstalk. How far is the red dot from the top your beanstalk? Measure the distance to the nearest quarter-inch.

My red dot is _____ inches from the top.

**3** Draw a red "X" more than one-third but less than five-sixths of the way up the beanstalk to show where Jim is climbing. Measure the distance to the nearest half-inch.

My X is _____ inches from the bottom.

**4** What else do you notice?

**138**

NAME | DATE

# Beanstalk Line Plot

Mrs. Englund's third graders were measuring their beanstalks again! This time they measured the leaves in centimeters and wondered how many of each leaf measurement they had. They decided to use a line plot to display their data.

**Leaf Measurements in Centimeters**

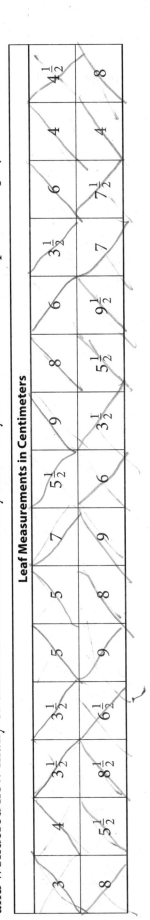

| 3 | 5 | 7 | $5\frac{1}{2}$ | 9 | $3\frac{1}{2}$ | 8 | 6 | $3\frac{1}{2}$ | 6 | 4 | $4\frac{1}{2}$ |
| 8 | 8 | 6 | 6 | $5\frac{1}{2}$ | $3\frac{1}{2}$ | $9\frac{1}{2}$ | 7 | $7\frac{1}{2}$ | 4 | 8 | |
| 4 | 5 | $3\frac{1}{2}$ | $6\frac{1}{2}$ | | | | | | | | |
| $5\frac{1}{2}$ | $8\frac{1}{2}$ | | | | | | | | | | |

Record the data on the line plot below.

**Beanstalk Measurements in Centimeters**

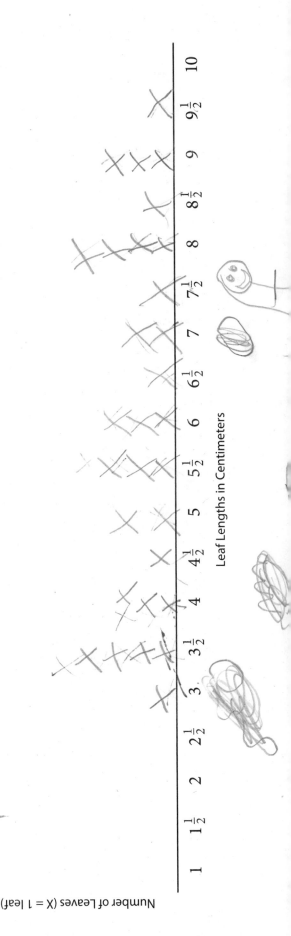

Number of Leaves (X = 1 leaf)

Leaf Lengths in Centimeters

1   $1\frac{1}{2}$   2   $2\frac{1}{2}$   3   $3\frac{1}{2}$   4   $4\frac{1}{2}$   5   $5\frac{1}{2}$   6   $6\frac{1}{2}$   7   $7\frac{1}{2}$   8   $8\frac{1}{2}$   9   $9\frac{1}{2}$   10

**NAME** _____ | **DATE** _____

# Another Beanstalk Line Plot

**1** Record all the leaf measurements from your beanstalk in the table below. Then complete the line plot using an X for each leaf.

| **My Leaf Measurement Data in Inches** (including fractions of an inch) | | | | | | | |
|---|---|---|---|---|---|---|---|
| | | | | | | | |
| | | | | | | | |
| | | | | | | | |

Beanstalk Leaf Measurements to the Nearest Quarter-Inch

Number of Leaves (X = 1 leaf)

$\frac{1}{4}$  $\frac{1}{2}$  $\frac{3}{4}$  1  $1\frac{1}{4}$  $1\frac{1}{2}$  $1\frac{3}{4}$  2  $2\frac{1}{4}$  $2\frac{1}{2}$  $2\frac{3}{4}$  3  $3\frac{1}{4}$  $3\frac{1}{2}$  $3\frac{3}{4}$  4  $4\frac{1}{4}$  $4\frac{1}{2}$  $4\frac{3}{4}$  5

Leaf Lengths in Inches

**2** Use the data on your line plot to help answer the questions below.

**a** How long was the longest leaf on your beanstalk? _____

**b** How long was the shortest left on your beanstalk? _____

**c** What was the most common measurement for your leaves? _____

**d** How many leaves did you have of that length? _____

**e** Did you have more leaves that were longer than $2\frac{1}{4}$ inches or shorter than $2\frac{1}{4}$ inches?

**f** How many of your leaves were longer than 3 inches? _____

**g** What does each x on your line plot stand for? _____

NAME _____    DATE _____

## 🎓 Beanstalk Measurements

Mrs. Englund's third graders measured how far Jim climbed up their beanstalks, using the nearest whole centimeters. The line below shows the heights Jim climbed.

**Beanstalk Leaf Measurements in Centimeters**

Number of Students (X = 1)

```
                                              X
                    X                   X     X
                    X           X   X   X   X X
            X       X       X   X   X   X   X X
        X   X       X       X   X   X   X   X X X X
    X   X   X   X   X       X   X   X   X   X X X X X
   30  31  32  33  34  35  36  37  38  39  40 41 42 43 44 45 46 47 48 49 50 51 52 53 54 55
```

**Heights Jim climbed in Centimeters**

Use the information from the line plot to answer the questions below.

**1** How high did most of the students have Jim climb the beanstalk? _____ 41cm

**2** How many students had Jim climb 42 cm or higher? _____ 15 Students

**3** How many students had Jim climb 41 cm or lower? _____ 18 Students

**4** What else did you notice?

NAME _____ | DATE _____

 # Measurement & Fractions

**1** A marble has 5 times the mass of a paperclip. Peter puts 3 marbles on one side of a pan balance scale.

How many paperclips should Peter put on the other side to balance with the marbles? Show your work.

Peter should put _____ paperclips on the other side of the balance.

**2** Tanner's dog dish has 4 times as much water as Lily's cat bowl. Lily's cat bowl has 200 milliliters of water in it.

How much water is in Tanner's dog dish? Show your work and label your answer with the correct units.

Tanner's dog dish has _____ of water.

**3** Mark and label the number line below with the following whole numbers and fractions: 0, 1, $\frac{3}{4}$, $\frac{1}{8}$, $\frac{1}{2}$, $\frac{1}{4}$, $\frac{7}{8}$.

**4** Winter wants to make 8 containers of orange paint for a school project. She is planning to fill each container with 4 liters of red paint and 7 liters of yellow paint to get the right shade of orange.

How much paint does Winter need in all? Show your work and label your answer with the correct units.

Winter needs _____ of paint in all.

**NAME** | **DATE**

 # Comparing Fractions

Fill in the shapes to show the two fractions. Then compare them using < or >.

| Show these fractions. | | Compare the fractions with < or >. |
|---|---|---|
| **ex** $\frac{1}{2}$ | $\frac{1}{4}$ | $\frac{1}{2} \quad > \quad \frac{1}{4}$ |
| **1** $\frac{1}{3}$ | $\frac{1}{2}$ | $\frac{1}{3} \quad < \quad \frac{1}{2}$ |
| **2** $\frac{2}{3}$ | $\frac{2}{4}$ | $\frac{2}{3} \quad > \quad \frac{2}{4}$ |
| **3** $\frac{3}{4}$ | $\frac{5}{8}$ | $\frac{3}{4} \quad \quad \frac{5}{8}$ |

NAME _____ | DATE _____

 **Thinking About Fours** page 1 of 2

**1** Write three mathematical observations about the Fours Chart. Include at least one observation about a row you *can't* see.

**a**

**b**

**c**

**2** Draw a line from each question on the left to the matching expression on the right. Then write the answer to each.

James saw 6 cars in the parking lot. How many wheels on the cars?

$5 \times 4 =$ _____

Jenny went to the pet shop to visit the rabbits. When she looked into the rabbit pen, she saw 12 legs. How many rabbits?

$16 \div 4 =$ _____

The kindergartners at our school have 5 little red wagons to use on the playground. How many wheels?

$7 \times 4 =$ _____

When Jeff went to the farm to visit the new piglets, he saw 16 little legs in the pigpen. How many piglets?

$6 \times 4 =$ _____

Lori went to the skateboard park with 6 of her friends. They all brought their skateboards. How many wheels?

$20 \div 4 =$ _____

Sara and Max went for a walk and saw 20 dog legs. How many dogs did they see?

$12 \div 4 =$ _____

NAME _____ | DATE _____

## Thinking About Fours page 2 of 2

**3** Every square has 4 sides. Fill in the ratio table to show how many sides different numbers of squares have.

| number of squares | 1 | 2 | 3 | | 5 | 8 | | 20 | 50 | |
|---|---|---|---|---|---|---|---|---|---|---|
| number of sides | 4 | | | 16 | 20 | | 40 | | | 400 |

**4** You will be circling and coloring in all the counting-by-4s numbers on the grid below.

**a** Do you think 100 will be one of the numbers you circle and color in? Why or why not?

**b** Now circle and color in all the counting-by-4s numbers on this grid.

| 1 | 2 | 3 | 4 | 5 | 6 | 7 | 8 | 9 | 10 |
|---|---|---|---|---|---|---|---|---|---|
| 11 | 12 | 13 | 14 | 15 | 16 | 17 | 18 | 19 | 20 |
| 21 | 22 | 23 | 24 | 25 | 26 | 27 | 28 | 29 | 30 |
| 31 | 32 | 33 | 34 | 35 | 36 | 37 | 38 | 39 | 40 |
| 41 | 42 | 43 | 44 | 45 | 46 | 47 | 48 | 49 | 50 |
| 51 | 52 | 53 | 54 | 55 | 56 | 57 | 58 | 59 | 60 |
| 61 | 62 | 63 | 64 | 65 | 66 | 67 | 68 | 69 | 70 |
| 71 | 72 | 73 | 74 | 75 | 76 | 77 | 78 | 79 | 80 |
| 81 | 82 | 83 | 84 | 85 | 86 | 87 | 88 | 89 | 90 |
| 91 | 92 | 93 | 94 | 95 | 96 | 97 | 98 | 99 | 100 |

**c** Is 100 one of those numbers? _____

**5** Jake says that counting-by-4s numbers have to be even and they can never be odd. Do you agree with Jake? Why or why not?

**145**

**NAME** | **DATE**

 # Writing Multiplication Equations

Write a count-by sequence and a multiplication equation to show the totals below.

| Group | Count-by-Sequence | Multiplication Equation |
|---|---|---|
| **ex** Three hands. How many fingers? | 5, 10, 15 | 3 × 5 = 15 fingers |
| **a** Six elephants. How many ears? | | |
| **b** Eight dimes. How many cents? | | |
| **c** Seven sea stars. How many arms? | | |
| **d** CHALLENGE Five egg cartons. How many eggs? | | |

**Multiplication Arrays**

**1** Complete the multiplication facts.

| 3 | 3 | 4 | 4 | 6 | 3 | 4 |
|---|---|---|---|---|---|---|
| ×4 | ×3 | ×6 | ×4 | ×3 | ×8 | ×9 |

| 6 | 3 | 5 | 3 | 5 | 4 | 8 |
|---|---|---|---|---|---|---|
| ×7 | ×9 | ×2 | ×5 | ×4 | ×7 | ×0 |

**2** Use the array to show how you could solve each fact.

**ex** 3 × 7 = 21

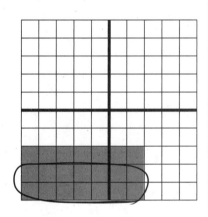

2 × 7 = 14
14 + 7 = 21

**a** 4 × 8 =

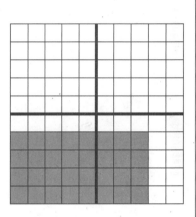

**b** 6 × 9 =

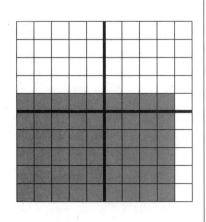

**c** 7 × 4 =

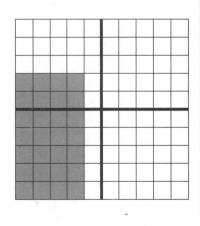

**Flowers, Shells & Cards**

**1** Lisa, Imani, and Carla were picking flowers for their aunt. If they each picked 8 flowers, how many flowers did they pick in all? Show all your work.

**2** Frank collected 18 beautiful shells for his 3 cousins. If he gave each cousin the same number of shells, how many shells did each cousin get? Show all your work.

**3** **CHALLENGE** Four friends were making cards to sell at the holiday sale. Each friend made 9 cards. They put all their cards together and then bundled them in groups of 6 cards to sell. How many bundles of 6 cards did they have to sell? Show all your work.

**NAME** | **DATE**

 ## Cats & Kittens

Pick the equation you could use to solve each problem. Then solve the problem.

**1** Ray's cat had 6 kittens. His neighbor adopted 2 of them. How many kittens does Ray have left?

○  6 ÷ 2 = ?          ○  6 + 2 = ?          ○  6 − 2 = ?          ○  6 × 2 = ?

Ray had _____ kittens left.

**2** Marsha's cat had 6 kittens. She gave all of them away by giving 2 kittens each to some of her neighbors. How many neighbors got 2 kittens?

○  6 ÷ 2 = ?          ○  6 + 2 = ?          ○  6 − 2 = ?          ○  6 × 2 = ?

_____ neighbors got 2 kittens each.

**3** One of Larry's cats had 6 kittens. Another one of his cats had only 2 kittens. How many kittens were there in all?

○  6 ÷ 2 = ?          ○  6 + 2 = ?          ○  6 − 2 = ?          ○  6 × 2 = ?

There were _____ kittens in all.

**4** Write a story problem to match this equation. 24 ÷ 3 = _____

Solve the story problem. Write your answer here: _____

NAME _____ | DATE _____

 **Solving Game Store Problems**

I am solving _____'s problem.

I estimate a reasonable answer will be: (circle one)

| less than 10 | 10 | 20 | 30 | 40 | 50 | 60 | 70 | 80 | 90 | 100 | greater than 100 |
|---|---|---|---|---|---|---|---|---|---|---|---|

The problem I am trying to figure out is:

Here's my equation:

This is my work:

**150**

# Work Place Instructions 5A Solving Game Store Problems

## This is an activity for 1 person. The student needs:

- 1 5A Solving Game Store Problems sheet
- copies of story problems written by classmates
- access to colored tiles and/or base ten pieces

**1** The student chooses a story problem that seems interesting, and estimates what a reasonable answer might be.

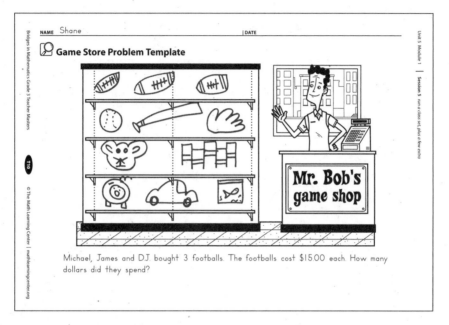

**2** The student records the name of the person who wrote the problem, and restates what the problem is asking. Then the student writes an equation to match the problem, with a box to stand for the answer.

**3** The student uses sketches, tiles, base ten pieces, or any other tools needed to to solve the problem.

**4** Then the student shows his or her thinking with numbers, labeled sketches, or words.

**5** Last, the student edits his or her work to be sure it meets the class guidelines.

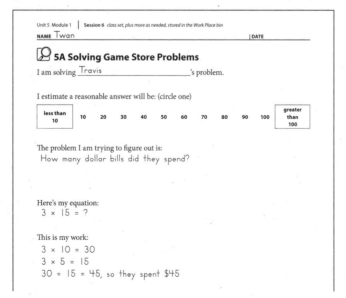

NAME _____ | DATE _____

 **Undersea Adventures**

**1** Chloe the clownfish is 4 inches long. There is a sea snake in the area that is 8 times as long as Chloe. How long is the sea snake? Show your work.

**2** Some brain coral nearby is 11 times as wide as Chloe is long.
How wide is the brain coral?

**3** Chloe swam behind a sea anemone that was 3 times as wide as Chloe is long.
Then Chloe saw a basket sea star that was twice as wide as the anemone.
How wide is the basket sea star?

**4** Use a dollar sign and decimal point to write the value of each group of coins.

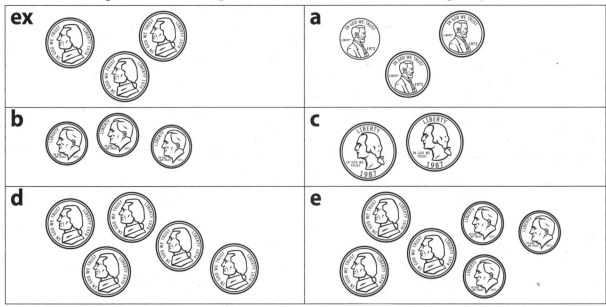

**NAME** | **DATE**

 # An Array of Fact Families

Label each array below with its dimensions. Then write a multiplication and division fact family to match.

| **ex** 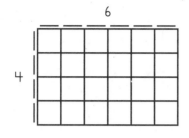 | **1** 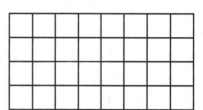 |
|---|---|
| $4 \times 6 = 24$  $24 \div 6 = 4$<br>$6 \times 4 = 24$  $24 \div 4 = 6$ | |
| **2** 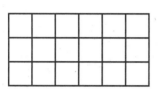 | **3** 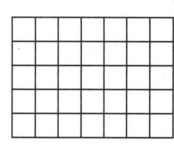 |
| **4** 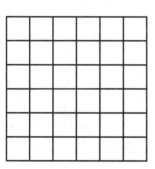 | **5** 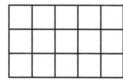 |
| **6** 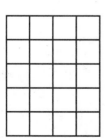 | **7** 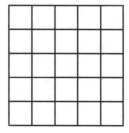 |

#  Work Place Instructions 5B Scout Them Out

## This is an activity for 1 person. The student needs:

- 1 5B Scout Them Out Multiplication & Division sheet
- a red and a blue colored pencil or crayon

**1** The student chooses one of the Scout Them Out sheets.

There are 8 different Scout Them Out sheets, lettered from A through H. Students can do them in any order.

**2** The student circles the first set of facts in blue and then uses regular pencil to record the answers. The student circles the second set of facts in red, and then uses regular pencil to record the answers.

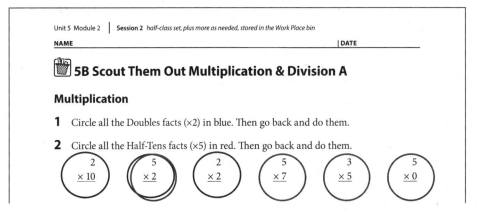

Circle x2 facts in blue and x5 facts in red.

**3** After the student has completed the multiplication facts, he uses the answers to help solve the division problems on the lower half of the sheet.

Students can use the Multiplication Table Student Book page they completed during Unit 2, Module 3, to check their own answers to the multiplication combinations.

**Fact Families & Missing Numbers**

**1** Write the multiplication and division fact family that belongs with each array.

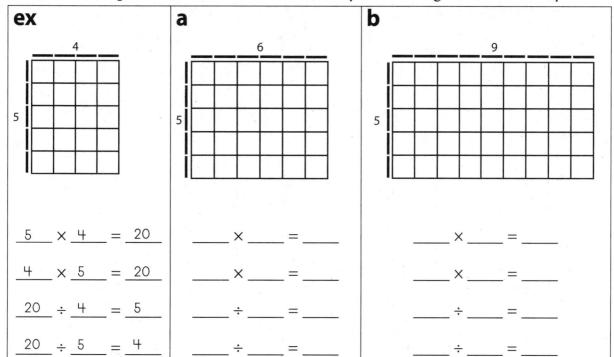

| ex | a | b |
|---|---|---|

**ex**

_5_ × _4_ = _20_

_4_ × _5_ = _20_

_20_ ÷ _4_ = _5_

_20_ ÷ _5_ = _4_

**a**

___ × ___ = ___

___ × ___ = ___

___ ÷ ___ = ___

___ ÷ ___ = ___

**b**

___ × ___ = ___

___ × ___ = ___

___ ÷ ___ = ___

___ ÷ ___ = ___

**2** Fill in the missing numbers below.

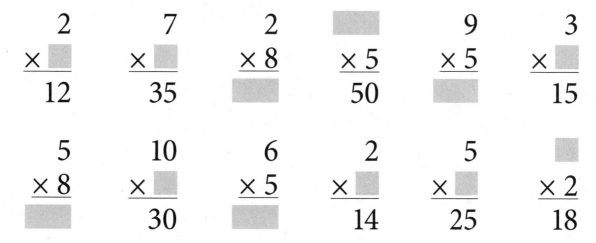

$\begin{array}{r} 2 \\ \times \blacksquare \\ \hline 12 \end{array}$  $\begin{array}{r} 7 \\ \times \blacksquare \\ \hline 35 \end{array}$  $\begin{array}{r} 2 \\ \times 8 \\ \hline \blacksquare \end{array}$  $\begin{array}{r} \blacksquare \\ \times 5 \\ \hline 50 \end{array}$  $\begin{array}{r} 9 \\ \times 5 \\ \hline \blacksquare \end{array}$  $\begin{array}{r} 3 \\ \times \blacksquare \\ \hline 15 \end{array}$

$\begin{array}{r} 5 \\ \times 8 \\ \hline \blacksquare \end{array}$  $\begin{array}{r} 10 \\ \times \blacksquare \\ \hline 30 \end{array}$  $\begin{array}{r} 6 \\ \times 5 \\ \hline \blacksquare \end{array}$  $\begin{array}{r} 2 \\ \times \blacksquare \\ \hline 14 \end{array}$  $\begin{array}{r} 5 \\ \times \blacksquare \\ \hline 25 \end{array}$  $\begin{array}{r} \blacksquare \\ \times 2 \\ \hline 18 \end{array}$

**3** Solve these equations.

$16 + 20 - (2 \times 4) =$ _____     $(7 \times 5) + 150 =$ _____     $(10 \times 10) - 79 =$ _____

NAME                                                                    | DATE

 **What's Missing? Bingo Board A**

| 4 | 6 | 7 |
|---|---|---|
| 9 | 8 | 5 |
| 10 | 2 | 3 |

| Fact Families |
|:---:|
|  |
|  |
|  |
|  |

NAME _____ | DATE _____

 **What's Missing? Bingo Board B**

| 3 | 9 | 2 |
|---|---|---|
| 5 | 10 | 6 |
| 8 | 7 | 4 |

| Fact Families | |
|---|---|
| | |
| | |
| | |
| | |

**157**

**Fact Families & More**

**1** Fill in the missing number in each equation below. Be sure that the number you write makes the equation true.

☐ × 7 = 7          ☐ × 9 = 72          6 × ☐ = 36

9 × ☐ = 45          6 × ☐ = 0          ☐ × 5 = 35

☐ × 6 = 18          4 × ☐ = 36          28 ÷ ☐ = 7

**2** Complete the fact families below.

| 9 × 3 = 27 |
| --- |
|  |
|  |
|  |

| 4 × 8 = 32 |
| --- |
|  |
|  |
|  |

| 7 × 6 = 42 |
| --- |
|  |
|  |
|  |

| 7 × 8 = 56 |
| --- |
|  |
|  |
|  |

**NAME** | **DATE**

 # More Missing Numbers & Fact Families

**1** Fill in the missing numbers below.

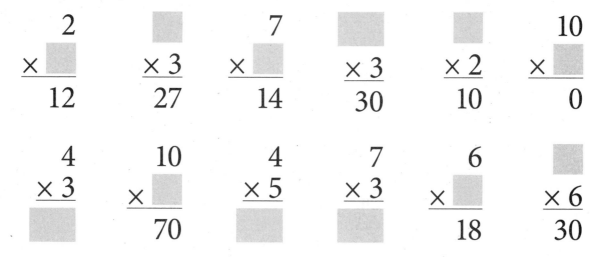

$$\begin{array}{r} 2 \\ \times\ \square \\ \hline 12 \end{array} \qquad \begin{array}{r} \square \\ \times\ 3 \\ \hline 27 \end{array} \qquad \begin{array}{r} 7 \\ \times\ \square \\ \hline 14 \end{array} \qquad \begin{array}{r} \square \\ \times\ 3 \\ \hline 30 \end{array} \qquad \begin{array}{r} \square \\ \times\ 2 \\ \hline 10 \end{array} \qquad \begin{array}{r} 10 \\ \times\ \square \\ \hline 0 \end{array}$$

$$\begin{array}{r} 4 \\ \times\ 3 \\ \hline \square \end{array} \qquad \begin{array}{r} 10 \\ \times\ \square \\ \hline 70 \end{array} \qquad \begin{array}{r} 4 \\ \times\ 5 \\ \hline \square \end{array} \qquad \begin{array}{r} 7 \\ \times\ 3 \\ \hline \square \end{array} \qquad \begin{array}{r} 6 \\ \times\ \square \\ \hline 18 \end{array} \qquad \begin{array}{r} \square \\ \times\ 6 \\ \hline 30 \end{array}$$

**2** Write the multiplication and division fact family that goes with each array. Use the arrays to find each product if you need to.

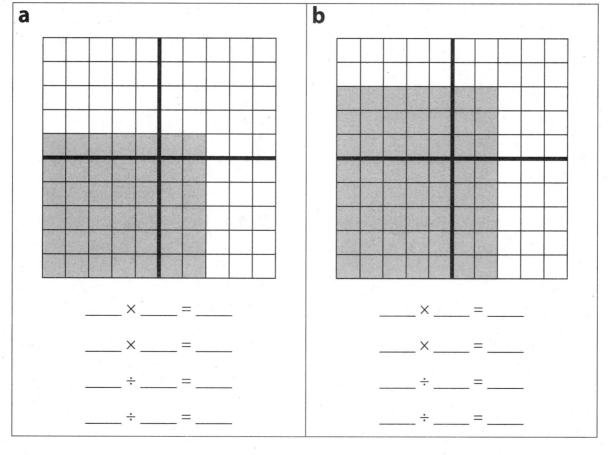

a

_____ × _____ = _____

_____ × _____ = _____

_____ ÷ _____ = _____

_____ ÷ _____ = _____

b

_____ × _____ = _____

_____ × _____ = _____

_____ ÷ _____ = _____

_____ ÷ _____ = _____

**159**

NAME _____ | DATE _____

 **Number Puzzles** page 1 of 2

**1** Read each of the equations below. If it is true, circle the T. If it is false, circle the F.

**a** $18 = 9 \times 2$      T    F         **e** $6 \times 10 = 12$      T    F

**b** $2 \times 4 = 4 \times 2$      T    F         **f** $2 \times 8 = 4 \times 4$      T    F

**c** $5 = 10 \div 2$      T    F         **g** $3 \times 2 = 12 \div 2$      T    F

**d** $2 \times 3 = 6 \times 5 = 30$    T    F         **h** $100 \div 2 = 25 \times 2$      T    F

**2** Fill in the missing numbers to make each equation true.

**a** $16 = 4 \times \boxed{\phantom{00}}$          **g** $25 \div 1 = \boxed{\phantom{00}}$

**b** $2 \times \boxed{\phantom{00}} = 4 \times 5$          **h** $60 = \boxed{\phantom{00}} \times 6$

**c** $\boxed{\phantom{00}} \times 10 = 30$          **i** $12 \div 2 = 6 \times \boxed{\phantom{00}}$

**d** $12 \div 2 = \boxed{\phantom{00}}$          **j** $18 \div 2 = \boxed{\phantom{00}} \times 3$

**e** $20 \div \boxed{\phantom{00}} = 4$          **k** $10 \times 10 = 50 \times \boxed{\phantom{00}}$

**f** $\boxed{\phantom{00}} \div 5 = 5$          **l** $10 \times 10 = 25 \times \boxed{\phantom{00}}$

**3** Sara has 3 bags of shells. Each bag has 10 shells in it. Her brother Max has 5 bags of shells. Each bag has 6 shells in it. Do Sara and Max have the same number of shells? Use labeled sketches, numbers, or words to prove your answer.

**NAME** | **DATE**

## Number Puzzles page 2 of 2

**4**  Briana and Bryan split 10 dollars evenly. Jody, Jamal, and Jasmin split 12 dollars evenly. Did all the kids get the same amount of money? Use labeled sketches, numbers, or words to prove your answer.

**5**  Write a word problem to go with each of the equations below.

**a**  $3 \times 5 = 15$

**b**  $20 \div 4 = 5$

**NAME** | **DATE**

 ## Fact Family Triangles

**1** $2 \times 4$ and $4 \times 2$ are 8. $8 \div 2 = 4$ and $8 \div 4 = 2$. Can you see how 2, 4, and 8 are related? That's why they're called a fact family. Each of the triangles below shows a fact family. Write 2 multiplication and 2 division facts for each family. The first one has been done for you.

**ex**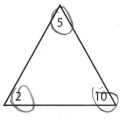

$2 \times 5 = 10$
$5 \times 2 = 10$
$10 \div 2 = 5$
$10 \div 5 = 2$

**a**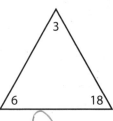

**b**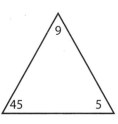

**c**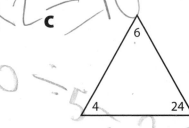

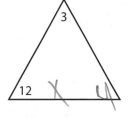 

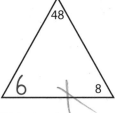 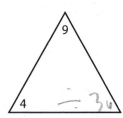

**2** Several Fact Families went to the amusement park. One member of each family got lost. Write in the missing member of each family. The first one has been done for you.

**ex**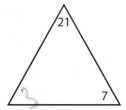

Write in 6 because
$6 \times 8 = 48$.

**a**

Hint: 3 times
what equals 12?

**b**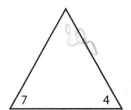

**c**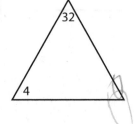

**d**

**e**

**f**

**g**

# 🔎 **More Story Problems** page 1 of 2

**1** Write your own story problem to fit this equation: $7 \times 5 = m$

**2** Write your own story problem to fit this equation: $35 \div 5 = n$

Solve each problem in your math journal. Show your thinking using numbers, labeled sketches, or words. Then write an equation that represents the problem and the solution on this page.

**3** Ms. Rowan has 6 tables in her classroom, and 24 students. If she divides the students evenly among the tables, how many students will sit at each table?

**4** Teresa has 24 stickers in her sticker book. Each page holds 6 stickers. How many pages does her sticker book have?

**5** Steve baked 36 cookies. He put 4 cookies in each bag. How many bags of cookies did he have?

**6** Craig gave his sister 4 boxes of new markers. She was happy to get 36 new markers. How many markers were in each box, if each box held exactly the same number of markers?

**7** Ms. Allyn was getting ready for a math investigation. Each student needed 8 paperclips. She had 32 paperclips. How many students were able to do the investigation?

*(continued on next page)*

## More Story Problems page 2 of 2

**8** The math club was going on a field trip. They were driving 8 school vans. If there were 32 students in the math club, and each van took the same number of students, how many students went in each van?

**9** Each student in the gym class gathered 4 tennis balls. There were 25 students in the class. Then, the gym teacher divided the balls evenly into 20 different buckets. How many balls are in each bucket?

Which equation would help you solve this problem?

- ○ $(4 + 25) \times 20 = b$
- ○ $(4 \times 25) + 20 = b$
- ○ $(20 \div 4) - 24 = b$
- ○ $(4 \times 25) \div 20 = b$

**10** **CHALLENGE** Mr. Garner gathered $6.50 from each student going to a music festival. He needed to divide the money evenly to pay the field trip helpers: the bus driver, the lunchroom lady, the person running the festival, and the photographer. He has 26 students going to the festival. How much money did he pay each field trip helper?

**NAME** _____ **DATE** _____

 # Division Practice

**1** Fill in the blanks.

$3 \times$ ___5___ $= 15$          $15 \div 3 =$ _____

$28 \div 7 =$ _____          $7 \times$ _____ $= 28$

_____ $\times 4 = 24$          $24 \div$ _____ $= 4$

$30 \div$ _____ $= 5$          _____ $\times 5 = 30$

$3 \times 2 =$ _____          _____ $\div 2 = 3$

_____ $= 8 \times 7$          _____ $\div 8 = 7$

$399 + 203 =$ _____          $302 - 198 =$ _____

**2** Solve the problems below. Show your thinking in words, numbers, or sketches.

**a** Mr. See has a collection of stamps. He has 45 total stamps, with 9 stamps on each page. How many pages of stamps does he have?

**b** Mrs. Kay has a photo album with 9 pages in it, and 45 photos. How many photos can she put on each page if she wants to put exactly the same number on every page in the album?

 **More Arrays** page 1 of 2

For the arrays in each pair below:

- Mark the array to show the number you started with (the dividend), the number you divided by (the divisor), and the answer (the quotient).
- Write an equation to represent the problem.
- Fill in the bubble to show whether you were trying to find the number in each group or the number of groups.

**1**  Steve baked 36 cookies. He put 4 cookies in each bag. How many bags of cookies did he have?

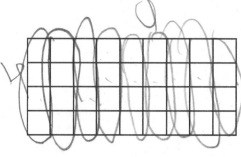

| **a**  Equation | **b**  The answer to this problem tells |
|---|---|
| $36 \div 4 = 9$ | ○ How many in each group<br>● How many groups |

**2**  Craig gave his sister 4 boxes of new markers. She was happy to get 36 new markers. How many markers were in each box, if each box held exactly the same number of markers?

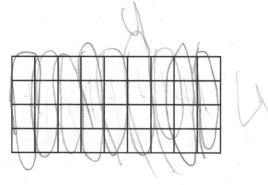

| **a**  Equation | **b**  The answer to this problem tells |
|---|---|
| $36 \div \boxed{9} = 4$ | ● How many in each group<br>○ How many groups |

**NAME** _____ | **DATE** _____

## More Arrays page 2 of 2

**3** Ms. Allyn was getting ready for a math investigation. Each student needed 8 paperclips. She had 32 paperclips. How many students were able to do the investigation?

| **a** Equation | **b** The answer to this problem tells |
|---|---|
| 32 ÷ =H | ⦿ How many in each group |
| | ○ How many groups |

**4** The math club was going on a field trip. They were driving 8 school vans. If there were 32 students in the math club, and each van took the same number of students, how many students went in each van?

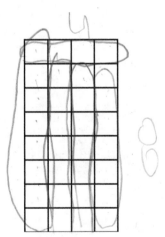

| **a** Equation | **b** The answer to this problem tells |
|---|---|
| 32 ÷ 8 = 4 | ○ How many in each group |
| | ○ How many groups |

NAME _____ | DATE _____

 **Mixed Operations & Story Problems**

**1** Fill in the blanks.

$6 \times \underline{7} = 42$ $\qquad$ $42 \div 6 = \underline{7}$ $\qquad$ $97 - \underline{42} = 55$

$54 \div 6 = \underline{9}$ $\qquad$ $6 \times \underline{9} = 54$ $\qquad$ $\underline{42} \div 8 = 3$

$\underline{19} + 87 = 101$ $\qquad$ $101 - 87 = \underline{14}$ $\qquad$ $3 \times 8 = \underline{24}$

**2** Write an equation for each problem. Be sure to include the unit in your final answer. Show your thinking in words, numbers, or sketches. Use your math journal if you need more room.

**a** Jeremy is setting up for a party. He has 63 cookies. He puts 7 cookies on each plate. How many plates does he use?

Equation: $\underline{63 \div ( = 9}$ Final Answer: _____

**b** Katina is helping to set up for the party. She puts 63 brownies on 7 different plates. How many brownies are on each plate?

Equation: _____ Final Answer: _____

**3** Write a story problem for each of these equations.

| $12 \times 4 = 48$ | $48 \div 4 = 12$ |
|---|---|
| They whtre 12 niss ek nis 4 Babhu niss hu nounu usmiss | |

# Work Place Instructions 5C Line 'Em Up page 1 of 2

**Each pair of players needs:**

- one 5C Line 'Em Up Record Sheet
- one 1–6 die and one 4–9 die
- about 100 colored tiles
- 12 red linear pieces
- base ten area and linear pieces (for Game Variation B)

**1** Players take turns rolling one die to see who goes first, and then write their names on the record sheet they're sharing.

**2** Player 1 rolls both dice, multiplies the two numbers, and writes an equation on his side of the record sheet to show the product.

**3** Player 1 counts out that many tiles and imagines they are bugs or anything else that might be divided into different numbers of lines.

**4** Player 1 divides his tiles into 2 lines first. Then he divides them into 3, 4, 5, and 6 lines.

- The player uses red linear pieces each time to show the number of lines he's making.
- Each time, he records an equation showing the division, making sure his partner is helping and agrees with his equations.

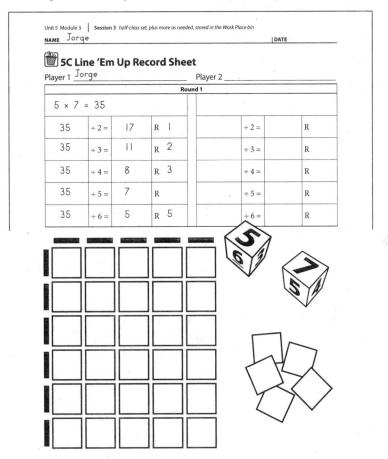

**5** Player 2 repeats steps 2–5.

**6** After both players have completed two rounds they each add up all their remainders. The player with the higher total wins.

# Work Place Instructions 5C Line 'Em Up page 2 of 2

## Game Variations

**A** Use 2 dice numbered 1–6 instead of 1 die numbered 1–6 and 1 numbered 4–9.

If the product of the roll is 5 or less, players won't be able to divide it into 6 equal lines, and the amount will be a remainder. For example, if a player rolls 2 × 2 for a product of 4, she won't be able to divide that amount into 5 or 6 equal lines, and will wind up with the following results:

- 4 ÷ 2 = 2
- 4 ÷ 3 = 1 R1
- 4 ÷ 4 = 1
- 4 ÷ 5 = 0 R4
- 4 ÷ 6 = 0 R4

**B** Use 2 dice numbered 4–9 instead of 1 die numbered 1–6 and 1 numbered 4–9.

If players use this game variation, they will need to use base 10 strips and linear pieces instead of the colored tiles and red linear pieces to model and solve at least some of the division combinations.

> *Connor OK, I rolled an 8 and a 9, and 9 × 8 is 72. Wow—that's a big number. Maybe I'll get some big remainders! I'm going to use the base ten pieces for this one—the tiles will take way too long.*

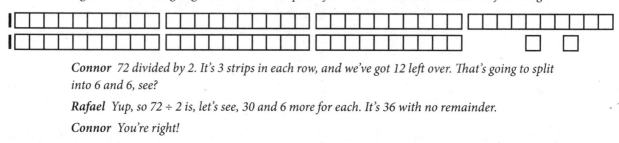

> *Connor 72 divided by 2. It's 3 strips in each row, and we've got 12 left over. That's going to split into 6 and 6, see?*
>
> *Rafael Yup, so 72 ÷ 2 is, let's see, 30 and 6 more for each. It's 36 with no remainder.*
>
> *Connor You're right!*

NAME _____ | DATE _____

 **Multiplication Review**

**1** Complete the multiplication facts.

| 10 | 3 | 5 | 9 | 4 | 5 | 6 |
|---|---|---|---|---|---|---|
| × 6 | × 1 | × 8 | × 0 | × 7 | × 3 | × 4 |
| 60 | 3 | 40 | 9 | 26 | 17 | 23 |

| 8 | 2 | 9 | 4 | 9 | 5 | 8 |
|---|---|---|---|---|---|---|
| × 2 | × 9 | × 10 | × 6 | × 3 | × 9 | × 4 |
| 24 | 10 | 40 | 33 | | | |

**2** Fill in the missing number in each fact. Then write a related division equation.

| ex          4  | a          ▮ | b          5 | c          ▮ |
|---|---|---|---|
| × 5 | × 2 | × ▮ | × 9 |
| 20 | 16 | 35 | 18 |
| 20 ÷ 5 = 4 | ___ ÷ ___ = ___ | ___ ÷ ___ = ___ | ___ ÷ ___ = ___ |

**3** **CHALLENGE** Use what you know about basic facts to complete these problems.

| 20 | 21 | 43 | 62 | 62 | 87 | 382 |
|---|---|---|---|---|---|---|
| × 10 | × 4 | × 2 | × 10 | × 5 | × 1 | × 0 |

| 24 | 14 | 14 | 63 | 52 | 10 | 24 |
|---|---|---|---|---|---|---|
| × 2 | × 10 | × 5 | × 2 | × 3 | × 69 | × 4 |

# Work Place Instructions 5D Division Capture page 1 of 2

## Each pair of players needs:

- 1 5D Division Record Sheet
- 1 clear spinner overlay
- 1 red and 1 blue colored pencil
- the completed Multiplication Table page from their Student Books (optional)
- colored tiles and red linear pieces (optional)

**1** Players take turns spinning the spinner. The player who gets the higher number goes first and decides whether he wants to play for red or blue.

**2** Player 1 spins the spinner, and uses the number he spins to fill in the answer to one of the division problems on the record sheet, using a pencil in the color he chose.

**3** Player 2 takes her turn, and then the players take turns back and forth.

- Each player tries to capture 3 or 4 boxes in a row—across, up and down, or diagonally.
- If the box a player needs is already filled, the player loses that turn and must wait until her next turn to try again.

**Note** Each number on the spinner has exactly 2 combinations on the grid that match. If a player spins a 3 and there are already two 3s written on the grid, she will not be able to find another and will lose that turn.

**4** Players continue to take turns until the record sheet is filled or neither player can use the number he or she spins 3 times in a row.

**5** Players each circle the places on the grid where they got 3 or 4 in a row, add up their points, and record their scores on the record sheet.

- Players get 1 point for each row of 3 they capture, and 2 points for each row of 4 they capture.

**6** The player with the higher total wins.

## Work Place Instructions 5D Division Capture page 2 of 2

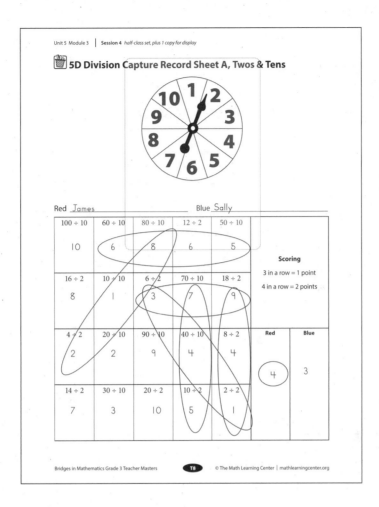

### Game Variations

**A**  Players can use the Multiplication Tables in their Student Books they completed during Unit 2 to help solve the division problems. They can also use the colored tiles and red linear units to help if they want.

**B**  Players take turns using a regular pencil to fill in the answers to the division problems until the grid is complete. Then they play the game as usual, but they find and circle the answers in their own color pencil instead of writing in the answers as they go.

This makes the game a little easier, because the players just have to search for the numbers they spin, instead of searching for the combinations that will give them those numbers.

**C**  There are five different Division Capture record sheets, each one a little more challenging than the one before it. Depending on players' needs, they can:

- Use the same record sheet more than once if they need practice with the facts on that sheet.

- Start with the first record sheet, and use the rest in order over several different Work Place times.

- Start with the record sheet that provides practice with the facts they most need to work on. For example, if both players know their division facts for 2, 3, and 10 pretty well already, they might choose to start with Record Sheet 4 or 5, instead of working through the sheets one by one, starting from 1.

**NAME** _____ **| DATE** _____

# All in the Family

**1** Fill in the missing number in each triangle. Then write the facts in the fact family.

| **ex** | **a** | **b** |
|---|---|---|

**ex**

Triangle: 16 (top), 2 (left), 8 (right)

$\underline{\;2\;} \times \underline{\;8\;} = \underline{\;16\;}$

$\underline{\;8\;} \times \underline{\;2\;} = \underline{\;16\;}$

$\underline{16} \div \underline{\;2\;} = \underline{\;8\;}$

$\underline{16} \div \underline{\;8\;} = \underline{\;2\;}$

**a**

Triangle: 21 (top), 7 (left)

$\underline{\quad} \times \underline{\quad} = \underline{\quad}$

$\underline{\quad} \times \underline{\quad} = \underline{\quad}$

$\underline{\quad} \div \underline{\quad} = \underline{\quad}$

$\underline{\quad} \div \underline{\quad} = \underline{\quad}$

**b**

Triangle: (top), 5 (left), 6 (right)

$\underline{\quad} \times \underline{\quad} = \underline{\quad}$

$\underline{\quad} \times \underline{\quad} = \underline{\quad}$

$\underline{\quad} \div \underline{\quad} = \underline{\quad}$

$\underline{\quad} \div \underline{\quad} = \underline{\quad}$

**c**

Triangle: 48 (top), 6 (right)

$\underline{\quad} \times \underline{\quad} = \underline{\quad}$

$\underline{\quad} \times \underline{\quad} = \underline{\quad}$

$\underline{\quad} \div \underline{\quad} = \underline{\quad}$

$\underline{\quad} \div \underline{\quad} = \underline{\quad}$

**d**

Triangle: (top), 8 (left), 4 (right)

$\underline{\quad} \times \underline{\quad} = \underline{\quad}$

$\underline{\quad} \times \underline{\quad} = \underline{\quad}$

$\underline{\quad} \div \underline{\quad} = \underline{\quad}$

$\underline{\quad} \div \underline{\quad} = \underline{\quad}$

**e**

Triangle: 18 (top), 3 (left)

$\underline{\quad} \times \underline{\quad} = \underline{\quad}$

$\underline{\quad} \times \underline{\quad} = \underline{\quad}$

$\underline{\quad} \div \underline{\quad} = \underline{\quad}$

$\underline{\quad} \div \underline{\quad} = \underline{\quad}$

**2** **CHALLENGE** Use multiplication and division to find the secret path through each maze. You can only move one space up, down, over, or diagonally each time. Write two equations to explain the path through the maze.

**ex**

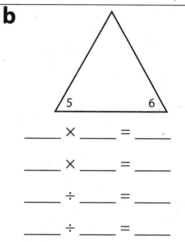

start
3
8—24  4  end
6

$3 \times 8 = 24$
$24 \div 6 = 4$

**a**

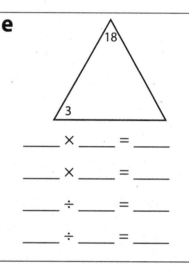

start
81
end  3  9  9
3

**b**

start
32
7  4  8
28
end

 **Grid Paper**

NAME

| DATE

 **More Multiplication Arrays**

**1** Complete the multiplication facts.

$$\begin{array}{r} 6 \\ \times 7 \\ \hline \end{array} \qquad \begin{array}{r} 3 \\ \times 8 \\ \hline \end{array} \qquad \begin{array}{r} 4 \\ \times 9 \\ \hline \end{array} \qquad \begin{array}{r} 9 \\ \times 9 \\ \hline \end{array} \qquad \begin{array}{r} 4 \\ \times 7 \\ \hline \end{array} \qquad \begin{array}{r} 3 \\ \times 9 \\ \hline \end{array} \qquad \begin{array}{r} 7 \\ \times 3 \\ \hline \end{array}$$

$$\begin{array}{r} 8 \\ \times 2 \\ \hline \end{array} \qquad \begin{array}{r} 2 \\ \times 9 \\ \hline \end{array} \qquad \begin{array}{r} 6 \\ \times 8 \\ \hline \end{array} \qquad \begin{array}{r} 3 \\ \times 6 \\ \hline \end{array} \qquad \begin{array}{r} 5 \\ \times 9 \\ \hline \end{array} \qquad \begin{array}{r} 6 \\ \times 6 \\ \hline \end{array} \qquad \begin{array}{r} 9 \\ \times 7 \\ \hline \end{array}$$

**2** Use the array to show how you could solve each fact if you didn't already know the answer.

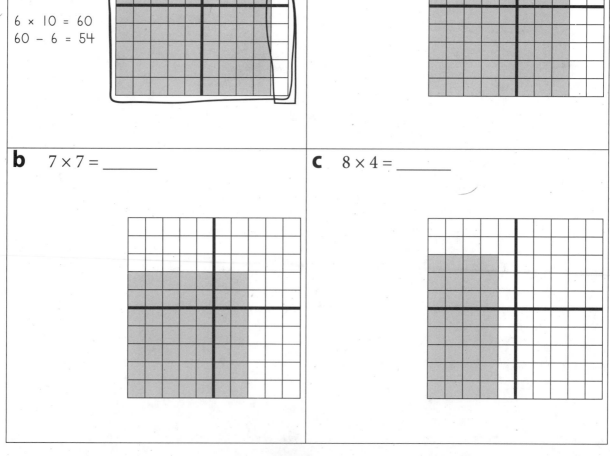

**ex** $6 \times 9 = \underline{54}$

$6 \times 10 = 60$
$60 - 6 = 54$

**a** $7 \times 8 = \underline{\qquad}$

**b** $7 \times 7 = \underline{\qquad}$

**c** $8 \times 4 = \underline{\qquad}$

NAME | DATE

 # Finding Areas Large & Small page 1 of 2

| Object | Your Estimate (in square units) | Approximate Measurement (in square units) | The Difference (in square units) |
|---|---|---|---|
| **1** Area of a large picture book | 6 | 6 | |
| **2** Area of a chair seat | 12 | 9 | |
| **3** Area of a desk or a small table | 12 | 34 | 18 |
| **4** Area of the top of a bookshelf | 12 | | |
| **5** Area of a piece of chart paper | 48 | | |

I noticed:

**NAME** _____ | **DATE** _____

## Finding Areas Large & Small page 2 of 2

**6** The rectangles below have already been marked with square units. Record the dimensions of each and then find the area. Write 2 different equations to show how you found the area of each.

**ex**

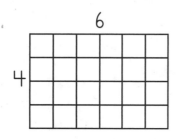

Area = __24__ square units

Equations:

6 + 6 + 6 + 6 = 24
4 × 6 = 24

**a**

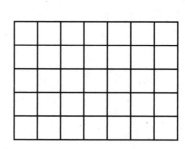

Area = _____ square units

Equations:

**b**

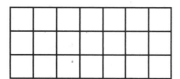

Area = _____ square units

Equations:

**c**

Area = _____ square units

Equations:

 **Grid Paper**

**179**

**NAME** _____ | **DATE** _____

 # Finding More Areas

You'll need a partner and some large square units made out of construction paper to do this sheet. Choose 5 different rectangular surfaces around the room to measure with the large square units. Be sure to estimate the area first.

| Object | Your Estimate (in square units) | Approximate Measurment (in square units) | The Difference (in square units) |
|---|---|---|---|
| **1** | | | |
| **2** | | | |
| **3** | | | |
| **4** | | | |
| **5** | | | |

180

**Measuring My Math Journal**

**1** Estimate the area of the front cover of your math journal in square inches.

Estimate: _____

**2** Using measurement tools from your classroom (ruler, tiles, grid paper, etc.), determine the area of the front cover of your math journal in square inches. Use words, labeled sketches, and numbers to explain how you got your answer.

Area of my math journal _____:

**3** **CHALLENGE** If you were to make a book cover for your entire math journal, front and back, approximately how many square inches of paper would you need? Explain your answer below.

**NAME** _____ | **DATE** _____

 ## Areas to Find

**1** Label each rectangle with its dimensions and area.

**a**

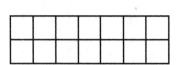

Area = _____ square units

**b**

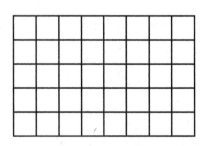

Area = _____ square units

**c**

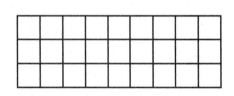

Area = _____ square units

**2** Multiply.

| 3 | 7 | 4 | 10 | 9 | 4 | 9 | 5 |
|---|---|---|----|---|---|---|---|
| × 4 | × 4 | × 5 | × 5 | × 5 | × 6 | × 9 | × 5 |

| 7 | 12 | 8 | 5 | 11 | 13 | 10 | 7 |
|---|----|---|---|----|----|----|---|
| × 7 | × 10 | × 2 | × 8 | × 9 | × 7 | × 15 | × 4 |

# Rainbow Rectangles

**1** Work with the students in your group to put the rectangles in order, from least to most area.

**2** After you've agreed on the order, write the colors of the rectangles where you think they belong in the boxes below.

| Least Area | | | | | Most Area |
|---|---|---|---|---|---|
| | | | | | |
| | | | | | |

**3** Estimate the area of each rectangle and then measure it in square inches. Remember to label your work with the correct units (square inches). Record your work on the chart below. (Hint: Use the red rectangle as a benchmark to help make your estimates.)

| Color Rectangle | Your Estimate in Square Inches (sq. in.) | Actual Area in Square Inches (sq. in.) |
|---|---|---|
| | | |
| | | |
| | | |
| | | |
| | | |
| | | |

**NAME** | **DATE**

 # Estimating & Measuring Area in Square Inches

**1** James says all you have to do to find the area of a 4" × 5" rectangle is multiply 4 × 5 Do you agree? Why or why not?

**2** For each object on the chart below:

- Estimate the area of the first object on the chart below in square inches.
- Record your estimate in square inches.
- Find the area of the object using 1-inch tiles or a ruler, and record the measurement.
- Find the difference between your estimate and the actual measurement. Record the difference in the last column.

Hint: Use what you know about the area of the first object to estimate the others.

| Object | Your Estimate (in square units) | Approximate Measurement (in square units) | The Difference (in square units) |
|---|---|---|---|
| **a** A notecard | | | |
| **b** This worksheet | | | |
| **c** Cover of a chapter book | | | |

**NAME** _____ **| DATE** _____

 # Finding More Small Areas

The rectangles below have already been filled with square units. For each pair of rectangles:

- Label the dimensions of the first one.
- Multiply the dimensions to find the area. Write an equation to match.
- Break the second rectangle into two smaller ones. Find the area of each of the smaller rectangles and add them. Write equations to show your work.

**ex**

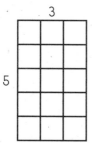

$5 \times 3 = 15$ _____ square units

$( \underline{\phantom{3}} \times \underline{\phantom{3}} ) + ( \underline{\phantom{2}} \times \underline{\phantom{3}} )$

$( \underline{3} \times \underline{3} ) + ( \underline{2} \times \underline{3} )$

$\underline{9} + \underline{6} = \underline{15}$ square units

**1**

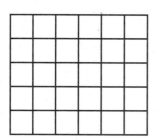

_____ square units

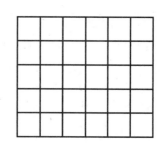

$( \underline{\phantom{xx}} \times \underline{\phantom{xx}} ) + ( \underline{\phantom{xx}} \times \underline{\phantom{xx}} )$

_____ + _____ = _____ square units

**2**

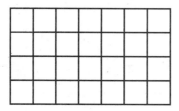

_____ square units

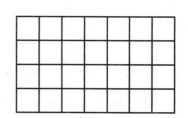

$( \underline{\phantom{xx}} \times \underline{\phantom{xx}} ) + ( \underline{\phantom{xx}} \times \underline{\phantom{xx}} )$

_____ + _____ = _____ square units

NAME | DATE

# Fractions Revisited

**1** Fill in the bubble next to the fraction that shows how much of each shape is filled in.

| | | | |
|---|---|---|---|
| **ex** ● $\frac{1}{2}$  ○ $\frac{1}{3}$  ○ $\frac{1}{4}$ | | **a** ○ $\frac{1}{2}$  ○ $\frac{1}{3}$  ○ $\frac{2}{3}$ | |
| **b** ○ $\frac{1}{2}$  ○ $\frac{3}{4}$  ○ $\frac{4}{3}$ | | **c** ○ $\frac{2}{1}$  ○ $\frac{1}{2}$  ○ $\frac{2}{2}$ | |
| **d** ○ $\frac{2}{4}$  ○ $\frac{2}{3}$  ○ $\frac{2}{2}$ | | **e** ○ $\frac{1}{3}$  ○ $\frac{2}{3}$  ○ $\frac{3}{3}$ | |

**2** Follow the instructions to color the array below.

- Color half the squares in the array red.
- Color one-fourth of the squares in the array blue.
- Color the rest of the squares in the array green.

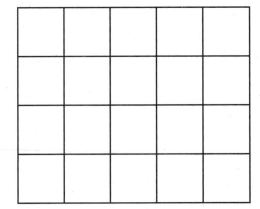

What fraction of the array is green?

**186**

NAME _____ | DATE _____

 **Mixed Review: Fractions, Multiplication & Division**

Solve each problem below. Show your work using numbers, sketches, or words.
Remember to label your answers with the correct units when you need to.

**1** Robin and Cody are collecting stamps. Their stamp books are exactly the same size, with the same number of pages. Robin's stamp book is $\frac{2}{3}$ full. Cody's stamp book is $\frac{3}{4}$ full. Whose stamp book is more full? How do you know?

**2** Robin has a page of her stamp book that is $\frac{1}{3}$ full. Cody has a page of his stamp book that is $\frac{2}{6}$ full. Whose page is more full? How do you know?

**3** One of Robin's pages has 6 out of 12 spaces full.

  **a** Write a fraction that represents how full the page is. _____

  **b** Write another fraction that tells how full the page is. _____

**4** On one page of Robin's stamp book, she has arranged her stamps in a 7-by-6 array. How many stamps are on this page?

**5** On one page of Cody's stamp book, he has 54 stamps. The stamps are organized in 6 groups. How many stamps are in each group?

NAME | DATE

# What Makes a Rectangle So Special?

All quadrilaterals have 4 sides and 4 corners. So, what makes a rectangle special?

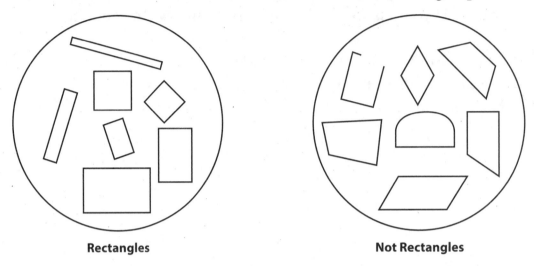

Rectangles                              Not Rectangles

**1** List at least 4 attributes that are shared by all of the shapes in the Rectangles group.

**2** List at least 4 reasons the shapes in the Not Rectangles group can't be in the Rectangles group.

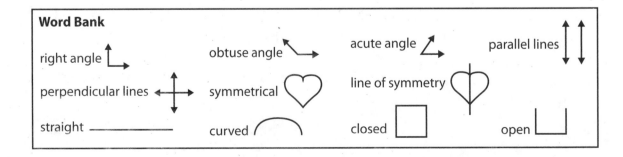

**Word Bank**

right angle | obtuse angle | acute angle | parallel lines

perpendicular lines | symmetrical | line of symmetry

straight | curved | closed | open

**188**

**NAME** | **DATE**

 **Shape Sorting**

**1** Walt sorted some shapes into these two groups.

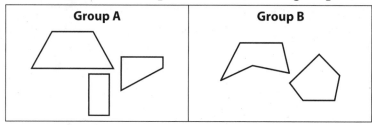

| Group A | Group B |
| --- | --- |

**a** Circle the shapes that belong in group B.

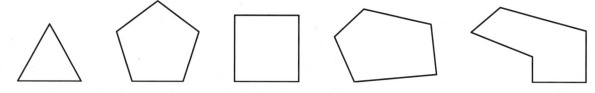

**b** What do the shapes in group B have in common?

**2** How can you tell if a shape is a hexagon?

**a** Circle all the hexagons.

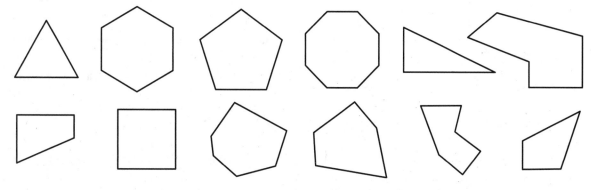

**Shape Poster Project**

You and your partner are going to make a poster about _____.

After someone reads your poster, they should know all about the attributes of your shape, and be able to tell what makes it a special quadrilateral.

Your poster must include:

- ○ A title that tells the name of your quadrilateral
- ○ The slip of paper from your teacher with examples and nonexamples of your quadrilateral
- ○ Words or labeled sketches to describe at least 4 attributes of your quadrilateral
- ○ Words or labeled sketches that give at least 4 reasons the shapes that are in the other group are not examples of your quadrilateral
- ○ Drawings that show 2 more examples of your quadrilateral and 2 more nonexamples of your quadrilateral
- ○ A sentence at the bottom that tells what sets your quadrilateral apart from all the other kinds of quadrilaterals and makes it special

Make your poster:

- • Neat
- • Colorful
- • Informative
- • Easy to read and understand
- • Fun!

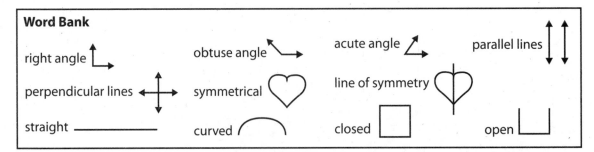

NAME _____ | DATE _____

 **Attributes of Quadrilaterals**

**1** Identify some of the attributes of the quadrilaterals below. Follow these instructions:

- Draw a blue loop around each shape that has 2 pairs of parallel sides.
- Make a red dot inside each shape that has at least 2 right angles.
- Draw a smiley face inside each square.
- Make a green dot inside each shape that has exactly 1 pair of parallel sides.
- Draw an X above each shape that has 4 sides that are exactly the same length.
- Draw a purple loop around each trapezoid.

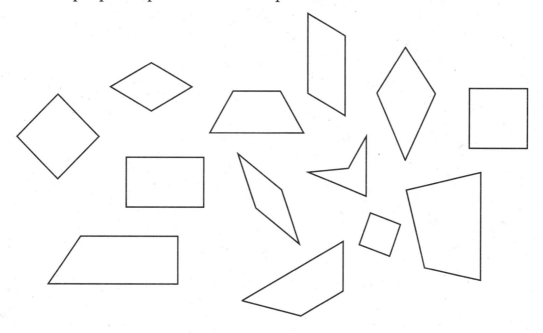

**2** Multiply.

| 3 | 4 | 5 | 8 | 6 | 2 | 10 |
|---|---|---|---|---|---|---|
| ×8 | ×4 | ×6 | ×4 | ×6 | ×8 | ×7 |


| 7 | 5 | 1 | 3 | 0 | 9 | 4 |
|---|---|---|---|---|---|---|
| ×3 | ×5 | ×9 | ×6 | ×10 | ×3 | ×6 |

**NAME** | **DATE**

 **Quadrilaterals**

**1** Cross out the figure that is *not* a parallelogram.

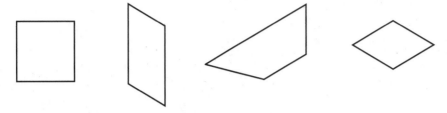

**2** Cross out the figure that is *not* a trapezoid.

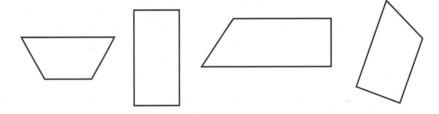

**3** How is a trapezoid like a parallelogram? Use labeled sketches and words to explain.

**4** How are a trapezoid and a parallelogram different? Use labeled sketches and words to explain.

**5** Solve the following problems.

| 39 | 278 | 54 | 108 | 379 | 914 | 19 | 635 |
|---|---|---|---|---|---|---|---|
| + 141 | + 46 | + 525 | + 52 | + 21 | + 36 | + 417 | + 45 |

| 872 | 143 | 87 | 105 | 121 | 243 | 216 | 87 |
|---|---|---|---|---|---|---|---|
| − 41 | − 28 | − 56 | − 28 | − 9 | − 7 | − 15 | − 47 |

#  Work Place Instructions 6A Tangram Polygons

**Each pair of players needs:**

- one 6A Tangram Polygons Record Sheet to share
- 2 sets of tangrams
- 2 rulers

**1** Players decide how many tangram pieces they want to use to build each shape. They write that number on the blank provided on the Tangram Polygons Record Sheet. Players can choose from 3, 4, 5, or 7 pieces.

Players have all 7 tangram pieces available to use, but will use only the number chosen to build each polygon. For example, if a player chooses to build with 4 pieces, any 4 pieces from the entire set may be used for each polygon. Players do not have to use the same 4 pieces every time.

**2** Players work together to build each of the polygons shown on the record sheet. Many have more than one solution.

**Note** One shape cannot be made with 5 pieces, and one shape cannot be made with 7 pieces.

**3** Players draw a sketch or sketches on the record sheet showing how they built each polygon.

- Players may use a ruler if they need help drawing straight lines.
- Players label the tangram pieces in their sketches with tangram piece letters, so other people can see how they solved the puzzles.
- Players show one or more ways they can find to build a shape.

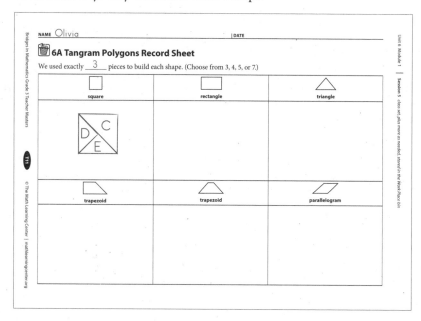

**4** Players can come back to this Work Place on other days, each time using a different number of pieces and a new record sheet.

## Game Variations

**A** Players may choose to work alone at this Work Place.

**B** After four visits to this Work Place, students may be interested in seeing what other polygons can be formed with 3, 4, 5, or 7 pieces. A wide variety of irregular polygons are possible. Students could create their own puzzle/record sheets for classmates to solve.

**NAME**             | **DATE**

 **Polygons**

**1** Two of the shapes below are polygons, and two are not.

   **a**   Circle the two polygons.

   **b**   Explain why the other two shapes are not polygons.

**2** Three of the shapes below are quadrilaterals, and one is not.

   **a**   Circle the three quadrilaterals.

   **b**   Draw two quadrilaterals that are not the same types as those you just circled.

**3** Multiply.

| 5 | 7 | 3 | 4 | 6 | 2 | 4 |
|---|---|---|---|---|---|---|
| × 6 | × 3 | × 8 | × 5 | × 6 | × 9 | × 7 |

| 10 | 9 | 4 | 7 | 7 | 10 | 7 |
|---|---|---|---|---|---|---|
| × 6 | × 3 | × 8 | × 5 | × 6 | × 9 | × 7 |

**4** **CHALLENGE** Multiply.

| 20 | 20 | 80 | 30 | 40 | 40 | 50 |
|---|---|---|---|---|---|---|
| × 3 | × 8 | × 5 | × 6 | × 6 | × 9 | × 7 |

**NAME** _____ | **DATE** _____

## Polygons & Time

**1** Two of the shapes below are rhombuses, and two are not. Circle the two rhombuses.

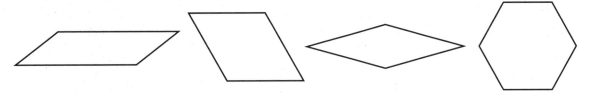

**2** Circle the two irregular polygons.

**3** Write the time shown on each clock.

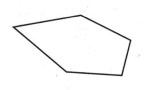   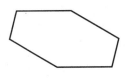

**4** Ava boards her school bus at 7:48 in the morning. She arrives at school at 8:07. How long does it take Ava to get to school? Show your work.

# Work Place Instructions 6B Geoboard Polygons

## Each student works alone and needs:

- 6B Geoboard Polygons Record Sheet (1 of 3 pages)
- geoboard and bands
- ruler

**1** Students choose one of the three pages of record sheets to work on, and record their name at the top of the page.

**2** Students read the polygon descriptions and build at least one example of each kind of polygon on their geoboard.

**3** Students copy their favorite example of each polygon on the record sheet, using a ruler to draw straight sides.

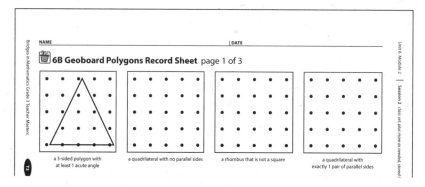

**4** Students check to make sure their drawing matches the polygon built on the geoboard before going on to the next polygon.

**5** Once students have completed a page, they can pair up with another student who has also finished and compare their polygons.

- Do students agree that each other's polygons fit the descriptions given on the sheet?
- If both students have built a polygon for the same descriptions, how are the polygons alike and different?

## Game Variations

**A** If some students have trouble building and describing their own polygons, invite them to build the polygons with a partner first and then describe them in collaboration.

**B** Students who are ready to work at a more challenging level might enjoy working in pairs, coming up with descriptions first and then challenging their partners to build polygons that match those descriptions.

NAME | DATE

 **Geoboard Polygons**

**1** On each geoboard below, draw an example of the polygon named.

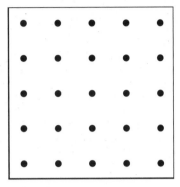

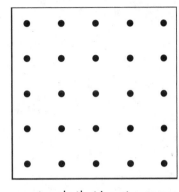

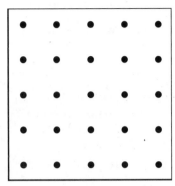

a square          a rectangle that is not a square          a rhombus

**2** Fill in every bubble beside a statement that is true about all three of the polygons you drew in problem 1.

○  All three of the polygons are quadrilaterals.

○  All three of the polygons have 4 sides that are congruent.

○  All three of the polygons are parallelograms.

○  All three of the polygons have 2 pairs of parallel sides.

**3** Multiply.

| 4 | 2 | 4 | 7 | 6 | 3 | 8 |
|---|---|---|---|---|---|---|
| $\times 3$ | $\times 7$ | $\times 4$ | $\times 5$ | $\times 4$ | $\times 9$ | $\times 8$ |

| 3 | 8 | 9 | 10 | 8 | 10 | 6 |
|---|---|---|---|---|---|---|
| $\times 3$ | $\times 7$ | $\times 4$ | $\times 8$ | $\times 4$ | $\times 9$ | $\times 8$ |

**4** **CHALLENGE** Multiply.

| 20 | 30 | 40 | 20 | 50 | 60 | 80 |
|----|----|----|----|----|----|----|
| $\times 8$ | $\times 7$ | $\times 4$ | $\times 5$ | $\times 4$ | $\times 9$ | $\times 8$ |

**NAME** | **DATE**

# Different Kinds of Quadrilaterals

A *quadrilateral* is a shape with 4 sides. Here are some different kinds of quadrilaterals.

| | |
|---|---|
| Trapezoid: a quadrilateral with exactly 1 pair of parallel sides 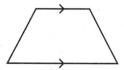 *Mathematicians use little arrows like these to show that two sides are parallel.* | Rectangle: a quadrilateral with 2 pairs of parallel sides and 4 right angles  *Mathematicians mark right angles with little squares like these.* |
| Rhombus: a quadrilateral with 4 sides that are all the same length 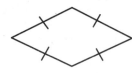 *When the sides of a shape are marked with little tic-marks like these, it tells you that the sides are equal.* | Square: a quadrilateral with 4 right angles and 4 sides that are all the same length  |
| Parallelogram: a quadrilateral with 2 pairs of parallel sides 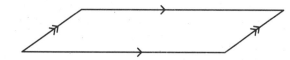 *When a shape has more than one pair of parallel sides, mathematicians use more arrow heads to show which pairs of sides are parallel.* | |

**1** Circle the word(s) that describe each shape.

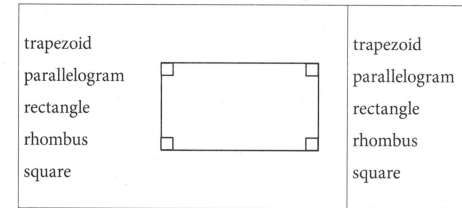

trapezoid
parallelogram
rectangle
rhombus
square

trapezoid
parallelogram
rectangle
rhombus
square

**2** Jackie circled all these words for this shape. Is she right or wrong? Explain your answer.

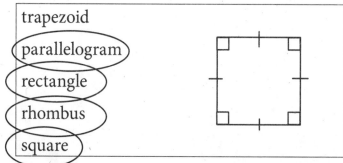

trapezoid
~~parallelogram~~
~~rectangle~~
~~rhombus~~
~~square~~

NAME _____ | DATE _____

 **Name that Quadrilateral**

**1** Fill in the bubbles to show all the names that could be used to identify this shape.

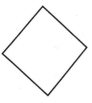

○ square          ○ rhombus          ○ quadrilateral          ○ parallelogram

**2** Fill in the bubbles to show all the names that could be used to identify this shape.

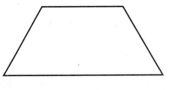

○ trapezoid          ○ parallelogram          ○ rectangle          ○ quadrilateral

**3** How do you know that the shape in problem 2 is not a parallelogram? Use labeled sketches or words to explain.

**4** Alejandro has a rock collection. His favorite rock has a mass of 123 grams. His next favorite rocks have masses of 188 grams and 209 grams. How much mass do Alejandro's three favorite rocks have together? Show your work.

**NAME** _____ | **DATE** _____

 # Know Your Quadrilaterals

**1** Draw a line from each description to **every** quadrilateral that has those attributes.

**Trapezoid**
a quadrilateral with exactly 1 pair of parallel sides

**Parallelogram**
a quadrilateral with 2 pairs of parallel sides opposite each other

**Rectangle**
a parallelogram with 4 right angles

**Rhombus**
a parallelogram with 4 congruent sides

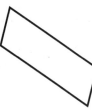

**Square**
a parallelogram with 4 congruent sides and 4 right angles

**2** Solve the following:

$$\begin{array}{r} 3 \\ \times\ \boxed{\phantom{0}} \\ \hline 15 \end{array} \qquad \begin{array}{r} 7 \\ \times\ 8 \\ \hline \boxed{\phantom{0}} \end{array} \qquad \begin{array}{r} 4 \\ \times\ \boxed{\phantom{0}} \\ \hline 28 \end{array} \qquad \begin{array}{r} 10 \\ \times\ 4 \\ \hline \boxed{\phantom{0}} \end{array} \qquad \begin{array}{r} 5 \\ \times\ \boxed{\phantom{0}} \\ \hline 30 \end{array} \qquad \begin{array}{r} 3 \\ \times\ 9 \\ \hline \boxed{\phantom{0}} \end{array} \qquad \begin{array}{r} 2 \\ \times\ \boxed{\phantom{0}} \\ \hline 16 \end{array}$$

**3** Complete the Mystery Number Line below.

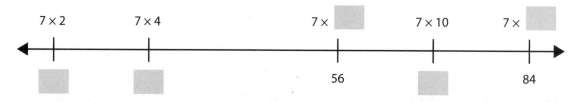

# Perimeter Record Sheet

**1** Label each figure on the Paper Quadrilaterals sheet with its name.

**2** Work with your partner to carefully cut out the 5 quadrilaterals. Then use your estimation skills to put them in order, from smallest to largest perimeter.

**3** After you've agreed on the order, write the letters of the quadrilaterals where you think they belong in the boxes below.

| Smallest Perimeter | ⟶ | | | Largest Perimeter |
|---|---|---|---|---|
| | | | | |

**4** Estimate the perimeter of each quadrilateral. Write your estimates on the chart below. Then measure the perimeter of each quadrilateral, and label the quadrilateral to show your work. Record the actual perimeters on the chart below.

| Quadrilateral Letter | Your Estimate in Centimeters (cm) | Actual Perimeter in Centimeters (cm) |
|---|---|---|
| | | |
| | | |
| | | |
| | | |
| | | |

**Perimeter Practice**

*Perimeter* is the total length of all sides of a shape. To find the perimeter, add the lengths of all the sides of a shape.

**1** Use a ruler marked in inches to measure the sides of the squares and rectangles. Label each side. Then find the perimeter of each shape. Show your work.

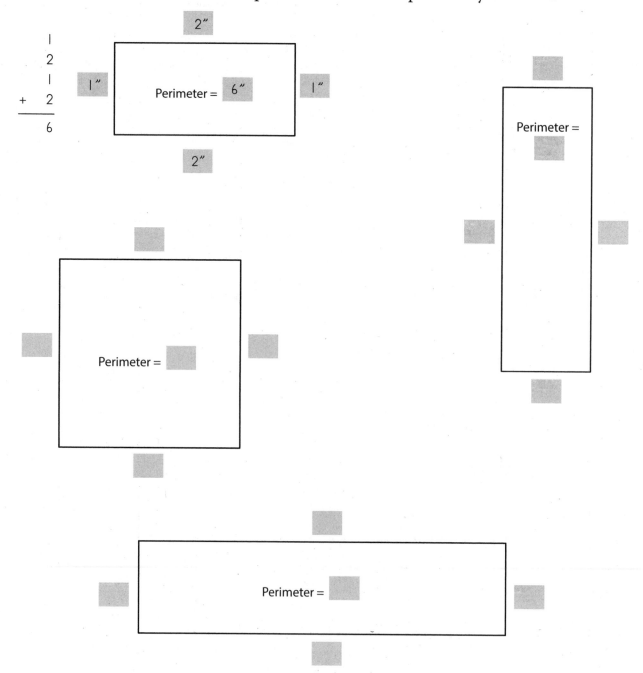

**NAME** _____ **| DATE** _____

 **Round the Table**

**1** Round these numbers.

| | to the nearest ten | to the nearest hundred |
|---|---|---|
| 329 | 330 | 300 |
| 184 | 1 | 200 |
| 2,532 | | |
| 467 | | |
| 251 | | |
| 485 | | |

**2** Emery Raccoon and his lunch guests used 329 spoons, 329 forks, and 329 knives. How many pieces of silverware did they use in all? Show your work.

**3** Multiply.

$$\begin{array}{c} 8 \\ \times 4 \\ \hline 3\cancel{2} \end{array} \qquad \begin{array}{c} 9 \\ \times 3 \\ \hline 27 \end{array} \quad 9 \qquad \begin{array}{c} 10 \\ \times 6 \\ \hline 60 \end{array} \qquad \begin{array}{c} 5 \\ \times 8 \\ \hline 40 \end{array} \qquad \begin{array}{c} 4 \\ \times 7 \\ \hline 28 \end{array} \qquad \begin{array}{c} 8 \\ \times 3 \\ \hline 24 \end{array} \qquad \begin{array}{c} 5 \\ \times 6 \\ \hline 30 \end{array} \qquad \begin{array}{c} 9 \\ \times 5 \\ \hline 45 \end{array}$$

**4** Add or subtract.

$$\begin{array}{c} 26 \\ + 18 \\ \hline 44 \end{array} \qquad \begin{array}{c} 297 \\ + 3 \\ \hline 300 \end{array} \qquad \begin{array}{c} 387 \\ + 13 \\ \hline 400 \end{array} \qquad \begin{array}{c} 475 \\ + 25 \\ \hline 500 \end{array} \qquad \begin{array}{c} 473 \\ - 52 \\ \hline 421 \end{array} \qquad \begin{array}{c} 80 \\ - 74 \\ \hline 6 \end{array} \qquad \begin{array}{c} 115 \\ - 108 \\ \hline 7 \end{array} \qquad \begin{array}{c} 527 \\ - 19 \\ \hline \end{array}$$

**5** **CHALLENGE** Emery tore up 10 sheets to make 330 napkins. How many napkins did he make out of each sheet? Show your work.

# Work Place Instructions 6C Guess My Quadrilateral

**Each pair of players needs:**

- 6C Guess My Quadrilateral Record Sheets (1 per player)
- 1 set of Quadrilateral Cards (use a set that belongs to one of the players)
- riddle booklets made by classmates

**1** Players work together to lay out all the cards from one of their sets of Quadrilateral Cards. Then they choose a riddle book written by a classmate.

**2** Players open the book for clue 1, read and discuss the clue, and set aside any of the Quadrilateral Cards that do not fit the clue.

Sample Clue: My quadrilateral has 2 pairs of parallel sides.

> *Cathy* *So we can get rid of anything that's not a square or a rectangle, right?*
>
> *Tyson* *We have to keep the parallelograms and the rhombus, too. They have 2 pairs of parallel sides.*
>
> *Cathy* *OK, so we'll get rid of the trapezoids and all the weird quadrilaterals.*

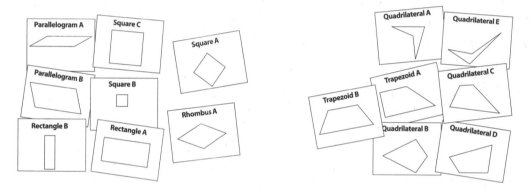

**3** Players continue reading one clue at a time, discussing and putting aside the quadrilaterals that do not match each clue, until only one is left.

**4** If players have more than one shape left, they look back over the clues to see if they forgot to put aside any of the shapes.

**5** Players compare their answer to the one on the back of the riddle booklet.

**6** Both players fill in the row on their record sheet for that riddle.

**7** Players push all their Quadrilateral Cards back together, trade their riddle booklet in for another one, and solve the next riddle in the same way.

**8** After players have solved at least five riddles, they answer the questions at the bottom of the record sheet.

## Game Variations

**A** Players may work alone to compete against a partner. Then players can compare answers after five riddles before checking answers on the riddle booklets. Players can assign one point for each correct riddle to determine a winner.

**B** Players create additional riddles for some of the Quadrilateral Cards in their set.

**C** Players determine the minimal number of clues necessary to identify a particular shape. In other words, which clues for each riddle were the most necessary? Could any have been eliminated?

NAME _____ | DATE _____

 # Game Night

Rodney Rabbit invited 17 of his pals over to play board games. Use tiles and red linear units to build as many different rectangular arrays as you can that allow all 18 game players to sit at the same table.

**1** Sketch each array on the grid below. Use a red colored pencil to mark the perimeter. Label the width and the length, and write an equation to show that the perimeter is 18 linear units. The first one is done for you as an example.

|   |   |   |   |   |   | 8 |   |   |   |   |   |   |   |   |   |
|---|---|---|---|---|---|---|---|---|---|---|---|---|---|---|---|

1 | [rectangle] | 1    1 + 8 + 1 + 8 = 18

8

**2** Record the dimensions, perimeter, and area of each of the rectangular arrays you built on the chart below.

**Note** The area of each array is the number of tiles it took to build it.

| Width (linear units) | 1 |  |  |  |  |  |
|---|---|---|---|---|---|---|
| Length (linear units) | 8 |  |  |  |  |  |
| Perimeter (linear units) | 18 |  |  |  |  |  |
| Area (Square units) | 8 |  |  |  |  |  |

**205**

NAME _____ | DATE _____

 **Metric Rectangles Record Sheet**

**1** Look at the six rectangles on the Metric Rectangles sheet. Write the letters of all the rectangles where you think they belong in the boxes below, in order from the smallest area to the largest area.

| Smallest Area | ⟶ | | | | Largest Area |
|---|---|---|---|---|---|
| A | B | C | D | e | F |

**2** Use your base ten pieces to find the area of each rectangle in square centimeters, and write an equation to show your work. Think of math shortcuts to help you determine the number of square centimeters, so you don't have to count each unit separately.

| Rectangle Letter | Write an equation to show how you found the area in square centimeters. | Area in square centimeters (sq. cm.) |
|---|---|---|
| A | | |
| B | 4 × 10 = | 40 |
| C | | |
| D | | |
| E | | |
| F | | |

**3** What do you think is the most efficient way to find the area of a rectangle? Use numbers, sketches, or words to describe your shortcut.

NAME _____ | DATE _____

 **Area & Perimeter**

**1** Find the area and perimeter of each rectangle. Area is the total amount of space covered by the rectangle. Perimeter is the distance around the rectangle.

| **ex** | **a** |
|---|---|
| 5 across, 3 down grid | 5 across, 4 down grid |
| Perimeter $3 + 3 + 5 + 5 = 16$ | Perimeter _16_ |
| Area $3 \times 5 = 15$ square units | Area _20_ |
| **b** | **c** |
| 6 across, 3 down grid | 7 across, 2 down grid |
| Perimeter _18_ | Perimeter _14_ |
| Area _18_ | Area _14_ |

**2** Find the area and perimeter of this shape. Show all your work.

Perimeter _20_

Area _29_

I Love you
Thies

**NAME** _____ | **DATE** _____

 **Bayard Owl's Borrowed Tables**

Emery Raccoon's new friend, Bayard Owl, is planning a birthday party for himself. He has borrowed 24 small square tables from Emery, and wants to push them together to make one large rectangular table where all his friends can sit together.

**1** Use your tiles to build as many *different* rectangular tables as you can. You have to use all 24 tiles for each table, and you can't leave any holes or gaps.

**a** Sketch each of the tables you make on the grid below. Label its side lengths, and write two equations: one to show what the perimeter is and how you found it, and another to show what the area is and how you found it.

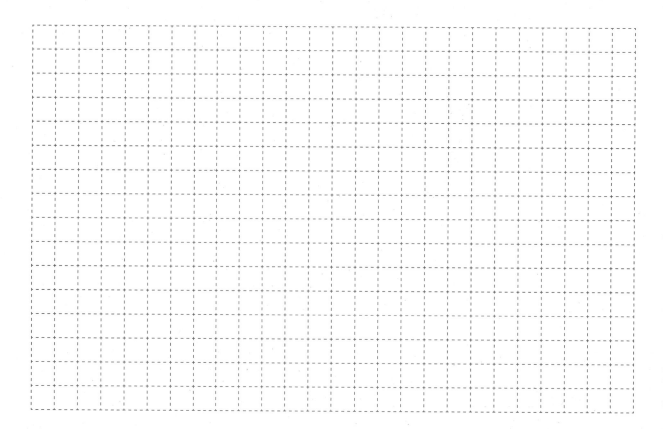

**b** Which table do you think Bayard Owl should use for his party? Why?

NAME _____ | DATE _____

 **Measuring to Find the Area & Perimeter**

Use the centimeter side of a ruler to measure each rectangle below. Label the dimensions of the rectangle, and use the information to find the area and perimeter. Show your work.

*Area* is the total amount of space covered by the rectangle, and perimeter is the total distance around the rectangle.

**ex**

3 cm

2 cm

Perimeter __2 + 3 + 2 + 3 = 10cm__

Area __2 × 3 = 6 square cm__

**1**

Perimeter _____

Area _____

**2**

Perimeter _____

Area _____

**3**

Perimeter _____

Area _____

**4** **CHALLENGE** Measure and label the figure below, then find its perimeter and area.

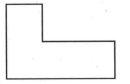

Perimeter _____

Area _____

**The Goat Twins' Table**

One day when Emery was in town doing errands, the Goat Twins, Zachary and Whackery, decided to surprise him. They got some of Emery's small square tables out of the shed and arranged them in an unusual way. When Emery got home, he laughed at the twins and said, "OK, if the two of you are so smart, can you tell me the area of this big new table you've arranged?"

**1** Help the twins. How can they find the area of the table they made without having to count all the small squares?

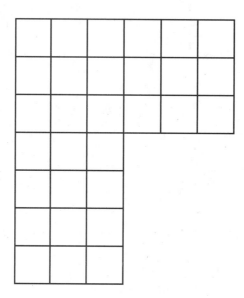

**2** Can you think of more than one way to solve this problem?

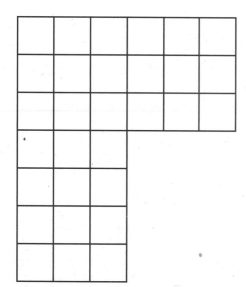
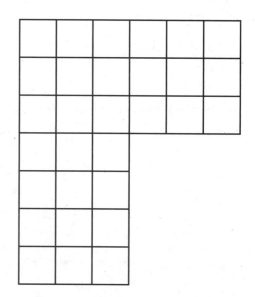

# Work Place Instructions 6D Area or Perimeter

## Each pair of players needs:

- 6D Area or Perimeter Record Sheets, 1 for each player
- 1 or more sheets of 6D Area or Perimeter Grid Paper
- 80 colored tiles *or* 2 sets of red linear units
  Players use *tiles* if rolling for area; they use *red linear units* if rolling for perimeter
- two 1–6 dice
- 1 colored pencil

**1**  Players decide together if they are going to roll for and keep the *area* or the *perimeter* the same for the rectangles they build. They each circle that word on their own record sheet.

**2**  One player rolls the dice. Using their individual record sheets, each player uses column 1 to record the numbers rolled and column 2 to record the product of the two numbers.

**3**  If players are working with area, they count out tiles to equal the product of the two numbers rolled. If they're working with perimeter, they count out red linear units to equal the product of the two numbers rolled.

**4**  Players lay their tiles or linear units out on the grid paper to form a rectangle.

- Players may need to use more than 1 sheet of grid paper to build some rectangles.
- The grid paper is optional for players working with area and using tiles. If players are working with perimeter and using the red linear pieces, they need to lay out the pieces on the grid paper.

**5**  Players record the dimensions, area, and perimeter of the rectangle they made on their record sheets.

Some products will not work as perimeters for rectangles. In that case, players just write "impossible" on the line for that roll.

**6**  Players work together to rearrange the tiles or red linear units to form another rectangle (with the same area or perimeter as rolled for the first rectangle) and record the information for it on the next line of the record sheet.

- Players keep rearranging and forming rectangles with that same area or perimeter until they can't make any more.
- Players use a colored pencil to draw a line across the table below the information for the last rectangle they were able to make for a pair of numbers.

**7**  Players roll the dice and build as many rectangles as they can for the new area or perimeter.

- Players must continue to work with the type of measurement they chose for that record sheet, rather than switching from area to perimeter or vice versa.
- If players roll two numbers they've already rolled today, or two numbers that make the same product, they roll again.

**8**  Players keep rolling and building rectangles until they fill the table or run out of time.

## Game Variations

**A**  Use one 1–6 die and one 4–9 die instead of two 1–6 dice.

**B**  Use two 4–9 dice instead of two 1–6 dice.

**NAME** _____ | **DATE** _____

 **More of the Twins' Tables**

**1** As soon as Emery had to go into town again, the Goat Twins, Zachary and Whackery, got up to their old tricks. Here are 4 different arrangements they made with Emery's small square tables. Find the area of each. Use lines or loops, along with numbers and equations to show how you got your answers.

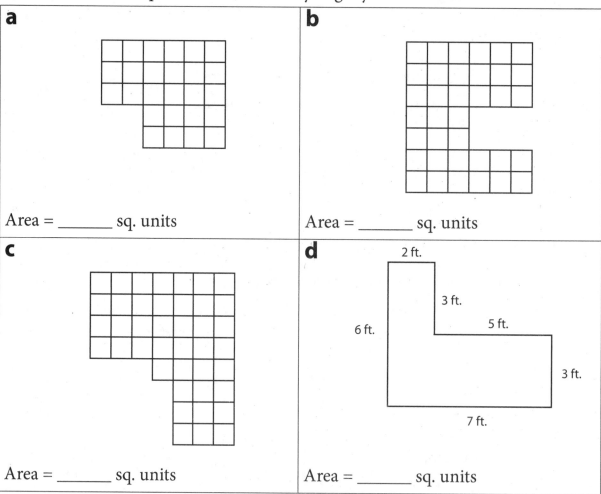

**a**

Area = _____ sq. units

**b**

Area = _____ sq. units

**c**

Area = _____ sq. units

**d**

2 ft.
3 ft.
6 ft.
5 ft.
3 ft.
7 ft.

Area = _____ sq. units

**2** Here is a little sketch map of Emery's rectangular backyard. The perimeter of the yard is 30 yards. Use that information, along with the picture, to figure out the length of the side labeled *s*.

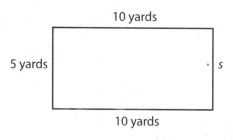

10 yards

5 yards

*s*

10 yards

Side *s* is _____ yards long.

**NAME** _____ |**DATE** _____

 **Geoboard Halves** page 1 of 2

How many different ways can you find to divide the square geoboard into halves?
Record them here. Put a star by the boards that show halves that are not the same shape
and size, but take up the same amount of area.

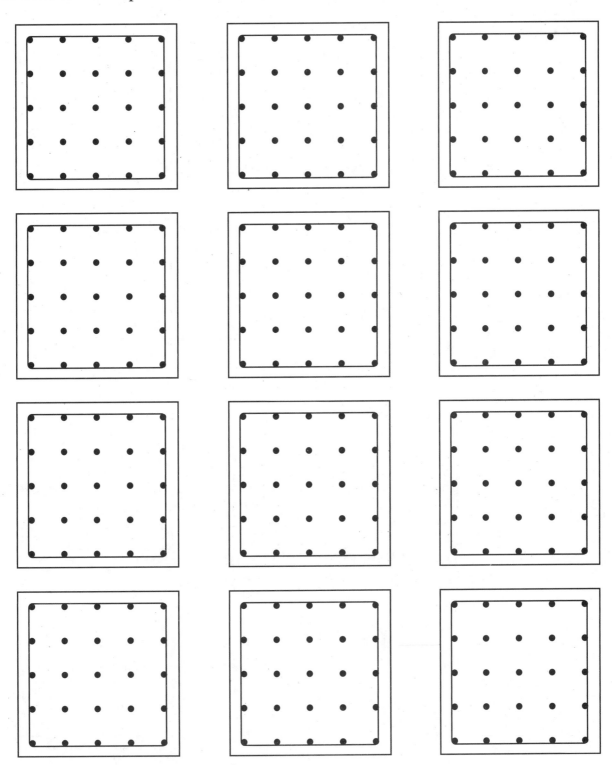

*(continued on next page)*

**213** © The Math Learning Center | mathlearningcenter.org

NAME | DATE

## Geoboard Halves page 2 of 2

How many different ways can you find to divide the square geoboard into halves? Record them here. Put a star by the boards that show halves that are not the same shape and size, but take up the same amount of area.

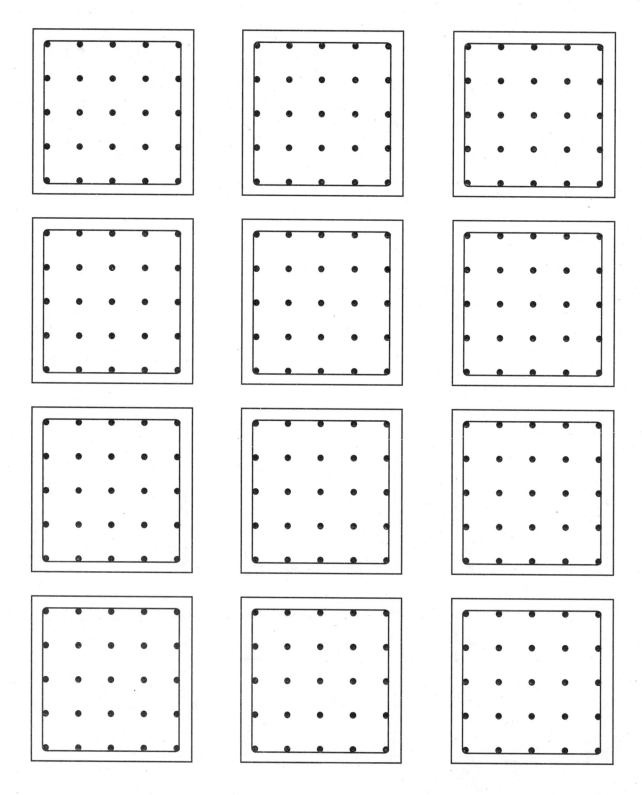

**NAME** _____ **| DATE** _____

 **Fractions of a Circle**

**1** Fill in the circle to show each fraction.

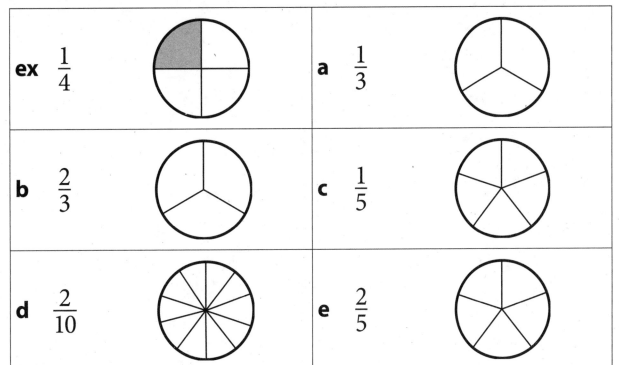

| | | |
|---|---|---|
| **ex** $\frac{1}{4}$ | | **a** $\frac{1}{3}$ |
| **b** $\frac{2}{3}$ | | **c** $\frac{1}{5}$ |
| **d** $\frac{2}{10}$ | | **e** $\frac{2}{5}$ |

**2** Look at the fractions you shaded in above. Use them to help complete each number sentence by writing <, >, or =.

| | | | |
|---|---|---|---|
| **ex** $\frac{1}{3}$ **>** $\frac{1}{5}$ | **a** $\frac{2}{5}$ $\frac{2}{3}$ | **b** $\frac{2}{3}$ $\frac{2}{10}$ |
| **c** $\frac{2}{10}$ $\frac{1}{5}$ | **d** $\frac{2}{5}$ $\frac{2}{10}$ | **e** $\frac{1}{4}$ $\frac{2}{10}$ |

**CHALLENGE**

| | | |
|---|---|---|
| **f** $\frac{1}{18}$ $\frac{1}{9}$ | **g** $\frac{2}{18}$ $\frac{1}{9}$ | **h** $\frac{1}{9}$ $\frac{2}{20}$ |

**NAME** _____ | **DATE** _____

 ## Geoboard Fractions

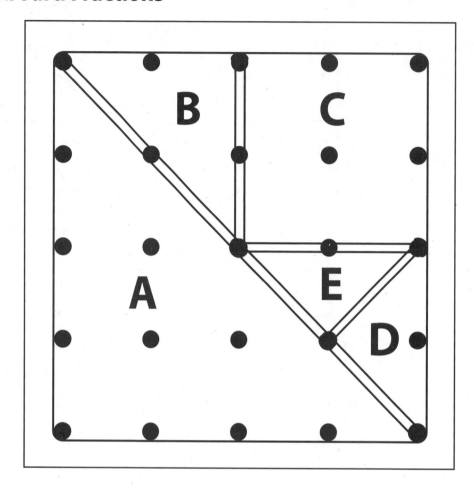

_____

_____

_____

_____

_____

_____

NAME _____  DATE _____

 **Fraction Draw & Compare**

**1** Divide each square into the number of pieces you need to model the fraction. Then shade in the correct amount.

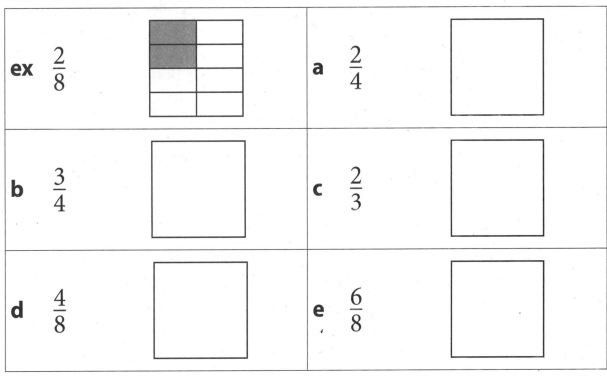

**2** Look at the fractions you shaded in above. Use them to help complete each equation by writing <, >, or =.

| ex | $\frac{4}{8}$ | $>$ | $\frac{2}{8}$ | a | $\frac{2}{4}$ | | $\frac{3}{4}$ | b | $\frac{6}{8}$ | | $\frac{2}{8}$ |
|----|---|---|---|---|---|---|---|---|---|---|---|
| c | $\frac{2}{4}$ | | $\frac{4}{8}$ | d | $\frac{1}{4}$ | | $\frac{1}{8}$ | e | $\frac{2}{4}$ | | $\frac{2}{8}$ |

**3** **CHALLENGE** Use what you know about fractions to complete each equation by writing <, >, or =.

| a | $\frac{1}{8}$ | | $\frac{1}{16}$ | b | $\frac{3}{16}$ | | $\frac{5}{16}$ | c | $\frac{2}{4}$ | | $\frac{8}{16}$ |
|----|---|---|---|---|---|---|---|---|---|---|---|

**Geoboard Quilt Blocks**

**1**  Build each quilt block design on your geoboard.

**2**  Write as many equivalent fractions as you can that describe how much area of the geoboard is shaded in each quilt block. *Remember that the geoboard is 1 whole unit.*

**3**  Then design your own quilt blocks on your geoboard and record your designs.

**4**  Write equivalent fractions for the shaded areas on your quilt block designs.

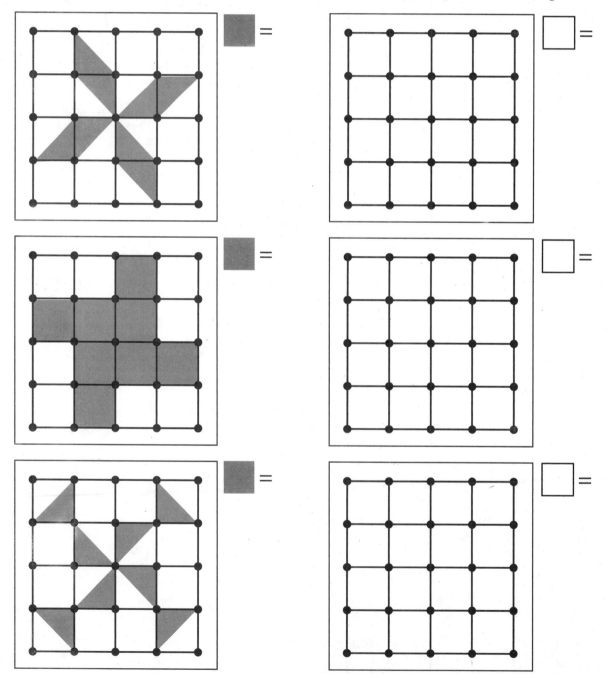

**218**

NAME _____ | DATE _____

 **Patchwork Fractions**

**1** Circle all the fractions that describe the shaded part of each geoboard patchwork quilt block, if the geoboard is 1 whole unit.

**a**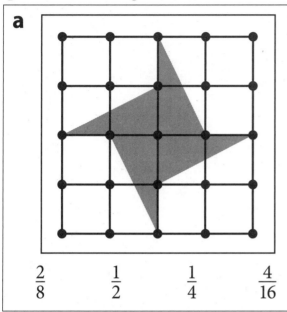

$\dfrac{2}{8}$    $\dfrac{1}{2}$    $\dfrac{1}{4}$    $\dfrac{4}{16}$

**b**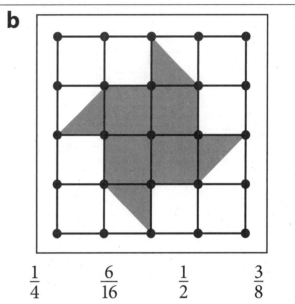

$\dfrac{1}{4}$    $\dfrac{6}{16}$    $\dfrac{1}{2}$    $\dfrac{3}{8}$

**2** Choose two fractions that you marked in part a above, and explain why they are equivalent.

**3** Fill in the bubble next to the equation that will help you solve each word problem. Then solve the problem. Show all your work.

**a** Rosa wants to buy a T-shirt for each of her 4 cousins. The T-shirts cost $12 each.

○  $4 + 12 = d$      ○  $4 \times 12 = d$      ○  $12 - 4 = d$      ○  $12 \div 4 = d$

Rosa will spend $ _____ on T-shirts for her cousins.

**b** Marco has some boxes of cookies. Each box has 6 cookies. There are 24 cookies in all. How many boxes of cookies does Marco have?

○  $6 + 24 = b$      ○  $6 \times 24 = b$      ○  $24 - 6 = b$      ○  $24 \div 6 = b$

Marco has _____ boxes of cookies.

## The 18¢ Problem

**1** What are all the different ways you can make 18¢ with pennies, nickels, and dimes?

   **a** Choose the strategy you will use to solve this problem.

    ○ Draw a picture

    ○ Guess and check

    ○ Make an organized list

   **b** Why does this strategy make the most sense to you?

   **c** Solve the problem with the strategy you picked. Show all your work.

**NAME** _____ |**DATE** _____

 # Skills Review: Area, Multiplication & Fractions

**1** Determine the area of each rectangle and write an equation to match.

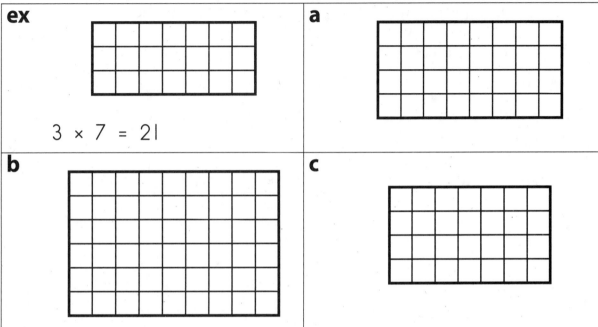

**ex**

$3 \times 7 = 21$

**a**

**b**

**c**

**2** Fill in the missing numbers below.

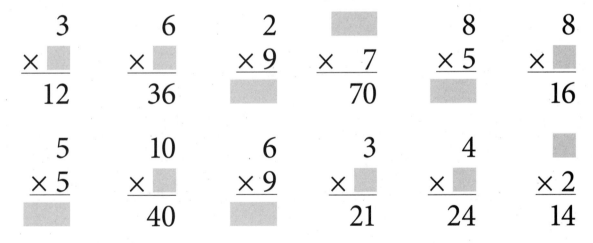

$$\begin{array}{r} 3 \\ \times \ \blacksquare \\ \hline 12 \end{array} \qquad \begin{array}{r} 6 \\ \times \ \blacksquare \\ \hline 36 \end{array} \qquad \begin{array}{r} 2 \\ \times \ 9 \\ \hline \blacksquare \end{array} \qquad \begin{array}{r} \blacksquare \\ \times \ 7 \\ \hline 70 \end{array} \qquad \begin{array}{r} 8 \\ \times \ 5 \\ \hline \blacksquare \end{array} \qquad \begin{array}{r} 8 \\ \times \ \blacksquare \\ \hline 16 \end{array}$$

$$\begin{array}{r} 5 \\ \times \ 5 \\ \hline \blacksquare \end{array} \qquad \begin{array}{r} 10 \\ \times \ \blacksquare \\ \hline 40 \end{array} \qquad \begin{array}{r} 6 \\ \times \ 9 \\ \hline \blacksquare \end{array} \qquad \begin{array}{r} 3 \\ \times \ \blacksquare \\ \hline 21 \end{array} \qquad \begin{array}{r} 4 \\ \times \ \blacksquare \\ \hline 24 \end{array} \qquad \begin{array}{r} \blacksquare \\ \times \ 2 \\ \hline 14 \end{array}$$

**3** **CHALLENGE** Solve each equation.

$16 + 25 - (6 \times 4) =$ $\qquad$ $(7 \times 7) + 175 =$ $\qquad$ $(10 \times 9) - 65 =$

**4** Place the following fractions on the number line below: $\frac{1}{4}$, 1, $\frac{3}{4}$, $\frac{3}{8}$, 0, $\frac{8}{8}$, $\frac{5}{8}$, $\frac{4}{8}$

**221**

## More Stickers & Beads page 1 of 2

**1** Sara bought a sheet of stickers with 2 rows of 5 stickers on it. The stickers cost 6 cents each. How much did Sara pay for the entire sheet of stickers?

**a** What is this problem asking you to figure out?

**b** Write an equation for the problem. Use a letter to stand for the unknown quantity.

**c** Solve the problem. Show all your work including numbers, words, or labeled sketches.

Sara paid _____ for the entire sheet of stickers.

**2** Jonah bought a sheet of stickers with 5 rows of 8 stickers on it. He gave 12 of the stickers to his little sister. How many stickers did he have left?

**a** What is this problem asking you to figure out?

**b** Write an equation for the problem. Use a letter to stand for the unknown quantity.

**c** Solve the problem. Show all your work including numbers, words, or labeled sketches.

Jonah had _____ stickers left.

*(continued on next page)*

NAME _____ | DATE _____

## More Stickers & Beads page 2 of 2

**3** Jasmine and her mother bought 2 boxes of beads to make some necklaces. One box was divided into 6 sections, with 10 beads in each section. The other box was divided into 4 sections, with 9 beads in each section. How many beads did they get in all?

**a** What is this problem asking you to figure out?

**b** Which equation best represents this problem? (The letter $b$ stands for beads in all the equations below.)

○ $(6 \times 10) + (4 \times 9) = b$

○ $(6 \times 10) - (4 \times 9) = b$

○ $2 + 6 + 10 + 4 + 9 = b$

○ $2 \times (6 \times 10) = b$

**c** Solve the problem. Show all your work including numbers, words, or labeled sketches.

**d** Does your answer make sense? How do you know?

**4** **CHALLENGE** Write a two-step story problem to match this equation: $(4 \times 25) - 28$. Then solve your own problem.

**NAME** _____ | **DATE** _____

 **Family Math Night**

**1** Flora is helping Mr. Jackson get ready for Family Math Night. Eight families are coming. Flora needs to count out 4 square pattern blocks and 3 triangle pattern blocks for each family. How many pattern blocks will she count out in all?

**a** What is this problem asking you to figure out? Underline any information that can help you solve the problem.

**b** Choose the equation that best represents this problem. (The letter $p$ stands for pattern blocks.)

○ $4 + 3 + 8 = p$

○ $(4 + 3) \times 8 = p$

○ $4 \times 3 \times 8 = p$

○ $(4 \times 3) - 8 = p$

**c** Solve the problem. Show your work.

**2** Jared is also helping Mr. Jackson get ready for Family Math Night. Jared needs to count out 5 red game markers and 5 blue game markers for each of the 8 families. How many game markers will he count out in all?

**a** Write an equation to represent the problem. Use a letter to stand for the unknown number.

**b** Solve the problem. Show your work.

**c** Is your answer reasonable? Why or why not?

224

## Multiplying by Eleven

**1** Solve the problems below. Use your base ten area pieces to help if you want.

$3 \times 11 =$ _____    $11 \times 5 =$ _____    $7 \times 11 =$ _____

$$\begin{array}{cccccc} 4 & 6 & 10 & 11 & 11 & 2 \\ \times 11 & \times 11 & \times 11 & \times 8 & \times 9 & \times 11 \end{array}$$

**2** Zack used his base ten area pieces to build this picture of $3 \times 11$. Jon used his base ten area pieces to build it a different way.

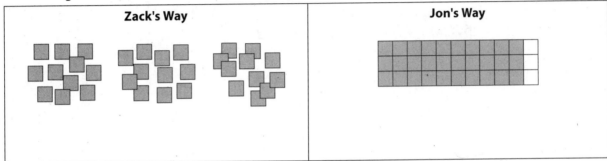

Zack's Way          Jon's Way

**a** Write an equation below the picture in each box to show the total number of units.

**b** Which way do you like better? Why?

**3** Jenna is starting a sticker book. There are 5 rows of stickers on each page, and each row has 11 stickers. So far, she's filled 2 pages. How many stickers is that in all?

**a** Write an equation for this problem. Use a letter to stand for the unknown quantity.

**b** Solve the problem. Show all your work including numbers, words, or labeled sketches.

**Multiplication, Division & Perimeter Practice**

**1** Complete the multiplication facts.

| 10 | 9 | 5 | 3 | 4 | 5 | 9 |
|---|---|---|---|---|---|---|
| × 8 | × 1 | × 7 | × 0 | × 8 | × 6 | × 2 |

| 2 | 9 | 4 | 3 | 5 | 4 | 10 |
|---|---|---|---|---|---|---|
| × 7 | × 5 | × 10 | × 4 | × 8 | × 7 | × 10 |

**2** Complete the division facts.

$40 ÷ 5 =$ _____          $12 ÷ 2 =$ _____          $90 ÷ 10 =$ _____

$8 ÷ 1 =$ _____          $25 ÷ 5 =$ _____          $14 ÷ 2 =$ _____

**3** Find the perimeter of each rectangle.

**a** Perimeter = _____

124 ft.

96 ft.

**b** Perimeter = _____

117 ft.

28 ft.

**4** What is the difference between the perimeters of the rectangles above?

**Multiplying by Twelve**

**1** Solve the problems below. Use your base ten area pieces to help if you'd like.

$4 \times 12 =$ _____          $12 \times 2 =$ _____          $5 \times 12 =$ _____

$$\begin{array}{r} 3 \\ \times\, 12 \\ \hline \end{array}$$          $$\begin{array}{r} 6 \\ \times\, 12 \\ \hline \end{array}$$          $$\begin{array}{r} 8 \\ \times\, 12 \\ \hline \end{array}$$          $$\begin{array}{r} 12 \\ \times\, 7 \\ \hline \end{array}$$

**2** For each problem below:
- Write an equation. Use a letter to stand for the unknown number.
- Solve the problem. Show all your work including numbers, words, or labeled sketches.

**a** Mrs. Green bought granola bars for the third grade field trip. There were 12 bars in a box. She bought 6 boxes and then found 4 more bars in her cupboard at school. How many bars did she have in all?

**b** Mr. Lee got 8 dozen pencils from the office. So far, he's given each of his third graders 3 pencils. He has 27 students. How many pencils does he still have left?

**NAME** | **DATE**

 # Meet the Elevens & Twelves Families

Write 2 multiplication and 2 division facts for each family. The first one has been done for you.

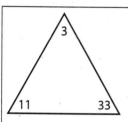

$$3 \times 11 = 33$$

$$11 \times 3 = 33$$

$$33 \div 3 = 11$$

$$33 \div 11 = 3$$

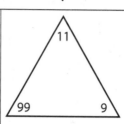

$$11 + a - \underline{\phantom{99}} 99$$
$$a + 11$$
$$99 \div 11 = 9a$$
$$11 \div a \ 11 = 9$$
$$= 99$$

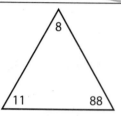

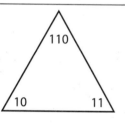

$$11 \times 121 = 11$$
$$121 \times 11 = 11$$
$$11 \div 121 =$$

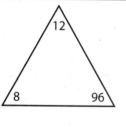

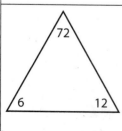

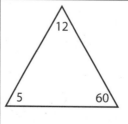

228  © The Math Learning Center | mathlearningcenter.org

**NAME** _____ | **DATE** _____

## 🔍 Explore Six

**1** Label the dimensions and area of the rectangle on each grid. Write a multiplication equation to match.

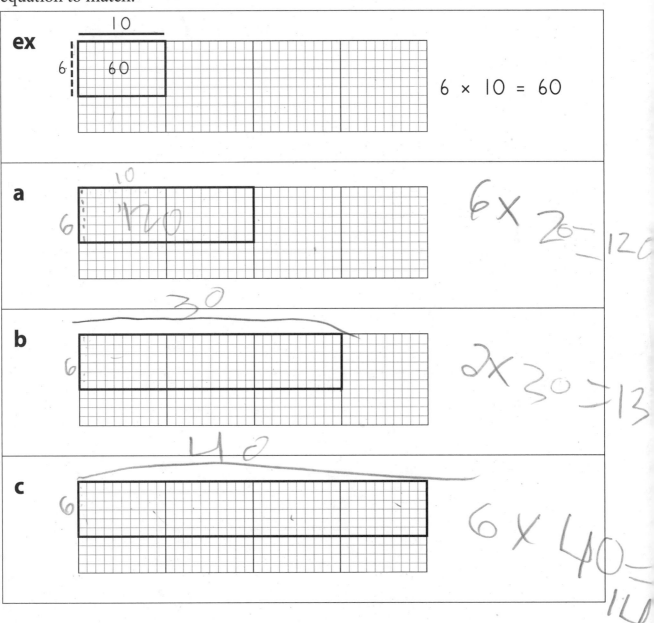

**ex**

10

6

60

$6 \times 10 = 60$

**a**

10

6

120

$6 \times 20 = 120$

**b**

30

6

$6 \times 30 = 13$

**c**

40

6

$6 \times 40 = 14$

**2** Use the information above to help solve these equations.

$6 \times 50 =$ _306_        $6 \times 60 =$ _360_        $6 \times 70 =$ _420_

$6 \times 80 =$ _480_        $6 \times 90 =$ _340_        $6 \times 100 =$ _700_

**NAME** | **DATE**

## 🔍 Explore More

**1** Choose a number between 4 and 9 (not 6) to multiply by 10 and multiples of 10. Draw the missing dimensions and the area of each rectangle. Write a multiplication equation to match.

**ex**
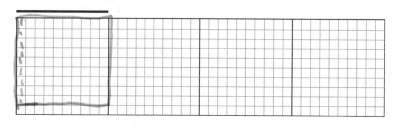

**a**
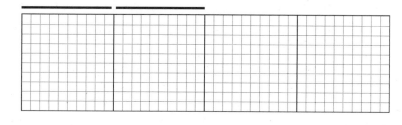

**b**
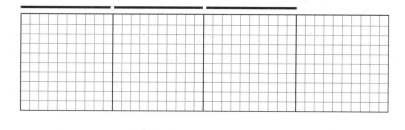

**c**
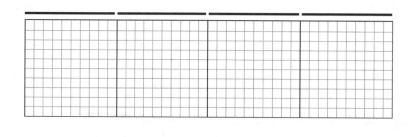

**2** Complete these equations using the number you chose.

◻ × 50 = ◻          ◻ × 60 = ◻          ◻ × 70 = ◻

◻ × 80 = ◻          ◻ × 90 = ◻          ◻ × 100 = ◻

**Multiplying by Multiples of Ten**

**1** Solve these problems in your head. Write the answers.

| 10 | 20 | 30 | 40 | 50 | 60 | 70 |
|---|---|---|---|---|---|---|
| × 3 | × 3 | × 3 | × 3 | × 3 | × 3 | × 3 |

| 80 | 90 | 100 | 1,000 | 10,000 | 100,000 |
|---|---|---|---|---|---|
| × 3 | × 3 | × 3 | × 3 | × 3 | × 3 |

**2** Jon says the problems above are easy. Do you agree with him? Why or why not?

**3** Solve these problems in your head. Write the answers.

| 10 | 20 | 30 | 40 | 50 | 60 | 70 |
|---|---|---|---|---|---|---|
| × 4 | × 5 | × 7 | × 2 | × 5 | × 4 | × 5 |

| 80 | 90 | 20 | 30 | 60 | 70 | 80 |
|---|---|---|---|---|---|---|
| × 4 | × 5 | × 8 | × 9 | × 8 | × 2 | × 5 |

| 40 | 30 | 50 | 60 | 50 | 70 | 70 |
|---|---|---|---|---|---|---|
| × 4 | × 6 | × 5 | × 9 | × 8 | × 4 | × 5 |

**CHALLENGE**

| 900 | 400 | 800 | 600 | 700 | 800 | 800 |
|---|---|---|---|---|---|---|
| × 9 | × 12 | × 9 | × 12 | × 11 | × 8 | × 12 |

# Sandwiches, Pizza & Books

**1** Rodney had a friend over on Saturday. His dad took them out for sandwiches. Each person (Rodney, his dad, and his friend) got a sandwich for $6. How much did they spend on sandwiches in all? Show all your work.

**2** Jasmine had a pizza party with 3 of her friends to celebrate the last day of school. They ordered 2 pizzas. Each pizza had 8 slices. They all ate the same amount of pizza and finished both pizzas. How many pieces did each person eat? Show all your work.

**3** CHALLENGE  There were 12,387 books in the school library. The librarian bought 445 more books to add to the library and put 126 books on the Give Away shelf near the office. How many books are in the library now? Show all your work.

**NAME** | **DATE**

 # Multiplication Practice

**1** Solve these problems in your head. Write the answers.

| 8 | 9 | 10 | 20 | 40 | 50 |
|---|---|---|---|---|---|
| × 3 | × 3 | × 3 | × 3 | × 3 | × 3 |
| 80 | 26 | 30 | 80 | 43 | |

| 60 | 70 | 80 | 90 | 100 | 1,000 |
|---|---|---|---|---|---|
| × 3 | × 3 | × 3 | × 3 | × 3 | × 3 |

**2** Explain how you figured out the answers to the problems above.

**3** Solve these problems in your head. Write the answers.

| 10 | 20 | 30 | 40 | 50 | 60 | 700 |
|---|---|---|---|---|---|---|
| × 4 | × 5 | × 7 | × 2 | × 5 | × 4 | × 5 |

| 80 | 90 | 20 | 30 | 60 | 70 | 80 |
|---|---|---|---|---|---|---|
| × 4 | × 5 | × 8 | × 9 | × 8 | × 2 | × 5 |

| 40 | 30 | 60 | 20 | 30 | 70 | 90 |
|---|---|---|---|---|---|---|
| × 4 | × 6 | × 5 | × 9 | × 8 | × 4 | × 5 |

**CHALLENGE**

| 900 | 400 | 800 | 600 | 700 | 800 | 800 |
|---|---|---|---|---|---|---|
| × 9 | × 8 | × 9 | × 10 | × 11 | × 8 | × 11 |

**NAME** | **DATE**

# Working with Equations

**1** Fill in the missing numbers to make each equation true.

$35 \div 7 = 20 \div \boxed{4}$ $\qquad$ $8 \times 3 = 40 - \boxed{\phantom{0}}$

$8 \times \boxed{\phantom{0}} = 36 + 28$ $\qquad$ $0 \times 67 = \boxed{\phantom{0}} \times 45$

$19 + \boxed{\phantom{0}} = 9 \times 5$ $\qquad$ $9 \times \boxed{\phantom{0}} = 668 - 587$

$3 \times 9 = 68 - \boxed{\phantom{0}}$ $\qquad$ $42 \div 6 = 63 - \boxed{\phantom{0}}$

**2** Use <, >, or = to complete each equation.

$54 \div 6 \boxed{<} 54 \div 2$ $\qquad$ $32 \times 10 \boxed{\phantom{0}} 13 \times 100$

$125 + 230 \boxed{\phantom{0}} 100 + 255$ $\qquad$ $144 \div 12 \boxed{\phantom{0}} 144 \div 6$

$197 + 326 \boxed{\phantom{0}} 284 + 139$ $\qquad$ $300 - 250 \boxed{\phantom{0}} 350 - 300$

**3** **CHALLENGE** Fill in the missing number to make each equation true.

$(20 \times \boxed{\phantom{0}}) \div 4 = 25$ $\qquad$ $(36 \div 4) \times \boxed{\phantom{0}} = 81$

$350 = (\boxed{\phantom{0}} \times 50) - 50$ $\qquad$ $1{,}826 = (10 \times \boxed{\phantom{0}}) - 100 - 74$

$(245 + \boxed{\phantom{0}}) \times 3 = 900$ $\qquad$ $(1{,}008 - 508) \div \boxed{\phantom{0}} = 5$

**4** **CHALLENGE** Use <, >, or = to complete each equation.

$(25 \times 4) \div 10 \boxed{\phantom{0}} 81 \div 9$ $\qquad$ $(514 - 489) \times 6 \boxed{\phantom{0}} 50 \times 3$

$(75 \times 2) - 51 \boxed{\phantom{0}} (100 \div 2) \times 4$ $\qquad$ $(328 + 22) - 150 \boxed{\phantom{0}} 500 \div 2$

$(739 + 261) \div 10 \boxed{\phantom{0}} 20 \times 5$ $\qquad$ $5 \times 5 \times 5 \boxed{\phantom{0}} (200 \div 2) + 50$

**234**

**NAME** _____ | **DATE** _____

 **Multiplication Review**

**1** Complete the multiplication facts.

| 10 | 30 | 50 | 90 | 40 | 50 | 60 |
|----|----|----|----|----|----|----|
| × 6 | × 2 | × 8 | × 3 | × 7 | × 3 | × 4 |

**2** Fill in the missing number to complete each multiplication equation. Then write a related division equation.

$4 \times 5 = 20$        $20 \div 5 = 4$

$\boxed{\phantom{0}} \times 2 = 16$        $\boxed{\phantom{0}} \div \boxed{\phantom{0}} = \boxed{\phantom{0}}$

$5 \times \boxed{\phantom{0}} = 35$        $\boxed{\phantom{0}} \div \boxed{\phantom{0}} = \boxed{\phantom{0}}$

$\boxed{\phantom{0}} \times 9 = 18$        $\boxed{\phantom{0}} \div \boxed{\phantom{0}} = \boxed{\phantom{0}}$

**3** Jenny made 3 bracelets with 8 beads each. Then she made 4 bracelets with 9 beads each. How many beads did she use in all?

**a** Write an equation to represent this problem. Use a letter to stand for the unknown quantity.

**b** Solve the problem. Show all your work.

**4** **CHALLENGE** Solve the following:

| 21 | 21 | 43 | 62 | 62 | 26 | 382 |
|----|----|----|----|----|----|-----|
| × 10 | × 5 | × 2 | × 10 | × 5 | × 3 | × 2 |

NAME _____ | DATE _____

 **Multiplication Equations**

**1** Multiply.

| 20 | 40 | 30 | 9 | 8 | 30 | 90 |
|---|---|---|---|---|---|---|
| × 6 | × 5 | × 7 | × 20 | × 40 | × 3 | × 2 |

**2** Circle T or F to show whether the equations below are true or false.

**ex** $4 \times 5 = 5 \times 4$    ⊤ F

**a** $3 \times 20 = 3 \times 2 \times 10$    T  F

**b** $6 \times 30 = 6 \times 3 \times 30$    T  F

**c** $(2 \times 5) \times 4 = 2 \times (5 \times 4)$    T  F

**d** $(2 \times 4) \times 6 = 2 + (4 \times 6)$    T  F

**3** Solve each pair of equations, and circle the one that seemed easier to solve.

**a** $(2 \times 5) \times 8 =$ _____    $2 \times (5 \times 8) =$ _____

**b** $(5 \times 2) \times 4 =$ _____    $5 \times (2 \times 4) =$ _____

**c** $(5 \times 4) \times 3 =$ _____    $5 \times (4 \times 3) =$ _____

**d** $(10 \times 3) \times 5 =$ _____    $10 \times (3 \times 5) =$ _____

**4** Rob says $4 \times 14$ is the same as $(4 \times 10) + (4 \times 4)$. Is he right? Explain why or why not.

**5** Solve each equation below. Show all of your work.

| $(5 \times 10) + (5 \times 3) =$ | $(6 \times 20) + (6 \times 2) =$ | $(3 \times 50) + (3 \times 2) =$ |
|---|---|---|
|  |  |  |

**Sixty Seconds in a Minute**

**1** **a** Fill in the tables below. Some of the answers have been filled in for you.

| × | 20 | 50 | 70 | 30 | 10 | 40 | 80 | 60 | 100 | 90 |
|---|----|----|----|----|----|----|----|----|-----|----|
| 6 | 120 | | | | | | | | | |

| × | 2 | 5 | 7 | 3 | 1 | 4 | 8 | 6 | 10 | 9 |
|---|---|---|---|---|---|---|---|---|----|---|
| 60 | | 300 | | | | | 480 | | | |

**b** What do you notice about your answers?

**2** There are 60 seconds in one minute.

**a** How many seconds are there in 3 minutes? _____

**b** How many seconds are there in 5 minutes? _____

**c** How many seconds are there in 10 minutes? _____

**d** How many seconds are there in 4 minutes? _____

**e** How many seconds are there in $1\frac{1}{2}$ minutes? Show your work.

There are _____ seconds in $1\frac{1}{2}$ minutes.

**3** **CHALLENGE** How many seconds are there in 1 hour? Show your work.

There are _____ seconds in 1 hour.

*(continued on next page)*

**NAME** _____ | **DATE** _____

## 🔍 Building & Sketching Unit Fractions

Build as many different unit fractions as you can using your egg carton, tiles, and yarn. Sketch each of them on this sheet, and label each sketch with the fraction it shows.

Don't forget to sketch the yarn as well as the "eggs" in these cartons. If you have extra cartons, see if you can find two or more different ways to build and sketch some of the fractions.

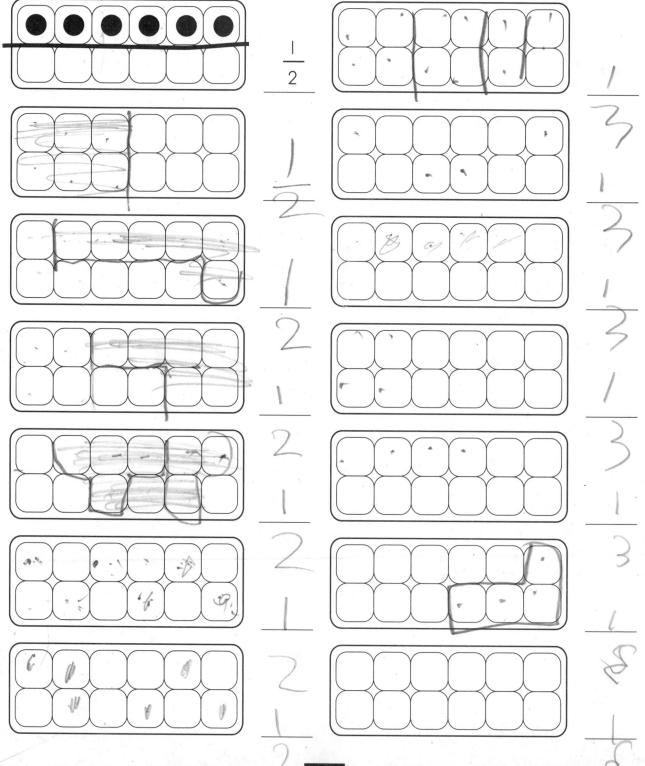

**Modeling Egg Carton Fractions**

**1** Use your egg carton, yarn, and tiles to build a model of each fraction. Then draw a sketch of each fraction you build.

| Build this fraction. | Sketch your model. |
|---|---|
| **ex** $\frac{1}{2}$ | |
| **b** $\frac{1}{4}$ | |

| Build this fraction. | Sketch your model. |
|---|---|
| **a** $\frac{1}{3}$ | |
| **c** $\frac{1}{6}$ | |

**2** Which is more, $\frac{1}{4}$ of a dozen cookies or $\frac{1}{3}$ of a dozen cookies?

**a** How many more cookies is that?

**b** How do you know? Use labeled sketches, numbers, or words to explain your answer.

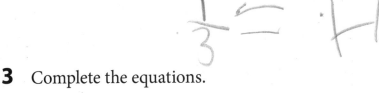

**3** Complete the equations.

$8 + \boxed{4} = 12$    $12 - \boxed{3} = 9$    $3 \times \boxed{4} = 12$    $2 \times \boxed{6} = 12$

$\boxed{7} + 5 = 12$    $4 \times \boxed{4} = 16$    $12 \div 4 = \boxed{3}$    $12 - \boxed{10} = 2$

$16 \div 2 = \boxed{8}$    $12 \div \boxed{2} = 6$    $12 + \boxed{6} = 18$    $16 - \boxed{4} = 12$

**4** **CHALLENGE** Write six different equations that each have 12 for an answer. You can use addition, subtraction, multiplication, or division, and numbers up to 1,000.

## 🔍 **Egg Carton Fractions** page 1 of 2

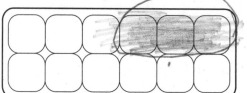

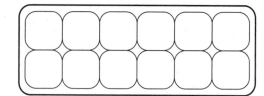

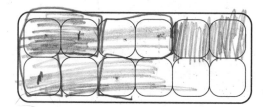
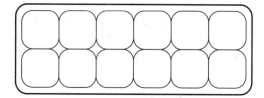

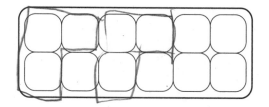
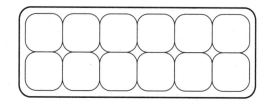

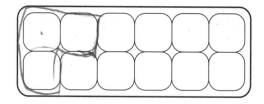
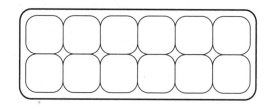

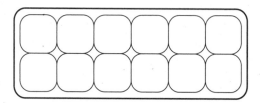
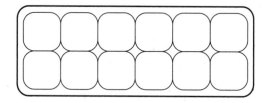

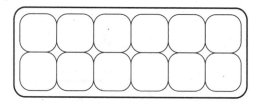
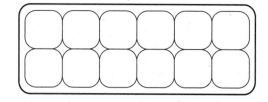

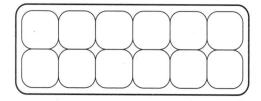
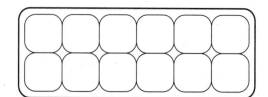

NAME | DATE

## Egg Carton Fractions page 2 of 2

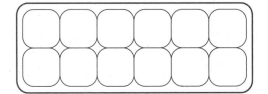

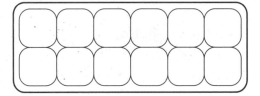

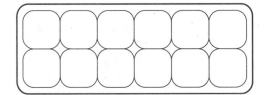

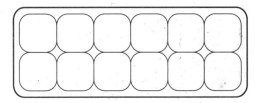

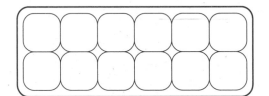

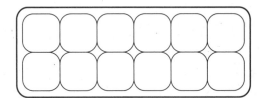

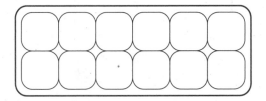

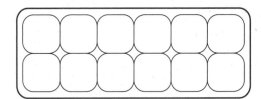

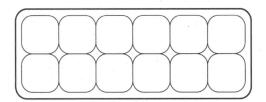

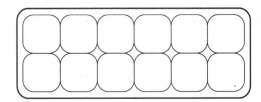

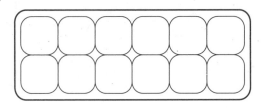

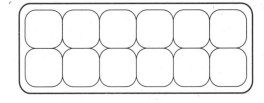

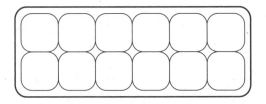

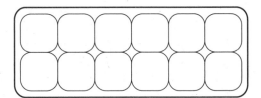

**NAME** _____ | **DATE** _____

 **Fraction Fill & Compare**

**1** Fill in the shapes to show each fraction.

| **ex** $\frac{1}{2}$ | **a** $\frac{1}{3}$ | **b** $\frac{1}{4}$ |
|---|---|---|
| **c** $\frac{1}{6}$ | **d** $\frac{2}{3}$ | **e** $\frac{5}{6}$ |

**2** Look at the fractions you shaded in above. Use them to help complete each number sentence by writing <, >, or =.

| **ex** $\frac{1}{4}$ > $\frac{1}{6}$ | **a** $\frac{1}{4}$ ☐ $\frac{1}{3}$ | **b** $\frac{1}{3}$ ☐ $\frac{2}{6}$ |
|---|---|---|
| **c** $\frac{1}{3}$ ☐ $\frac{2}{3}$ | **d** $\frac{3}{3}$ ☐ 1 | **e** $\frac{3}{6}$ ☐ $\frac{3}{4}$ |

**3** Fill in the shapes to show each fraction.

| **ex** $\frac{1}{3}$ | **a** $\frac{1}{4}$ | **b** $\frac{1}{6}$ |
|---|---|---|
| **c** $\frac{1}{8}$ | **d** $\frac{3}{8}$ | **e** $\frac{7}{8}$ |

**4** Write each of these fractions where they belong on the number line: $\frac{1}{4}$, $\frac{1}{6}$, $\frac{7}{8}$, $\frac{2}{3}$.

0 ←————————————— $\frac{1}{2}$ ————————————— 1 →

**Fraction Fiction**

Solve the story problems below. Use numbers, sketches, or words to show your work.

**1** Sophia is writing and illustrating a picture book about chickens. The book will have 12 pages in all. She has finished 6 pages. What fraction of the book has Sophia finished?

**2** On one page, Sophia shows chickens' nests in the henhouse. There are 12 nests. Chickens are sitting in 9 of the nests.

**a** What fraction of the nests have chickens sitting in them?

**b** What fraction of the nests are empty?

**3** On another page, Sophia shows 12 eggs in a bowl in the kitchen. Two-thirds of the 12 eggs will be used in a cake. How many eggs are for the cake?

**4** On another page, Sophia has written a story problem for her friends to solve. It says, "Last week, 5 of my chickens laid 1 egg, 3 of my chickens laid 2 eggs, and 4 of my chickens laid 3 eggs. How many eggs in all?"

**a** Write an equation to represent Sophia's story problem. Use a letter to stand for the unknown number.

**b** Solve the problem. Show all your work.

NAME | DATE

 # Introducing Dozens of Eggs

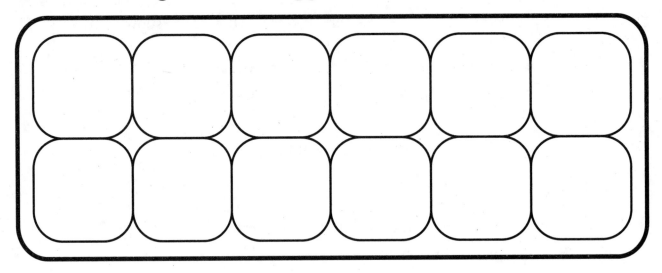

| Teacher | Students |
|---|---|
| 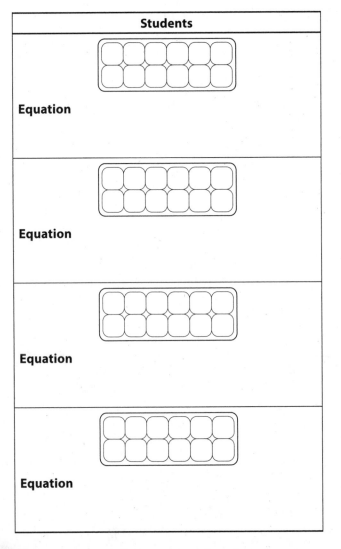 | |
| **Equation** | **Equation** |
| **Equation** | **Equation** |
| **Equation** | **Equation** |
| **Equation** | **Equation** |

**244**

# Work Place Instructions 7A Dozens of Eggs page 1 of 2

## Each pair of players needs:

- 2 Dozens of Eggs Record Sheets
- 1 deck of Dozens of Eggs Fraction Cards
- 1 egg carton
- 6 pieces of string or yarn
- 12 colored tiles
- colored pencils or crayons

**1** Players shuffle the fraction cards and lay them face-down in a stack. Each player draws one card. The player with the larger fraction goes first. Players put the cards just drawn at the bottom of the stack.

Players may build fractions on the Egg Carton Diagram if needed to determine which fraction is larger.

**2** Player 1 draws a card from the top of the deck, reads the fraction out loud, and uses string and colored tiles to build a model of the fraction in the egg carton. Player 2 checks Player 1's work.

> *Jasmine Wow! I got a really big fraction on my first turn. So I'm going to divide the egg carton into 3 equal parts, and fill 2 of them, like this.*

> *Sara I agree that $\frac{2}{3}$ of the egg carton is 8 eggs, because there are 4 eggs in one-third of a carton.*

**3** Player 1 draws circles to represent that number of eggs in one of the diagrams on her record sheet and records that number of twelfths as a fraction on the sheet.

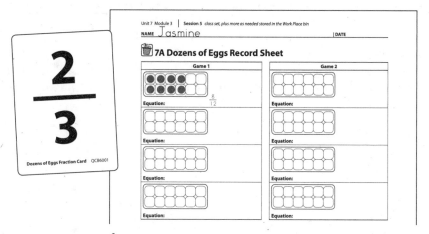

> *Jasmine I have to change $\frac{2}{3}$ into twelfths, but that's easy, because each egg is one-twelfth of the carton, so I got $\frac{8}{12}$ on my first turn. I only need 4 more twelfths to fill this carton.* Player 1 empties the egg carton diagram and puts the card in a discard stack. Then Player 2 takes a turn.

**4** Players continue to take turns until one person has filled in all four cartons on the record sheet. Players should use a different color to record each new turn.

When all the cards in the deck have been used, shuffle the deck and use it again.

**5** On each turn, players must put all of the eggs in one carton. However, players may begin to fill another carton before the first is completely filled.

**6** If the fraction drawn does not fit into one of the cartons, the player misses that turn.

*(continued on next page)*

## Work Place Instructions 7A Dozens of Eggs page 2 of 2

**7** When a carton is filled, the player writes an equation by inserting plus signs between the fractions for that carton and showing them equal to 1 whole.

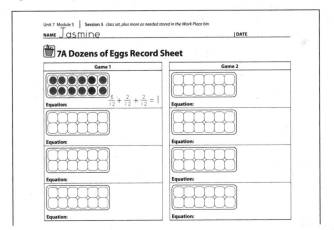

**8** The winner is the first player to fill all four cartons on his record sheet. If Player 1 is the first to fill all four cartons, Player 2 may take one last turn.

## Game Variations

**A** Players work together to fill all four cartons on a single record sheet rather than playing against each other.

**B** Players begin with all four cartons filled, by drawing 12 circles in each of the cartons and writing $\frac{12}{12}$ at the start of each equation line. Then each player subtracts the fractions that are written on the cards they get, crossing out that many eggs and subtracting that many twelfths. Players must subtract the entire fraction from one carton rather than splitting the fraction between two or more cartons. The winner is the first player to get rid of all the eggs from all four cartons.

NAME _____ | DATE _____

 **Fraction Review**

**1** Lincoln has several chickens. Every day, he gathers eggs and puts them in a 12-egg carton. On Monday, he collected 3 eggs. On Tuesday, he collected 4 eggs. On Wednesday, he collected 2 more eggs.

    **a** What fraction of the egg carton did Lincoln fill on Monday? How do you know?

    **b** What fraction of the egg carton did Lincoln fill on Tuesday? How do you know?

    **c** If Lincoln put all of the eggs he gathered on Monday, Tuesday, and Wednesday into an egg carton, what fraction of the carton would be full? Show your work.

    **d** How many eggs does Lincoln need to take out so the egg carton will be only half full? How do you know?

**2** Write each of these fractions where they belong on the number line: $\frac{1}{3}$, $\frac{1}{1}$, $\frac{1}{6}$, $\frac{5}{8}$, $\frac{6}{12}$, $\frac{1}{2}$.

0

# Work Place Instructions 7B Racing Fractions page 1 of 2

**Each pair of players needs:**

- 7B Racing Fractions Game Board (1 copy per player)
- 5 red game markers
- 5 blue game markers
- 1 deck of Number Cards with the 0s, 5s, 7s, 9s, 10s, and wild cards removed

**1** Players decide who will play with the red game markers and who will play with the blue markers. Then both players place one of their game markers at the beginning of each number line on their own game board.

**2** Players shuffle the Number Cards and lay them face-down in a stack. Each player draws two cards, and uses them to form a fraction. The player with the larger fraction goes first. Players put the cards just drawn at the bottom of the stack.

Players must use the smaller of the two numbers they drew as the numerator, and the larger as the denominator now and throughout the game.

**3** Player 1 draws two new cards, uses them to form a fraction, and moves one or more game markers the distance shown on the card. Player 2 checks Player 1's work.

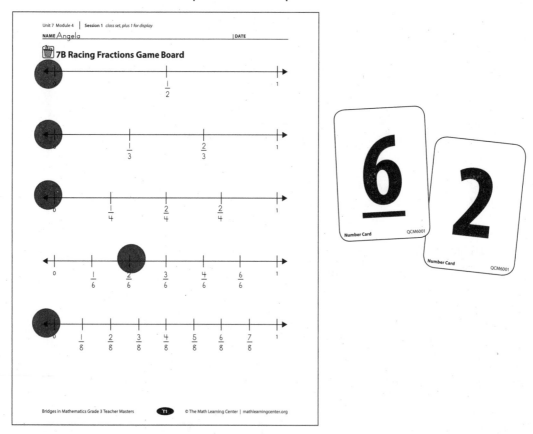

*Player 1* OK, I got a 6 and a 2. I have to use the smaller number on the top of the fraction, so that's two-sixths. I think I'm just going to move the marker on the line for the sixths—one-sixth, two-sixths, your turn!

*(continued on next page)*

## Work Place Instructions 7B Racing Fractions page 2 of 2

**4** Then Player 2 draws two Number Cards and takes a turn. Player 1 checks the second player's work.

**5** Players continue to take turns and check each other's work until one player's game markers are all on 1. If Player 1 is the first to get all of her markers on 1, Player 2 may take one last turn.

- If a player cannot find a possible move for a card he has drawn, the player loses the turn.

- Players may also move game markers backward. For example, if a player gets the cards 2 and 3 to make the fraction $\frac{2}{3}$, she can move one marker up $\frac{1}{3}$ and another back $\frac{2}{6}$. The sum of the moves still needs to equal the value of the fraction.

- Players must go out exactly. In other words, if a player has all his markers except one on 1, with just $\frac{1}{4}$ left to go on one line, and he draws a 1 and a 2 to form the fraction $\frac{1}{2}$, he loses the turn.

## Game Variations

**A** Play cooperatively. Players can work together and help each other finish the track in a certain time period.

**B** Both players place one of their game markers at the end of each number line on their own game board. Then they race to see who can be first to get the markers on all their lines back to 0.

**C** Players can use either of the cards they draw on a given turn as the numerator or the denominator. For example, if a player draws the cards 6 and 3, she can arrange those cards to form either $\frac{3}{6}$ or $\frac{6}{3}$.

NAME | DATE

 **Garden Patch Problems**

**1** Liam wanted to put a fence around his vegetable garden patch. His brother asked him to put a fence around his garden patch too. Liam's garden patch was 5 feet wide and 10 feet long. His brother's patch was 6 feet wide and 7 feet long. How many feet of fencing will Liam need? Show all your work.

**2** Liam bought too much fencing and had 26 feet of it left over. He and his brother decided to make a rectangle-shaped garden patch for their little sister. They wanted to use all the extra fencing to outline her garden patch. What could be the dimensions of the patch they make for their sister? (Use only whole numbers of feet.) Show all your work.

**3** **CHALLENGE** Draw and label two other ways Liam and his brother could use all 26 feet of fencing for their sister's garden.

| DATE

 ## Sharing Pizzas Record Sheet

Write the number of kids your team is working with in the spaces provided. Then solve each problem using the paper pizzas. Glue the paper pizza pieces in the boxes to show how you divided the pizzas evenly between the kids. Include a sentence telling how much pizza each kid gets.

My team is dividing pizzas evenly between _____ kids.

**1** What happens when _____ kids share 2 pizzas?

**2** What happens when _____ kids share 3 pizzas?

**3** What happens when _____ kids share 4 pizzas?

**251**

**NAME** | **DATE**

 **Pizza Problems**

**1** You can use some of your leftover paper pizzas to help you solve these problems or you can draw your own circles.

**a** Jim and Emma were eating pizza for lunch. Jim ate $\frac{2}{6}$ of the pizza. Emma ate $\frac{3}{6}$ of the pizza. How much pizza did they eat in all? Use labeled sketches, numbers, or words to explain how you got the answer.

**b** Rosa and Carmen made two mini-pizzas for lunch. They cut both pizzas into fourths. Rosa ate $\frac{3}{4}$ of a pizza. Carmen ate $\frac{3}{4}$ of a pizza. How much pizza did they eat in all? Use labeled sketches, numbers, or words to explain how you got the answer.

**c** **CHALLENGE** Carl and his brother Noel ordered a pizza. Carl ate $\frac{1}{4}$ of the pizza. Noel ate $\frac{2}{4}$ of the pizza. How much of the pizza did they eat in all? Use labeled sketches, numbers, or words to explain how you got the answer.

**2** Write each of these fractions where they belong on the number line: $1$, $\frac{2}{3}$, $\frac{3}{4}$, $\frac{1}{3}$, $\frac{5}{6}$, $\frac{3}{3}$, $1\frac{1}{2}$.

## Student Survey

**1** Here is the question I want to ask my classmates:

**2** Here are the answer choices (please provide two or three possible answers):

**a**

**b**

**c**

**3** Here are my predictions about the results of this survey:

**4** Ask exactly 12 classmates your question. Record and organize their answers below or on another piece of paper.

NAME | DATE

 ## Circle Graph Record Sheet

**Title**_____

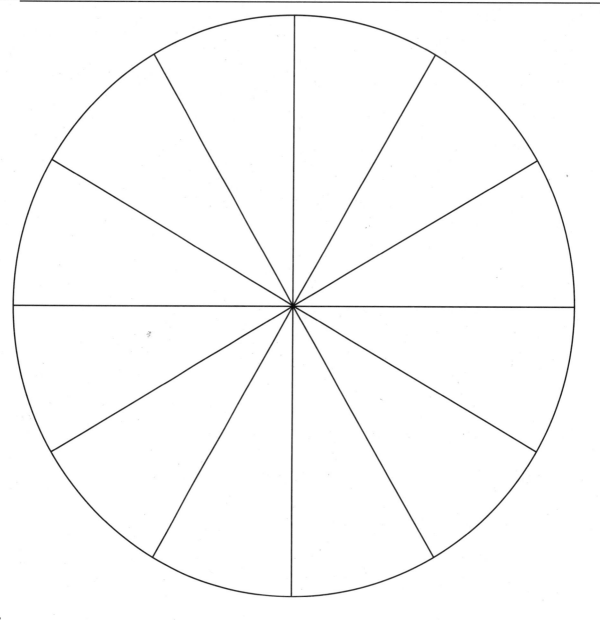

**Key**

**Fraction Action**

Solve each story problem below. Use the example to see how to show your work.

**ex** Sam and Sophia are playing basketball. Sophia has scored 16 points. Sam has scored half as many points as Sophia.

**a** Make a labeled sketch to show how many points Sam has scored.

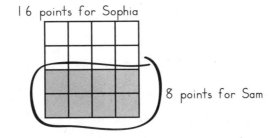

**b** How many points has Sam scored? Sam scored 8 points.

**1** Sam and Sophia play basketball again. This time, Sophia scored 12 points and Sam scored one-third as many points as Sophia.

**a** Make a labeled sketch to show how many points Sam scored.

**b** How many points did Sam score?

**2** On another day, Sam and Sophia play soccer. Sam scored 8 points. Sophia scored one-fourth as many points as Sam.

**a** Make a labeled sketch to show how many points Sophia scored.

**b** How many points did Sophia score?

**3** Solve the following problems:

$(5 \times 10) \times 2 =$ _____ $(2 \times 5) \times 10 =$ _____ $3 \times (6 \times 10) =$ _____ $6 \times (3 \times 10) =$ _____

**255**

## 🔍 Pull & Graph Record Sheet

Put 8 green and 4 yellow tiles in a bag. Shake the bag well. Pull out a tile and record its color by filling in 1 section on the circle graph below. Return the tile to the bag, shake well, pull out another tile, and record the color on the circle graph below. Do this 12 times.

*Be sure to put the tile back in the bag and shake it again each time.*

What do you predict will happen? Why?

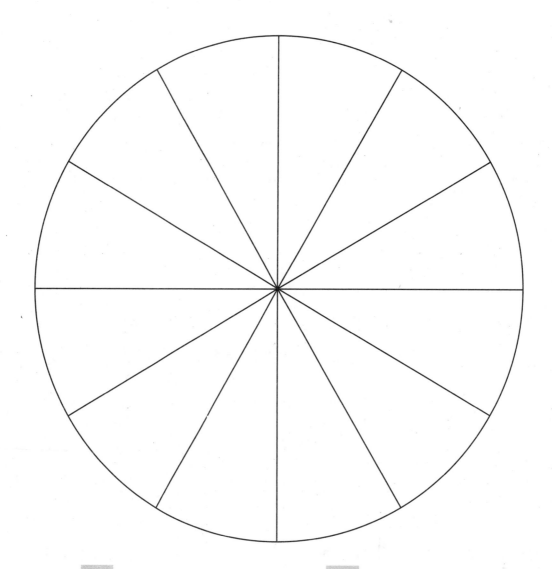

Green came out $\frac{\phantom{00}}{12}$ of the time. Yellow came out $\frac{\phantom{00}}{12}$ of the time.

NAME _____ | DATE _____

 ## Comparing Fractions on a Number Line

When you are comparing fractions, it can help to think about how close those fractions are to landmarks like one whole and one-half. Use the number line to help complete the problems below.

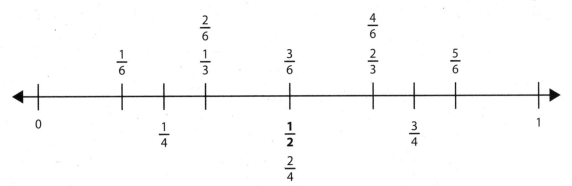

**1** Complete the table.

| Circle the fraction that is greater than $\frac{1}{2}$. | | Write an expression showing which fraction is greater. |
|---|---|---|
| **ex** $\left(\frac{4}{6}\right)$ $\frac{1}{4}$ | | $\frac{4}{6} > \frac{1}{4}$ |
| **a** $\frac{2}{6}$ $\frac{2}{3}$ | | |
| **b** $\frac{3}{4}$ $\frac{1}{4}$ | | |

**2** Complete the table.

| Circle the fraction that is closest to 1. | | Write an expression showing which fraction is greater. |
|---|---|---|
| **a** $\frac{3}{4}$ $\frac{2}{4}$ | | |
| **b** $\frac{2}{6}$ $\frac{2}{3}$ | | |
| **c** $\frac{3}{4}$ $\frac{3}{6}$ | | |

**NAME** _____ | **DATE** _____

 **Lemonade & Bracelets**

**1** Philipe is making lemonade with his dad to serve at their party. Their recipe makes 6 glasses of lemonade. The recipe calls for 4 lemons, 1 cup of sugar, and 6 cups of water.

**a** If they want to make enough lemonade for 30 people to drink a glass, how many lemons will they need to buy?

**b** Use words, numbers, or pictures to explain how you know your answer above makes sense.

**2** Lisa is making bracelets for four of her friends. She needs 18 beads for each bracelet.

**a** How many beads does she need in all?

**b** Use words, numbers, or pictures to explain how you know your answer above makes sense.

**c** **CHALLENGE** If each bead costs 15¢, how much would it cost for Lisa to buy all those beads? Show your work.

`258`

**NAME** _____ | **DATE** _____

 # How Long Is That Bridge?

**1** Study the chart below and then solve the problems.

| Notable Bridges | |
|---|---|
| Bailey Bridge in India | 98 feet |
| Lugou Bridge in China | 874 feet |
| Blue Wonder Bridge in Germany | 920 feet |
| Victoria Falls Bridge in Zimbabwe | 650 feet |
| Union Chain Bridge in Scotland | 449 feet |
| Ponte di Rialto in Italy | 157 feet |
| Bridge to Nowhere in New Zealand | 130 feet |

**a** What is the difference in feet between the longest and the shortest bridge? Show your work.

**b** If you walked across the Union Chain Bridge and then across the Ponte di Rialto Bridge, how far would you have walked in all? Show your work.

**c** If you walked 230 feet every minute, how long would it take you to cross the Blue Wonder Bridge? Show your work.

**d** **CHALLENGE** Which bridge is 5 times as long as another bridge? How do you know?

**2** Solve the problems below.

$5 \times$ _____ $= 65$        _____ $\div 3 = 9$        $46 =$ _____ $\times 2$        $90 = 15 +$ _____

**NAME** | **DATE**

 # Work Place Instructions 8A Weight Lifting

**1** At the Weight Lifting event station, Player 1 and Player 2 both plan their weight lifts.

- Each player gets a copy of the 8A Weight Lifting Record Sheet.
- Each player chooses an item to weight lift and records the item chosen on the record sheet.
- Each player estimates the mass of 1 item and records their estimate on the record sheet.
- Using the pan balance and metric weights, each player measures the mass of 1 item and records it on the record sheet.

    *If measuring the mass of 1 item is difficult, measure the mass of 10 items and divide to find the mass of 1.*

- Each player estimates how many of this item she can grab in one hand, then estimates the mass of that many of the item and records that estimate on the record sheet.

    **Jami** *I think I can grab 30 of these little cubes. Each cube has a mass of 1 gram, so I'm going to put 30 grams.*

    **Rick** *The dice are bigger than the cubes, but I bet I can grab 30 of them anyway. One of them is about 5 grams, so I'm going to put 150 grams for my estimate.*

**2** Player 1 grabs as many of her chosen item as she can hold in one hand. Then she counts the items, finds their total mass, and records the total mass on the record sheet.

**3** Player 2 repeats this process with his chosen item.

**4** Players calculate the difference between their estimates and the actual mass they grabbed and record the differences in the table.

**5** The winner is the player whose grab came closest to their estimate.

**6** Players repeat the game, choosing new items to grab.

**NAME** _____ | **DATE** _____

# Work Place Instructions 8B Wacky Discus

**1** Each player gets an 8B Wacky Discus Record Sheet and records the Wacky Discus area on the sheet.

- Players use the area posted at the station. If no area is posted, players agree on an area to use for the event.

**2** Each player writes all of the possible pairs of dimensions for the chosen area on their record sheet.

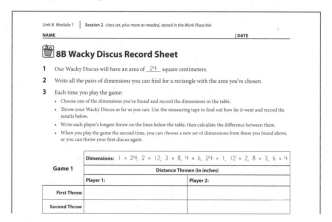

**3** Each player chooses one of the pairs of dimensions to make their Wacky Discus and records the dimensions in the table. Then each player measures the dimensions onto a sheet of paper and cuts out their Wacky Discus.

**4** Each player throws their Wacky Discus three times. Players record the results on their record sheets.

- When throwing, the players stand with toes just barely on the starting line.
- After throwing, players use the measuring tape to measure a straight line from the starting line to the nearest edge of the discus.
- Players record the measurement to the nearest quarter-inch.

**5** Each player calculates the difference between his best distance and the other player's best distance and records that difference on the record sheet.

**6** Players repeat the event. They can either keep the same discus, or make a new discus with the same area but different dimensions.

## Game Variation

**A** Make a triangle, trapezoid, or parallelogram discus instead of a rectangle.

**NAME** _____ | **DATE** _____

 ## How Big Is That School?

José made a scale model of his school, Roebling Elementary. A drawing of the model is shown below.

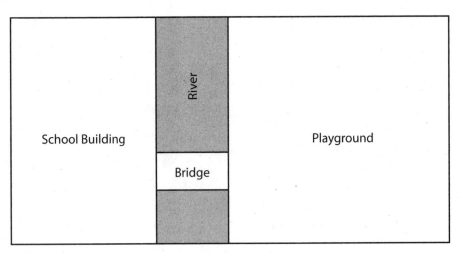

**Roebling Elementary School**

**1** Using centimeters, measure the dimensions of the school building, playground, river, and bridge.

- Record the dimensions of each part of the model in the table below.

- Find the area of each part of the model and record the areas in the table below.

*Hint: Remember that the river runs underneath the bridge.*

|   |                 | Dimensions (in centimeters) | Area |
|---|-----------------|-----------------------------|------|
| **a** | School Building |                         |      |
| **b** | Playground      |                         |      |
| **c** | River           |                         |      |
| **d** | Bridge          |                         |      |

**e** What is the area of the entire model of Roebling Elementary School? Show your work.

**2** Solve the problems below.

$5 \times \underline{\hspace{1cm}} = 90$     $\underline{\hspace{1cm}} \div 15 = 6$     $\underline{\hspace{1cm}} \times 3 = 45$     $90 = 2 \times \underline{\hspace{1cm}}$

NAME _____ | DATE _____

 ## How Big Is That Bridge?

**1** Ariana and Maya built the model beam bridges shown below.

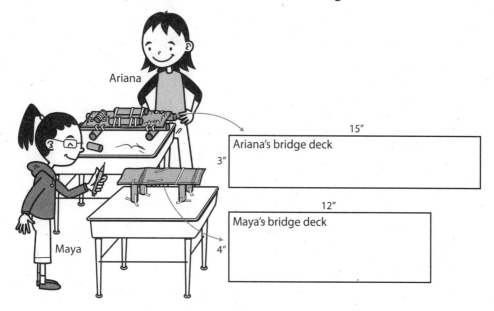

**a** What is the area of Ariana's bridge deck? Show your work.

**b** What is the area of Maya's bridge deck? Show your work.

**c** What is the difference between the areas of the two decks? Show your work.

**d** Ariana's bridge spanned $10\frac{1}{2}$ inches. Maya's bridge spanned $8\frac{1}{2}$ inches. How much longer was Ariana's span? Show your work.

**2** Solve the problems below.

$20 \times \underline{\hspace{1cm}} = 120$    $\underline{\hspace{1cm}} \div 8 = 9$    $45 = \underline{\hspace{1cm}} \times 5$    $90 = 30 \times \underline{\hspace{1cm}}$

**NAME** _____ **| DATE** _____

 # How Much Weight Does That Bridge Hold?

**1** Mr. Weldele's class made small beam bridges out of craft sticks and paper. Examine the data in the table and answer the questions below.

| Team | Weight (grams) | Area (square inches) | Load per square inch |
|------|----------------|----------------------|----------------------|
| A | 88 | 4″ | 22 grams per square inch |
| B | 24 | 8″ | |
| C | 48 | 6″ | |
| D | 36 | 9″ | |
| E | 54 | 6″ | |

**a** How much more weight did Team E's bridge hold than Team C's bridge? Show your work.

**b** In bridge design, one important factor is load per square unit—the amount of weight that an area of the bridge can hold. Team A calculated the load per square inch of their bridge as follows:

88 grams ÷ 4 square inches = 22 grams per square inch

Calculate the loads per square inch of the bridges made by the other teams and enter them on the table above. Use the space here to do your calculations.

**2** Solve the problems below.

$5 \times 60 =$ _____     _____ $\times 4 = 28$     $120 =$ _____ $\times 4$     _____ $\div 4 = 14$

NAME | DATE

# Arch Bridges Bar Graph

Make a bar graph to represent the data from the Arch Bridges table. Write the team name below each bar, and write the actual number of grams above each bar.

**Weight Data for Each Team**

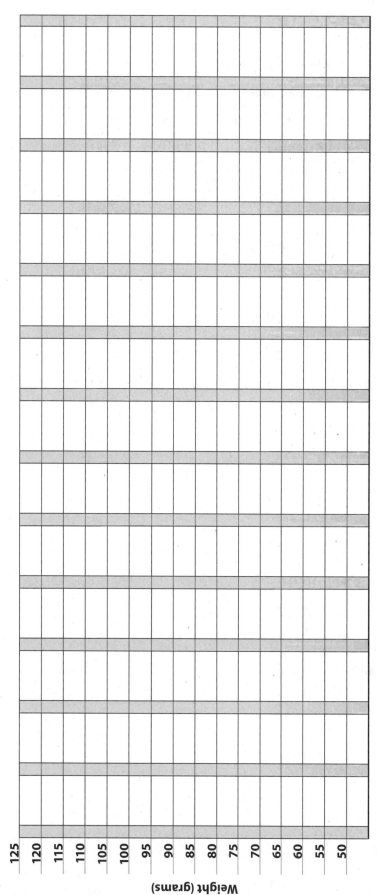

Weight (grams): 125, 120, 115, 110, 105, 100, 95, 90, 85, 80, 75, 70, 65, 60, 55, 50

Team Names

NAME _____ | DATE _____

 **Arch Bridge Data on a Line Plot**

**1**  Ms. Fisher's class made arch bridges out of books and card stock. Every bridge had the same size of arch and the same type of deck. Here is the data they collected.

| Builder | Weight (grams) |
|---------|----------------|
| Gayle   | 83 ✓           |
| Sharon  | 91             |
| Dan     | 83             |
| Rick    | 85             |
| Ryan    | 86             |
| Ken     | 65             |
| Lisa    | 89             |
| Dennis  | 85             |
| Greg    | 83             |

| Builder | Weight (grams) |
|---------|----------------|
| Gary    | 81             |
| Jami    | 85             |
| Dixie   | 83             |
| Ted     | 86             |
| Glenda  | 85             |
| Ana     | 84             |
| Martha  | 83             |
| Ty      | 74             |
| Susan   | 85             |

**a**  Draw an X for each team's data on the line plot below. Gayle's data has been added to the line plot already.

**Arch Bridge Data**

X

65 66 67 68 69 70 71 72 73 74 75 76 77 78 79 80 81 82 83 84 85 86 87 88 89 90 91 92 93 94 95
**Grams**

**b**  Write two things you notice about the data on the line plot.

**2**  Solve the problems below.

$10 \times$ _____ $= 1,000$     _____ $\div 100 = 10$     $200 =$ _____ $\times 10$     _____ $\div 20 = 10$

# Work Place Instructions 8C Speed Skating

## Each pair of players needs:

- 8C Speed Skating Record Sheets, 1 per player
- 1 gram cube
- 2 rulers
- two 30 cm lengths of string
- scratch paper or copy paper

**1** Each player creates a quadrilateral skating track with a perimeter of 30 centimeters. Players draw a sketch of their track on the recording sheet, labeling the length of each side.

- Players use a ruler to keep the sides of the quadrilateral straight and to make sure their lengths add up to 30 cm.
- Players measure the sides of their quadrilateral and label each side, then mark a starting point on the skating track.

**2** Player 1 places a gram cube at the starting line of his speed skating track, then gently blows the cube along the line until it has gone around the track three times and come back to the starting line.

- Players can gently turn the record sheet to change the angle at which their breath hits the cube to keep it on track.
- If the cube leaves the track, the player must take a 1-minute penalty and put the cube back where it left the track, then continue skating it around the track.
- If the cube tends to abruptly fly across the paper, the player is blowing too close to the cube or using sharp puffs of air that are too strong. Try blowing steadily from a distance of 3–6 inches, pausing for breath as needed.

**3** While Player 1 skates the cube around his track, Player 2 serves as timekeeper.

- The timekeeper records the time to the nearest minute when the skating begins, then records the time again when three laps are complete.
- If the skating player's cube leaves the track, the timekeeper adds a 1-minute penalty and records it on the record sheet.
- Players calculate and record the elapsed time on their record sheets, adding any penalties.

**4** Player 2 repeats the process, using his own track, while Player 1 keeps time.

**5** The player with the shorter (faster) time wins. Calculate the difference between the faster and slower times and record the difference on the record sheet.

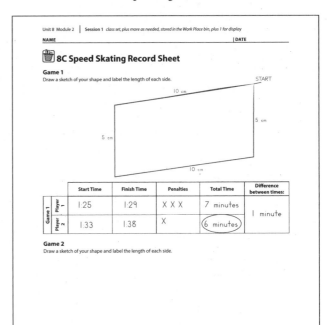

## Game Variations

**A** Make a track that is not a quadrilateral. Try tracks with 3, 5, 6, or 7 sides.

- To make more complex shapes, players can use the 30 cm length of string to make a polygon on the paper, then trace it.

**B** Make an oval or circular track, or one that has some curved sides.

- In this case, players do not need to mark the lengths of the track's sides, but the perimeter of the track must still be 30 cm. Use the length of string to make sure.

#  Work Place Instructions 8D Curling

## Each pair of players needs:

- 10 gram cubes
- 2 rulers
- 8D Curling Record Sheet (1 per player)
- 8D Curling: Rectangle, Square, and Triangle (1 of each per player)
- copy paper (to make curling sheets for Variation B)

**1** Players play three games, one on each curling sheet. Together players choose a sheet for the first game.

**2** Players partition their targets into parts. See the table below for the number of parts for each target.
- Players can use rulers to measure the targets' lengths and widths, then calculate areas, in order to ensure equal partitions. Partitions do not need to have equivalent shapes, but must have equal areas.

**3** Players take turns curling. To curl, players place a gram cube on the starting line, then give it a tap with the ruler to send it gliding toward the target.

**4** Players evaluate the results of their curl and record their current score on the record sheet:
- Each partition with a cube in it is worth a fraction of a point, as shown in the table below.
- Each partition of the target may only be scored once. For example, if two cubes are in one-fourth of the rectangle, that part is still worth only $\frac{1}{4}$ point.
- A cube outside the target, or touching any of the lines of the target, scores no points.

**5** Each player curls another gram cube, aiming for or avoiding their previous cube as they like.
- Later cubes may strike cubes already on the sheet. In this way, players may use later cubes to push an earlier cube into the target, or into a different part of the target. Cubes may also be pushed off the target.
- After each curl, players evaluate their current score and record it on the record sheet. Each turn has a new score; there is no "total."

**6** Play continues until one player scores 1 full point (at least one cube in each partition of the target). The first player to achieve this is the winner.

**7** Players repeat the game with the other two curling sheets.
- To play a more competitive game, players partition their targets in the exact same way.
- To play a more strategic game, players partition their targets in a way they think will give them an advantage in gameplay and scoring (each part must still be of equal area).

| Target | Partitions | Point value per partition |
|--------|------------|---------------------------|
| Rectangle | 4 | $\frac{1}{4}$ point |
| Triangle | 2 | $\frac{1}{2}$ point |
| Square | 3 | $\frac{1}{3}$ point |

Points are scored only for cubes that are within a partition at the end of each turn. Cubes touching more than one partition do not score any points.

## Game Variations

**A** Players agree on a different number of partitions for the curling target, such as 4 partitions for the rectangle or 3 partitions for the triangle, and score accordingly.

**B** Using a blank sheet of paper, players make a curling target with 4 sides that is not a rectangle, or even a shape with more than 4 sides, then partition and assign points accordingly.

NAME _____ |DATE _____

 **Fractional Parts**

**1** **a** Measure (in centimeters) and divide these rectangles into 3 equal parts. Do it two different ways.

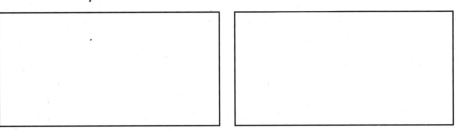

**b** What fraction can you use to describe one of the parts of each rectangle? _____

**c** What are the dimensions (length and width) of one part in centimeters?

**2** **a** Measure (in centimeters) and divide the squares into 4 equal parts. Do it two different ways.

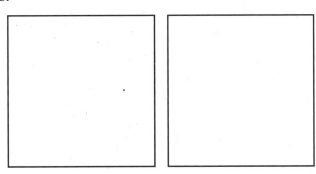

**b** What fraction can you use to describe one of the parts of each square? _____

**c** What is the area of one part in square centimeters?

**3** Divide these rectangles into 4 equal parts, then color in $\frac{3}{4}$ of each rectangle. Do it two different ways.

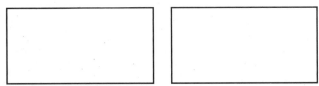

**4** Write < , =, or > to make each expression true.

$3\frac{1}{2}$ ☐ $3\frac{1}{4}$         $2\frac{1}{2}$ ☐ $2\frac{2}{4}$         $4\frac{1}{8}$ ☐ $4\frac{1}{3}$         $5\frac{4}{6}$ ☐ $5\frac{2}{3}$

**Capacity in Daily Life**

**1** Javier brought a Thermos of tomato soup for lunch. He estimates that he brought about $\frac{3}{4}$ of a liter. His friend insists he brought about $\frac{3}{4}$ of a milliliter. Who is correct? Why? Explain your answer using numbers, pictures, or words.

**2** Julene is making fruit punch for her scout troop. There are 10 girls in the troop, and each one will drink at least 1 glass of punch. Should she use 2 milliliters, 2 liters, 20 liters, or 200 liters of juice? Why? Explain your answer using numbers, pictures, or words.

**3** Jillian is planning to keep a container of water with her electric teakettle so that she can make tea without having to go to the sink each time. The kettle makes 2 teacups of tea. Should she use a container that holds 10 milliliters, a container that holds 100 milliliters, a container that holds 1 liter, or a container that holds 10 liters? Why? Explain your answer using numbers, pictures, or words.

**4** Solve the problems below.

$100 \div$ _____ $= 2$      $20 \times$ _____ $100$      _____ $\div 5 = 20$      $50 \times$ _____ $= 100$

NAME

DATE

# Plotting Bridge Lengths

Title: _____

271

**NAME** | **DATE**

 **Estimate & Reason with Water**

**1** **a** Troy wants to provide bottles of water for the soccer team's family members to drink while they watch the game. There are 15 kids on each team, and 2 teams will play. Troy thinks that 2 cases of water bottles, with 24 bottles in each case, will be enough for all the family members. Do you think he's right? Why or why not?

**b** How many 24-bottle cases would you tell Troy to buy? _____

**2** A cat drinks about half as much water as a cocker spaniel. Tasha has noticed that her cocker spaniel, Pal, drinks about 15 ounces of water a day. Tasha plans to adopt a cat, and wants to put out a 32-ounce fountain for the cat to drink from (in a spot Pal can't reach). She expects to refill the fountain twice a week. Is Tasha's plan reasonable? Why or why not?

**3** Jhong needs to clean out and refill his hot tub. He knows the hot tub holds about 750 gallons of water. He also knows that using his garden hose, he can fill the hot tub with about 12 gallons every minute. He calculates how long he'll need to refill the tub with this equation:

$$(750 \text{ gallons} \div 12 \text{ gallons/minute}) = m$$

**a** What does the $m$ in Jhong's equation represent?

**b** **CHALLENGE** Use letters and numbers to write an equation that shows how to convert $m$ (from Jhong's equation) into hours.

NAME _____ | DATE _____

## Graphing Our Bridge Collection

**1** Create a bar graph of our class data. Then use your graph to answer the questions below.

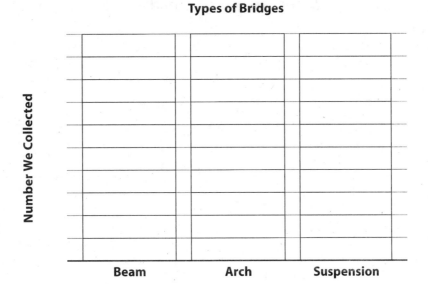

**Types of Bridges**

Number We Collected

Beam          Arch          Suspension

**a** How many images did we collect in all?

**b** Which bridge type has the most images?

**c** How many more images does it have then the other two types of bridges?

**2** Draw a picture of your favorite bridge. Label as many of its parts and features as you can. Use your math journal if you need more room.

**NAME** _____ **|DATE** _____

 **Favorite Bridges**

**1** Ms. Gibbons' class read about beam bridges, arch bridges, and suspension bridges. Then the class took a survey of their favorite of the three types of bridge, and recorded the results in a table.

| Favorite Type | Students |
|---------------|----------|
| Arch | 11 |
| Beam | 6 |
| Suspension | 13 |

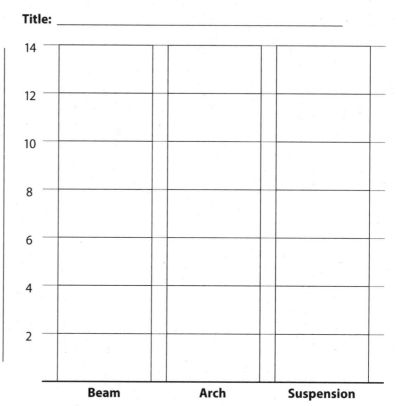

**Title:** _____

**a** Show the information from the table on the bar graph. Title the graph and label the *y*-axis.

**b** How many students were surveyed?

**c** What bridge type was most popular?

**d** After reading about truss bridges, 7 students changed their favorite type of bridge to truss bridge. Of those 7 students, 3 had previously preferred suspension bridges, and 1 had previously preferred arch bridges. How many students still liked beam bridges best after the changes?

**2** Solve the problems below.

$9 \times$ _____ $= 270$          _____ $\div 8 = 9$          $720 =$ _____ $\times 9$          _____ $\div 3 = 9$

**274**

**Finding Shapes in Bridges** page 1 of 2

**1** Describe the shapes you see in the beam bridge below.

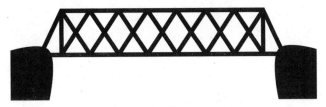

**a** Outline a parallelogram in blue.

**b** Use red to partition a rhombus into equal triangles.

**c** Use a purple color to outline a trapezoid.

**2** Look at the two bridges below.

 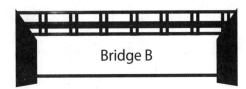

**a** Describe the shapes in this bridge:

**b** Describe the shapes in this bridge:

**c** Which bridge do you think is stronger? Why?

**d** Which shapes could you change to make the weaker bridge stronger? Draw a picture and describe your changes.

## Finding Shapes in Bridges page 2 of 2

**3** Look at the arch bridge below. Outline and label three different types of quadrilaterals on the bridge.

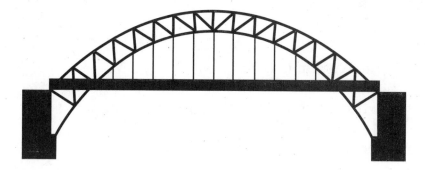

**4** Create your own strong bridge to span the opening below. Use at least four different shapes and label an example of each in your drawing.

**NAME** _____ | **DATE** _____

## Triangle Perimeters

**1**  Use the measurements shown to help you fill in the missing numbers.

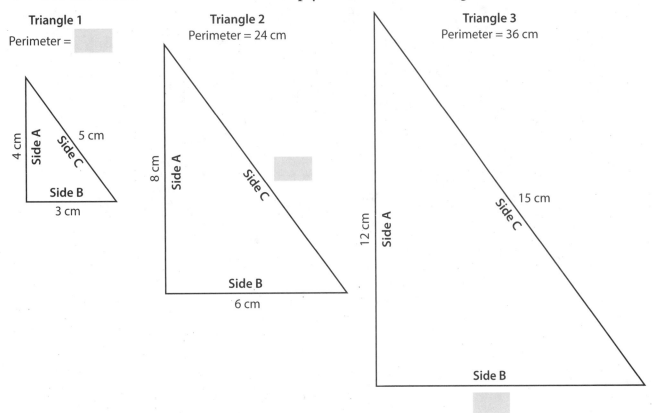

**Triangle 1**

Perimeter = [        ]

Side A  4 cm
Side C  5 cm
Side B  3 cm

**Triangle 2**
Perimeter = 24 cm

Side A  8 cm
Side C  [        ]
Side B  6 cm

**Triangle 3**
Perimeter = 36 cm

Side A  12 cm
Side C  15 cm
Side B  [        ]

**2**  Fill in the dimensions for Triangles 1, 2, and 3 below.

| | Dimensions (cm) | | | Perimeter (cm) |
|---|---|---|---|---|
| | **Side A** | **Side B** | **Side C** | |
| **Triangle 1** | | | | |
| **Triangle 2** | | | | |
| **Triangle 3** | | | | |
| **Triangle 4** | | | | |

**3**  Describe at least two patterns you see in the table.

**4**  Can you predict the measurements of Triangle 4? Sketch and label it in your math journal or on a spare sheet of paper. Fill in its dimensions and perimeter in the table above.

**NAME** _____ **| DATE** _____

 **How Much Time Does He Need?**

**1** Joshua has one hour to work on his race car today.

- He needs 5 minutes to set up tools.
- It will take him twice as long to clean up as it takes to set up the tools.
- He wants to spend half his time working on building his car.
- He needs the remaining time to make drawings of his building plans.

**a** How many minutes can he spend on each task? Show your work.

- Set up tools _____
- Make drawings of building plans _____
- Work on building the car _____
- Clean up tools _____

**b** If he begins at 4:35 in the afternoon, at what time should he begin each task?

- Set up tools _____
- Make drawings of building plans _____
- Work on building the car _____
- Clean up tools _____

**2** Solve the problems below.

$60 \div \underline{\hspace{1cm}} = 15$　　　$3 \times 20 = \underline{\hspace{1cm}}$　　　$\underline{\hspace{1cm}} \div 5 = 12$　　　$15 \times \underline{\hspace{1cm}} = 120$

**NAME** _____ | **DATE** _____

 **The Class Party**

The students in Mr. Frisbie's class are having a party today. Answer the questions about the party activities. You can use the number line below to keep track of each activity.

**1**  School ends at 3:00, and the party starts 1 hour and 15 minutes before the end of school. What time does the party start?

**2**  As soon as the party starts, the students need 5 minutes to pass out the party treats. What time will it be when everyone has their treats?

**3**  The class is going to enjoy their treats for 20 minutes and then go outside to play games. What time will they go outside?

**4**  They get to play games outside for 30 minutes. Then it's time to return to the classroom. What time will they return to the classroom?

**5**  When students return to the classroom, they'll sing the song they've been practicing in music this year for Mr. Frisbie. The song is 4 minutes long, and they need 2 minutes before they start to get everyone ready. What time will it be when they're done singing?

**6**  After singing, the class will clean up and get ready to go home. How much time do they have to do this before school is over?

NAME

# Strength Graph

DATE

Title _____

_____

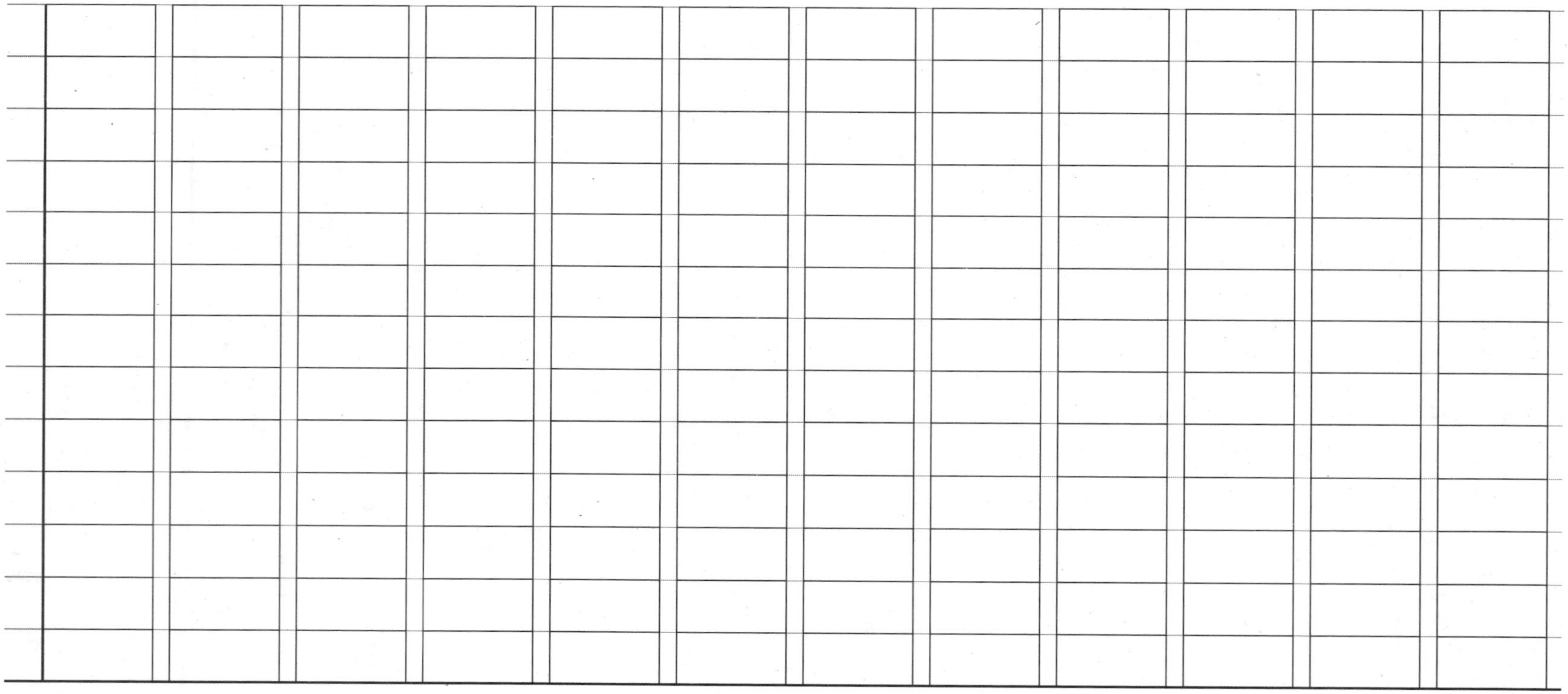

**Key to Bridge Types**

Beam

Arch

Suspension

NAME _____ | DATE _____

 # Graphing Shapes in Our Bridges

One team in Mr. Carson's class counted the shapes they found in their bridge and entered the data in the table below.

| Shapes in Our Bridge | Number of Shapes |
|---|---|
| Rectangle | 13 |
| Parallelogram | 11 |
| Square | 5 |
| Trapezoid | 16 |
| Triangle | 18 |

**1**  Draw the number of shapes the team found in their bridge in the picture graph below. Make each shape you draw represent 4 shapes. The rectangle data has been entered as an example.

### The Shapes in Our Bridge

| Rectangle | Parallelogram | Square | Trapezoid | Triangle |
|---|---|---|---|---|

Each picture = 4 shapes

**Quadrilaterals & Perimeters**

**1** Label the missing side lengths on each polygon below.

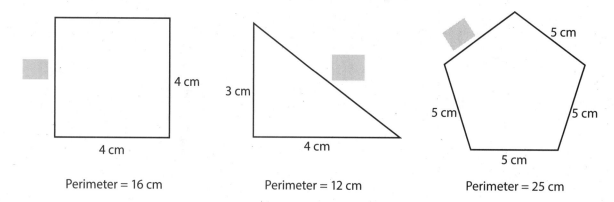

Perimeter = 16 cm       Perimeter = 12 cm       Perimeter = 25 cm

**2** Label each figure below with its name and perimeter.

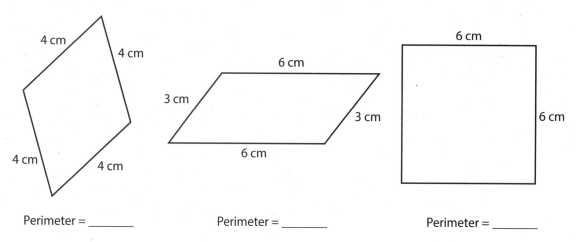

Perimeter = _____      Perimeter = _____      Perimeter = _____

**3** Label each figure below with its name and area.

**CHALLENGE**

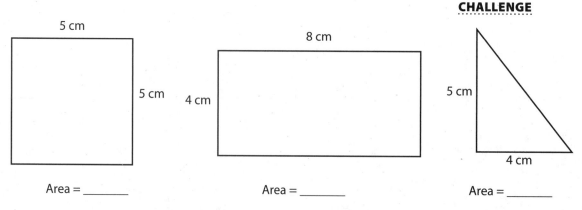

Area = _____      Area = _____      Area = _____

**4** Draw a quadrilateral that has a different name than any of those shown above, and label it with its name.

**NAME** _____ | **DATE** _____

 **Plot the Data**

**1** The students in Mr. Frisbie's class measured their bridges' deck thickness. The measurements are below:

| Team | Deck Thickness (in inches) |
|---|---|
| Purple | $2\frac{1}{4}$ |
| Green | $4\frac{3}{4}$ |
| Gray | 5 |
| Yellow | $3\frac{1}{2}$ |
| Blue | 3 |

| Team | Deck Thickness (in inches) |
|---|---|
| Teal | $2\frac{1}{4}$ |
| Pink | $3\frac{1}{4}$ |
| Orange | 3 |
| Red | $2\frac{1}{2}$ |
| Fuschia | 4 |

**a** Draw a line plot to represent the class data. Remember to give the line plot a title and labels.

**Title** _____

**b** What do you notice about the data? Write at least two observations.

**2** Write < , =, or > to compare each pair of mixed numbers.

$2\frac{1}{2}$ ___ $2\frac{1}{4}$          $3\frac{1}{3}$ ___ $3\frac{1}{4}$          $5\frac{2}{8}$ ___ $5\frac{2}{3}$          $1\frac{4}{6}$ ___ $1\frac{2}{3}$

**NAME** _____ **| DATE** _____

# 🔍 Considering Our Data

**1** How many of each type of bridge is represented on the scatter plot?

Arch bridge:

Beam bridge:

Suspension bridge:

**2** Calculate the mean, or average, deck width of each bridge type.

Arch bridge:

Beam bridge:

Suspension bridge:

**3** Was your bridge thicker or thinner than the average for its type? Write an expression using >, =, or < to show how your bridge's deck thickness compares to the average.

**4** Fill in the blanks.

**a** The bridge with the thinnest deck had a span of _____ inches.

**b** The longest bridge's deck was _____ inches thick.

**c** The longest bridge was a(n) _____ type of bridge.

**d** The bridge with the thinnest deck was a(n) _____ type of bridge.

**NAME** _____ | **DATE** _____

 # The Javelin Throw

Sam and Tanisha are playing a new Measurement Olympics game called Javelin Throw. Using two fingers, they each throw a straw "javelin" five times and measure the distance the straw flew to the nearest whole inch. The winner is the player whose average distance is the highest. Sam and Tanisha threw their javelins the following distances:

| Sam | 21 inches | 25 inches | 33 inches | 34 inches | 37 inches |
|---|---|---|---|---|---|
| Tanisha | 20 inches | 39 inches | 19 inches | 19 inches | 33 inches |

**1** Draw a line plot to represent their data.

- Give the line plot a title and labels.

- Use a different color for Sam than for Tanisha, and fill in the legend to show which color is for which thrower.

**Title** _____



| Key | ☐ Sam | ☐ Tanisha |

**2** **CHALLENGE** Sam calculated his average throw using the following expressions, but got stuck at the end. Complete his work to show his average throw.

$$21 + 25 + 33 + 34 + 37 = 150$$

$$150 \div 5 =$$

**3** **CHALLENGE** Write equations that Tanisha can use to calculate her average throw, then solve them.

**Lemonade Stand**

Philipe is making lemonade to serve at a lemonade stand. His recipe makes 6 glasses of lemonade. The recipe calls for 4 lemons, 1 cup of sugar, and 6 cups of water. For Friday at the lemonade stand, Philipe wants to make enough lemonade to serve 1 glass each to 30 customers.

**1** How many lemons does he need? Use words, numbers, or pictures to show your work.

**2** When Philipe makes the lemonade, he gets 1 cup of lemon juice out of every 4 lemons. How many cups of liquid (lemon juice and water together) will be in his whole batch of lemonade?

**3** **CHALLENGE** Philipe expects to have more customers on Saturday since more people will be playing outside. He thinks he might serve as many glasses of lemonade as he did Friday, plus half again that many. How many recipes of lemonade should he make for Saturday? Use words, numbers, or pictures to explain your reasoning.

NAME _____ |DATE _____

 **How Much Water?**

**1** One team in Mr. Frisbie's class said the load limit of their bridge was 800 liters. Another team says it was 800 milliliters. Who is correct? Why? Explain your answer using numbers, pictures, or words.

**2** Another team is measuring the water the whole class will need for the load-limit tests. There are 10 teams in the class, and each team will need at least 1 water bottle full of water. Should they measure out 5 milliliters, 5 liters, 50 liters, or 500 liters of water? Why? Explain your answer using numbers, pictures, or words.

**3** A third team has already built an early version of their bridge design and is measuring its load limit. They hung a bottle containing 65 milliliters from the bridge, then hung another bottle from that one. At first, the second bottle held 50 milliliters, but the bridge still held it, so they added more water to it. Their bridge held 145 milliliters of water before collapsing. How much water was in the second bottle when the bridge collapsed? Show your work.

**4** Solve the problems.

$3 \times$ _____ $= 36$    _____ $\div 4 = 9$    $36 =$ _____ $\times 2$    _____ $= 3 \times (5 + 7)$

$(2 + 8) \times 10 =$ _____    _____ $= 4 \times (4 + 5)$    _____ $= 4 \times 10 \times 2$    $6 \times (3 + 3) =$ _____

**NAME** _____ | **DATE** _____

 **More Bridge Patterns**

**1** Cassandra built some truss bridges using trapezoids for the trusses. She made sketches of her bridges like those shown below.

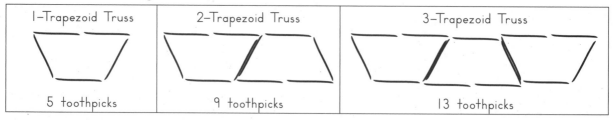

How many toothpicks will it take to build a truss bridge with 8 trapezoids? Explain your answer using labeled sketches, numbers, and words.

**2** Cassandra wanted to make her truss bridges stronger, so she added toothpicks to turn the trapezoids into triangles.

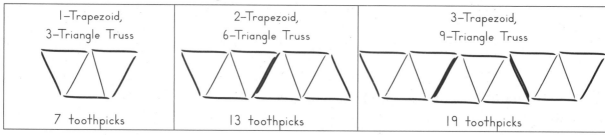

**a** Fill in the table to show the new relationships of toothpicks to trusses.

| Trapezoids | 1 | 2 | 3 | 4 | 5 | 6 | 7 | 8 |
|---|---|---|---|---|---|---|---|---|
| Triangles | 3 | 6 | 9 | | | | | |
| Number of Toothpicks | 7 | 13 | 19 | | | | | |

**b** How many triangles will it take to build a truss bridge with 10 trapezoids?

**c** How many toothpicks will Cassandra need to build the bridge with 10 trapezoids?

Solve the problems below.

$\_ \times 9 =$ _____     $8 \times (5 + 3) =$ _____     $(5 + \_\_\_) \times 9 = 54$     $(8 \times 5) + (\_\_\_ \times 3) = 64$

NAME

DATE

# Graphing the Final Bridges

Title

Key to Bridge Types

Beam

Arch

Suspension

**NAME** _____ | **DATE** _____

 **How Much Time?**

**1** Mr. Frisbie's class has 1 hour and 10 minutes to work on their bridges.

- They need 5 minutes to gather materials.
- It will take them twice as long to clean up.
- They want to spend 30 minutes building and testing their bridges.
- They need the remaining time to draw a picture of the bridge.

How many minutes can they spend on each task? Show your work below.

**2** Ms. Delawney's class has 25 minutes to prepare for a bridge design showcase. They'll start their preparations at 2:15 p.m.

- They will first use 10 minutes to write statements explaining their designs.
- Next, they will spend half as long making covers for their folders.
- Last, they will use the remaining time to plan activities and games for the showcase.

At what time will they need to start each task? Show your work below.